Praise for A GOOD HARD KICK IN THE ASS

"Learn from our scars—and maybe yours won't run so deep."
—Mike Betzer, CEO, Ineto

"For once, here are real-world examples that *really* illustrate the fundamentals of market validation, team-building, and market traction. This book is a must-read for all first-time entrepreneurs—and a great refresher for startup veterans."
—Gary Neill, cofounder and CEO, Covasoft, Inc.

"Perfect for the experienced leader and the entrepreneurial novice alike, this book is a hard-hitting meat-and-potatoes road map to success. Think of it as required reading for all those brave souls who venture into the entrepreneur's world."
—C. J. "Gabe" Gabriel, President and CEO, Newgistics, Inc.

"This is a book for new and old economy entrepreneurs alike. Its 'head-on' style challenges the readers to question the very essence of their business mission—the healthiest step they can take. Adams has diamond-sharp insight into what you need to succeed in the entrepreneurial world. I'll recommend this book to any student considering a career as an entrepreneur or an investor."
—Philip C. Zerillo, Graduate Dean and Associate Dean
of Executive Education, University of Texas

"Everyone from the independent entrepreneur to the corporate manager can benefit from this practical guide. Read *A Good Hard Kick in the Ass*—and learn how to build the truly entrepreneurial organizations of the future."
—Alisa Nessler, founder and CEO, Lane15 Software

"Think of Adams's advice as marching orders for entrepreneurs—the kick-start every entrepreneur needs to succeed in a competitive world."
—Peter Simon, founder and president,
Simon Management Group

"Where the heck was this book while I was making all these mistakes? I've been a startup CEO six times. These lessons could have saved me lots of scar tissue—and kept me from having to do it six times before I got it right!"
—Michael Bennett, former CEO and chairman,
Mission Critical Software

A GOOD HARD KICK IN THE ASS

ROB ADAMS

KICK

IN THE ASS

BASIC TRAINING FOR ENTREPRENEURS

CROWN
BUSINESS
NEW YORK

Published by Crown Business, New York, New York.
Member of the Crown Publishing Group, a division of Random House, Inc.

www.randomhouse.com

Crown Business is a trademark and the Rising Sun colophon is a registered trademark of Random House, Inc.

Printed in the United States of America

Design by Lindgren/Fuller Design

Library of Congress Cataloging-in-Publication Data
Adams, Rob (Robert J., Jr.), 1959–
   A good hard kick in the ass: basic training for entrepreneurs / Rob Adams.
   Includes index.
   1. Entrepreneurship. I. Title.
HB615.A33 2002
658.4'21—dc21   2001042467

ISBN 0-609-60950-5

10 9 8 7 6 5 4 3 2 1

First Edition

For Anne, Kyle, and Megan

CONTENTS

FOREWORD

When Bill Gates and Steve Ballmer recruited me to work at Microsoft, I really had no idea what I was in for. I'd been an executive at IBM for many years, and I assumed I'd be there until I retired. I didn't particularly *want* to leave Big Blue. To this day, I count my IBM years as a wonderful and rewarding experience. It seemed almost crazy to forsake a sure, steady, still-challenging gig at one of the world's finest companies—and crazier still to jump headfirst into a business that was just getting its legs. Still, there was *something about* those guys and their vision. I found myself becoming more and more intrigued. Finally I decided to take the plunge. (To give you an idea where I was coming from, during our hiring negotiations I was as concerned about my vacation time as I was about the stock package. See? I had no idea. . . .)

Well, what I was in for at Microsoft—what we were *all* in for—was to participate in one of the most effective execution machines in the history of business. We demonstrated, first-hand, the value of targeting the best and the brightest for our team; it made the difference between success and failure. We pursued market opportunities aggressively, using a tough evaluation process to vet ideas and determine whether a particular product would fly in the market. We designed clear, targeted product and marketing strategies. Throughout, we never lost touch with the customer. Some things failed; others took multiple tries to get right. In every case, though, we kept a clear focus on the goals we had set. And we worked our fannies off.

Microsoft isn't the only company that has executed in this way. Certainly, IBM has done it too—although a younger company is, by definition, less bureaucratic and easier to mold. Many of today's companies—and *all* of the successful ones—have performed with the same tenacity. And in the pages of this book, you are about to meet some *very* young companies who are doing it right now.

You're also about to receive, in a single source, many of the lessons that can help you do it in your own business. When I read this book, I was astonished by how strongly it resonated with my own experience. I was struck by how thorough an account Rob Adams gives of the issues that are important—not just to the startup, but to *any* company, big or small, that wants to keep innovating and competing. And I was gratified to see how strongly he defines and debunks the myths and illusions that have tripped up so many infant businesses in recent years.

Now that my tenure at Microsoft is over, I serve on the boards of several new businesses. I'll strongly suggest that they all buy this book, and that they read it cover to cover. You would be smart to do the same, because Rob Adams understands—and this book describes—what entrepreneurs *really* need to know (and do!) so that their companies will play in today's economy.

—Mike Maples,
Executive VP of Products,
Microsoft Corporation (retired)

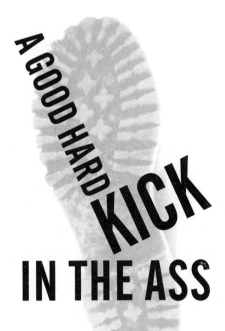

A GOOD HARD KICK IN THE ASS

READY FOR A GOOD HARD KICK IN THE ASS?

I run a boot camp for entrepreneurs that gets their companies up and running. I can't tell you how often I hear people say things like:

"I have an idea for a new product that'll make a billion-dollar business."

"I've spent ten years working in this business, and I know what customers really want."

"All I need to do now is write a killer business plan and raise a whole lot of money fast."

"My company will go public in a couple of years."

When entrepreneurs talk like this, I want to give them a swift kick in the pants. Why? Because these notions are BS. They have nothing to do with what it really takes to start a successful company. They're myths. They're illusions. And in this book, I'll tear them down. If you subscribe to them, I'll rearrange your thinking. In the process, I'll prepare you for the winner-take-all firefights of the marketplace.

I've been involved with new businesses for all of my working life, and I'm incredulous that the entrepreneurial path has been so polluted. Who believes all this junk? Believe me, it's not just the techno-hip I-wanna-retire-by-thirty crowd. I hear experienced corporate executives say things like, "The Internet represents a $50 billion market, and we will capture one-half of one percent of that." People who've spent decades building sophisticated technology will say, "All I need for marketing is some advertising." Or consider this, from a Fortune 500 stalwart spinning out a new business unit: "We have no competition." What *I* say is "Dream on!"

Snap out of the hype—or wind up in the tank.

All of a sudden, a lot of startups are looking like armadillos on a country road in Texas. Spawned by the feeding frenzy of the late 1990s, many of these companies went public well before they should have. Even the ones that never IPO'ed hired hundreds of employees, sat them in ergonomically correct desk chairs, and spent money like screaming banshees before they hit the wall with no skid marks. First, it was the business-to-consumer startups that bombed—especially those whose revenues *(what* revenues?) relied solely on website advertising, community, or referral fees. Then, like dominoes, many of the business-to-business exchanges—startups linking companies up to do business over the Internet—began to collapse. Plenty of other categories started teetering as well.

Who founded all these companies, anyway? A bunch of bozos? No. Mostly they were intelligent, technically astute people who intended to build great businesses and make everybody rich. Problem was, they used a process that was fundamentally broken. They didn't start by defining their market and determining how best to serve that market. Instead, they got their hands on all-too-readily-available wads of capital, built their products, then tried to figure out how to reach the market. They used what I call the "ready, fire, aim" approach to business. They blew through huge stockpiles of money—unbelievably quickly—without stopping to think how their resources could be used to build value. Profitability never crossed their minds. The result? Their companies (not to mention shareholders) have been taking it right between the eyes.

Who's next to bite the dust? No telling. But if you read this book—and follow the principles in it—you're upping your chances it won't be you.

At AV Labs, the accelerator venture fund I run in Austin, our entrepreneurs get the help they need to clear an extremely high bar—the venture bar. They're quickly disabused of the notion that all they need is a good (read, "unique") idea. In these pages, you'll receive the same education they get. You'll find out ideas are a dime a dozen. Successful businesses don't depend on unique ideas. Instead, they rely on a team's ability to execute—to build, market, and sell a product that's better, faster, or cheaper, and to do so to near-superhuman perfection.

Here you'll learn that *every* product has competition—even if it's just "I want to keep my money." If you believe yours doesn't, then you haven't analyzed your market adequately. Or maybe your product or service is not that great to begin with.

Think you need to get your paws on a big fat bankroll to get your business off the ground? Most of our AV Labs entrepreneurs thought so too. That is, until we gave them a potent dose of reality. When it comes to raising money, *a little bit* suffices in the earliest days. Then, funding events can be timed around execution milestones that raise your company's value. The alternative? Morale- and wealth-destroying dilution of ownership.

In short, this book will help you calibrate your BS meter. It will help you let go of all the crap people believe about the startup enterprise. You're about to learn—as our entrepreneurs have learned—that there is only one path to success in a startup. What's that? Hard work—and adherence to the fundamentals.

My motto: Back to the fundamentals—or you're roadkill.

We started AV Labs in 1999, which was, as everyone now knows, the apex of the "new economy" boom. We were founded as a spin-off from Austin Ventures, the largest venture fund in the Southwest. With all the infant businesses sprouting in the area, Austin Ventures knew most of those startups needed seasoning—and some risks removed—before they were ready for multimillion-dollar investments.

What was required? An environment like AV Labs to prepare entrepreneurs for the bloody battles of the marketplace. At AV Labs, we're much more than an early-stage venture fund. We give new companies the initial "seed" funding they need to get off the ground, but we also roll up our sleeves and break a good hard sweat with them, getting through some crucial milestones:

• *Validating the market.* Who's my customer, anyway? (Think you know? Think again.)
• *Designing a profitable business model.* How can I make money? (Not with a "killer product," that's for sure.)
• *Hiring a great team.* Who's most likely to help me succeed? (Sorry, it might not be your college roommate.)
• *Lining up strong follow-on investors.* What quality investors will advise and support me moving forward? (No, good ones *won't* demand a quick return.)
• *Making sure the product can be built in our lifetimes.* Is the product technologically feasible? (Wowing the world is not your goal—your goal is to get to market with a salve for customers' pain.)

We have been successful, particularly when you consider the times we've operated in. AV Labs was spawned right along with many other "startup incubators" and "startup accelerators," all of whom had the goal to help ignite brand-new (usually Internet-related) businesses. Most of these high-flying IPO-funded or corporate-backed incubators have gone down the tubes—right behind the dot-coms and B2Cs and B2Bs and all the other junk they backed.

AV Labs, on the other hand, is still standing. So, as it happens, are most of the companies that have "graduated" from the Labs.

Why? Because from the start, we've stuck to the fundamentals. We have forced our entrepreneurs—kicking and screaming a lot of the time—to spend time validating their customers, finding out who those people are and what their reddest-hot pain is around a problem. Only then can a startup even begin to design a solution the market will accept.

We have gone back to the drawing board time after time with our entrepreneurs to develop straightforward, profit-producing business models. You wouldn't believe how hard it can be to pound the message home: *You have to make money.* For way too long, this was *not* the no-brainer you might think.

We've coached our entrepreneurs to bring on the right executive and investor talent for growing the company. Execution intelligence is the #1 deciding factor for a team's success. If that means somebody other than the founder should take the helm as CEO, then so be it.

From day one at AV Labs, we've eaten our own dog food. We've kicked *ourselves* in the ass, plenty of times. Before we even got started, we analyzed the market. We asked the people in the trenches, entrepreneurs and investors alike: *What do startups need the most? Where's the most scorching pain?* At the time, capital was so plentiful it was a mere commodity. What was the scarce resource? Executive talent. That, then, became the core AV Labs value proposition: to supply our portfolio companies with solid management expertise, along with the process needed to build solid companies. We've attracted a stable of talented executives over time, people with plenty of fast-growth and startup scar tissue. They've made a critical difference for our companies.

Now, of course, as the markets have returned to reality, funding is a whole lot harder to come by as well. With capital no longer the commodity it once was, AV Labs has *three* compelling value propositions—in addition to the management talent and startup acceleration process, the dollars these companies have to have.

Have we had doubts about sticking to the fundamentals? You bet. Especially in the early days, we wondered constantly if we were doing things the right way. Take business-to-consumer investments, for example. When we got started, *everybody* was throwing money at these companies. We were tempted, believe me. But we forced ourselves through the validation process: *Who's the customer? What's the pain? How in the world can you make money at this?* We couldn't answer these questions in ways that got us very excited. So we passed. We also avoided awarding the sky-high, artificially inflated valuations that startups typically received in those days.

It was tough, but we wouldn't let ourselves believe the myths. And we wouldn't let our entrepreneurs believe them either.

We were vindicated when the entire scene crashed around our ears and AV Labs—along with our companies—remained standing. Now, in more decaffeinated times, we know our strategy of sticking to the fundamentals was the right one.

Who is Rob Adams, anyway? And why should you listen to me?

AV Labs is built on the same principles I espouse in these pages—principles I've learned, sometimes the hard way, through a business career focused on the entrepreneurial journey.

An engineer with an MBA, I've had the privilege of working for some awesome software companies. I cut my teeth at Lotus Development in its early days, joining it just after it went public. I saw the founders bring in seasoned management. Firsthand, as the company grew its markets beyond 1-2-3 to Notes and its revenues from a few million a year to billions, I learned how critical great management can be. I knew Lotus from the inside in its heyday, and I reveled in the experience.

In an effort to recapture the glory days of Lotus, in the early '90s (the "slow days" of venture capital) I co-founded a venture-backed startup, Business Matters. By the standards of the last few years, the company was wildly successful. But those were more staid times, and Business Matters—with real customers, great venture backers, and a strong team—wasn't able to survive. In the end, I learned an invaluable lesson, one I apply today in working with the AV Labs teams: If the market for your product costs too much to capture, no sales-and-marketing model on earth can get you to profitability.

After Business Matters, I was VP of marketing at Pervasive Software. At Pervasive, I saw a startup thrive in the market with an existing product and an innovative channel model. In the case of Pervasive, the same qualities that were present in Business Matters— great customers, financial backers, and team—produced a winner that culminated in a successful IPO and secondary offering.

Throughout my career, I've had a lot of experience with funding issues. I was involved with acquisitions at Lotus, and with venture capital at both Business Matters and Pervasive. I have talked and strategized with countless business associates while they were in the process of raising capital. A couple of years ago, I took a seat on the other side of the money-raising table. Now I sign the front of checks instead of the back. I've had an opportunity to see thousands of business plans and meet hundreds of entrepreneurs. I've invested, directly or indirectly, in dozens of businesses. I'm a software guy, and AV Labs is a software fund; our companies are all building software.

Somewhere along the way, I began to recognize undeniable patterns in the startup landscape. I saw a set of known risks with common themes. There were, I realized, certain risk variables a startup could control: market, business model, team, investors. What, I asked myself, if I could describe these variables for others? What if I could develop them into coherent principles and practical advice?

The result is this book. These pages contain much of what I've learned in startups and venture firms over the years. They also reflect my experience as an adjunct professor of entrepreneurship at the University of Texas Graduate School of Business and other business grad schools. In the classroom, I've discovered that the best learning occurs around war stories like the ones presented here.

Get a swift kick—and lose your illusions.

If you've picked up this book, you might be thinking of starting a business yourself. Or maybe you're building a new division in an established company. Perhaps you want to reengineer your existing business to take advantage of the Internet or some other new technology. Or you might just want to learn about what *really* works for businesses in these confusing, hype-ridden, fast-changing economic times.

Whatever brings you to these pages, I bet you're smart. You're also pretty sophisticated, am I right?

All the same, I'd wager you have some fairly goofy ideas about starting a business. Go back to the start of this introduction. Take a look at some of the stuff I've heard so many people say. Does any of this ring a bell? I thought so.

Where did all these fallacies come from, anyway? From a lot of places. But I think one of the primary culprits—in our day, at least—has been the business media.

The business media produces an endless avalanche of articles, anecdotes, and speculations about the startup enterprise. I have a name for much of this output: business porn. Like the other kind, the business variety can be entertaining. But like the other porn, it doesn't much resemble the real world.

Business porn: titillating fantasies—not much reality.

There are now around 700 business-related magazines in publication, up from half as many in 1990. Many focus exclusively on the growth of the Internet, displaying an obsessive fascination with startups. Even *Forbes* and *Fortune* jumped on the startup bandwagon in the late '90s, with *Fortune's* ever-growing Silicon Valley office generating the magazine's most active segment. The Internet itself, of course, came to host literally thousands of sites dedicated to business and finance. And let's not forget cable TV, with the MSNBC and CNBC business channels, where all day and all night, stock-market pundits and business analysts spout the latest theory or market projection *du jour.*

The business media really had a field day at the height of the so-called "new economy." Publications loved to exaggerate the "overnight" part of all the dot-com successes—Amazon.com, eBay, etc. etc. etc. But they somehow managed to downplay the hard work behind those companies' success. Pundits and analysts salivated over the latest crop of dot-com millionaires, whose baby-faced mugs smiled out at us from the covers of everything from *Fast Company* to *Red Herring.* Founding a startup began to look easy. In many ways, it *was* easy—way *too* easy, at least when it came to funding. Undergrads (translation: teenagers) got bankrolled in their dorm rooms. People who had no retail experience started online pet-food companies. And to further legitimize the trend, *Fortune*-class companies birthed e-commerce spin-off after e-commerce spin-off, all hyped endlessly in the media.

It is really no wonder, then, that thousands of perfectly sane, intelligent people jumped on the startup bandwagon. Far too few of them had any real understanding of the entrepreneurial task. They believed, plain and simple, the business porn. They mistook the fantasy for reality.

And you know what? *They still do.*

The myths generated in the heyday continue to infect the minds and imaginations of countless folks I've encountered in the past few years. Seasoned businesspeople hold as tenaciously to their illusions as naïve twentysomethings. So pervasive are these wacky ideas, so entrenched in the popular imagination, that entrepreneurs know—or think they know—*exactly* what to do.

Most of the time they're flat-out wrong.

Real-life startups: walking the walk.

If you've paid much attention to business porn in the last few years (and who hasn't?), this book will wake you up. Along with the AV Labs entrepreneurs whose stories appear in these pages, you'll lose your attachments to startup myths and misconceptions. You'll embrace, like them, fundamental business principles.

You'll realize there's nothing magical about it—just sound principles, applied in new ways. You'll watch our teams put those principles to the test. You'll feel the optimism and experience the naïveté. You might even identify with some of the predicaments. All the while, you'll get plenty of practical information about how to start and run a company.

Keep in mind that some of our startups are creating products that are technically very sophisticated. One is building software for managing a brand-new network architecture, for example. Another, tools that help businesses monitor what are known as "transaction processes" in complex e-business environments. I've tried in these pages to give you an overview of the technology. I've also included a "Cast of Characters" appendix you can refer to for a bird's-eye overview. But unless you're a software geek like me, you might not completely understand the nitty-gritty ins and outs of what these startups are doing, technologically speaking. If that's the case, don't tear your hair out. The technology is not really what's important here. What is? The *business* lessons these entrepreneurs have learned on their journey through the startup landscape.

*Big-company sidebars: Startup fundamentals keep working,
and working, and working. . . .*

Another feature I've included in the book are shaded sidebars
describing established companies, to show you that *these principles
are not just for startups.* In a company's early stages, the entrepreneur
sets the stage for what is to follow. But the astute team does not simply abandon startup principles once a company reaches a certain
size. The companies that have been most successful—like the ones
appearing in this book—are those that have continued to apply these
principles over time.

Having said that, I can already hear some of the groans from people flipping through *A Good Hard Kick in the Ass* for the first time.
*Here we go, yet another write-up on Dell. Do I really have to read
about Microsoft again? Haven't we already seen enough stuff about
Cisco? And Amazon—if I see another word about them, I'll gag.*

Not so fast. Bear with me here. You might *think* you've read
everything there is to read about Dell, Microsoft, Cisco, and Amazon. I don't really blame you if you perceive them as overly cited.
But what you'll get here is a fresh twist—a new way to think about
an old dog.

This is a crucially important point. *To be successful, big companies
should act more like startups.* Which is precisely why, in addition to
the big-company asides scattered throughout the book, I devote a
final chapter to some of our AV Labs' entrepreneurs' thoughts on the
issue. I also include a sprinkling of sidebars that showcase how
emerging leaders—such as Austin's Vignette Corporation and the
public relations firm Blanc & Otus—are applying the principles in
the book as they solve customers' problems and achieve prominence
in their markets.

Takeaways: summing it all up.

In addition to the sidebars, each chapter of *A Good Hard Kick in the Ass* has its key points consolidated in end-of-chapter takeaways. Included as convenient summaries, the takeaways encapsulate core ideas.

Are the fundamentals a guarantee? *No.*

A little earlier, I talked about all the businesses out there that have fizzled. But while they've been crashing, plenty of other startups have done just fine. Fact is, many of the companies ignited during the heady "new economy" heyday continue to thrive. Granted, their stock prices may not be as over-the-top as they were in early 2000. But they're hanging in there, marching toward profitability if they're not already there. What's more, as this book amply illustrates, new companies are coming on the scene every day. Many of those are equally promising.

What's the difference? *I reiterate: The successful entrepreneurs are the ones who've adhered to the fundamentals.* And right now, the only businesses getting funded are the ones that are sticking to the fundamentals.

Essentially, flourishing new companies turn on the same wheels that have propelled "old" businesses for a century or more. Despite what you hear, it is easier to *start* a company today than it's ever been. But it's harder than ever to grow one. Value propositions have to be built and proven, not just written on napkins. Quality teams have to be acquired thoughtfully, not just slapped together and given inflated titles and salaries. The "good times" will come and go. But the tenets of business that apply during times of hype are the same ones that continue to work when the hype has burnt itself out. *Companies that stick to the fundamentals will be good companies.*

Does that mean they will never fail? *No. There are no such guarantees.*

Take the companies you're about to meet in this book, for example. I don't know whether they'll make it or not. What *do* I know? They have solid foundations. They have met one of the highest bars out there. They've received financing from top-tier venture investors and strategic partners. Still, remember this: The "V" in "VC" stands for "venture." Investing in new companies is by definition a risk. No one is omniscient—venture capitalists included. The numbers suggest that 90% of startups fail. If we're lucky, we'll do better than that, but only time will tell. What I *can* say is, the companies you'll read about are minimizing the risks that can kill a new business. And they provide great examples of how you can mitigate your company's risk.

Remember, *there are no magical formulas.* You need to learn how to manage known risks. Validate the market. Assemble a great team. Develop a profitable business model. Execute as perfectly as possible. All the while, know this: If you step up to the plate to start a company, you're taking a chance you'll strike out. *No matter what you do.* While there are variables you can control, there are many you can't.

The commonsense rules in this book will (usually) get you a ticket to play. These principles might not guarantee anything, but one thing's for sure: If you don't stick to them, you'll probably never make it to the game.

Ready to get started? The next chapter will disabuse you once and for all of the notion that good ideas are scarce. Turn the page and get ready for your first kick!

GOOD IDEAS ARE A DIME A DOZEN

Nothing beats an ice-cold beer on a blazing hot day in Austin, Texas. And nothing leads entrepreneurs down more ratholes than the myth that *good ideas are scarce.* Both these facts were driven home to me one late summer evening, as I shared a round of draughts with Mike Turner and Mark McClain in the air-conditioned bar of Louie's 106, a local deal-making hot spot around the corner from our offices.

This was shortly after AV Labs got underway. Mike and Mark had started with us to pioneer the role of Venture Fellow, a position allowing experienced executives to mentor infant businesses while exploring their own startup ideas. Both ex-VPs at Tivoli Systems, they'd been hard at work trying to pinpoint an idea they could make fly in the marketplace. Together with Kevin Cunningham and Bill Kennedy, ex-Tivoli directors who'd agreed to be part of a new company, they'd been talking to people, researching the Internet, and reviewing industry analyst reports. So far, they hadn't found the right concept—but judging from the positive attitudes that flowed along with the cold beer that afternoon in Louie's, they were having a great time.

"We've coined a new term, Rob," said Mark, his gray eyes thoughtful behind wire-rimmed glasses. "Web-roaching."

"What's that?" I asked.

"We've been using the Internet to research different concepts. We've found out that the minute you hit on an idea you think is unique, four or five roaches scurry out from underneath a rock."

At that point Mike jumped in. "We thought we were really out there when we hit upon application firewalls. We figured, hey, what if you could fire up a Web-based application and partition it, then let different outsiders access only certain parts? We thought this was a really unique notion—until Kevin and I found five companies that were already doing it."

Now pretty fired up themselves, they told me they'd decided to pursue their one and only idea that seemed to be one-of-a-kind: the next great sensory input to the Internet. I must have looked confused (perhaps because I was). "Smell, Rob, *smell,*" Mark explained. "Face it—we have sight, and we have sound. Now, the Internet needs smell. Our company will make it possible to point to something on the Internet and get an odor."

"Cool, huh?" said Mike, grinning as he watched the reaction on my face. Then they both started laughing. I was relieved to know these guys weren't serious about pursuing such an outlandish idea. Unique, undoubtedly, but totally off-the-wall. Of course nobody was doing this—and no wonder!

I knew Mike and Mark would soon find a way to put their talents to the entrepreneurial test. In the meantime, as we finished our beers, I promised to pass on any ideas that crossed my mind, and to watch for any interesting trends suggested by the press or analysts. You can imagine how we all laughed when, not long after, I plopped a *Money* magazine on the conference table at a meeting. In that issue, *Money* ran a story about a startup on the West Coast. That company's mission—you guessed it—was to provide olfactory input and output over the Internet.

Think your idea has to be unique? You're deluded.

If Mike and Mark's experience tells you anything, it should tell you this: There *really is* nothing new under the sun. You wouldn't believe how many would-be entrepreneurs believe otherwise. They come into our office and swear they've got some new, radically cool, killer idea. They expect us to be impressed. They're surprised, even offended, when we're not.

Even intelligent, aware, knowledgeable people—people like Mark and Mike—believe a good idea is like the Hope Diamond. A good idea, they think, is rare in its brilliance and perfection. It is utterly unique in the universe. To be successful, entrepreneurs are *supposed* to have an idea like that, aren't they?

No! The idea does not have to be unique. The idea itself is really not that big a deal.

It wasn't long before Mike and Mark perceived this for themselves. At Louie's that day, they'd already gotten a whiff (if you will) of the truth. I knew it was only a matter of time before they figured it out. I was right. "We spent a month," Mark now says, "trying to come up with an idea no one had thought of, something you couldn't find commercially. I have to say that honestly, it's hard to find, if not impossible. Ultimately, what we learned was, there is no new idea."

Mike, Mark, Kevin, and Bill went on to form Waveset Technologies, one of Austin's most promising startups. And—surprise, surprise—the idea they finally zeroed in on was similar to the firewall concept they'd discarded early on, when four or five "Web roaches" scurried out from underneath the rock. Using the Waveset solution, companies can give outside partners and customers Internet access to internal data and applications, while managing this access in a secure manner.

Unique? Not by a long shot. In fact, the Waveset team got wind of several competitors early on. (Those dang roaches, all over the place.) What distinguishes Waveset is *not* the idea. Something else entirely will propel this company beyond the competition. What's that? The team's *execution intelligence.* In this chapter, I will explore what I mean by "execution intelligence." You will learn an important lesson:

Good ideas are not scarce; what's rare is a team that can execute.

But before we dive in to that discussion, let's debunk the notion that good ideas are scarce, once and for all.

In love with your idea? Get over it. Ideas are commodities.

If you come see us at AV Labs, we'll be able to tell if you're wrapped around the axle on your idea. First, you'll ask us to sign a nondisclosure agreement. Then you'll claim you're going to be "first to market." Then you'll tell us you have "no competition." We'll probably continue to listen politely. But your credibility will be zero.

Let's talk a little bit about each of these entrepreneurial delusions—all sub-myths of the Big Lie that "a unique idea is the key to my success."

Want me to sign a nondisclosure? Instead, say: "I'm clueless."

If I had a nickel for every entrepreneur who's walked into my office and asked me to sign a nondisclosure agreement, I could chuck it all and move to Tahiti. Every time this happens, I see a huge red flag pop out of the top of their head: *Warning! Careful! Don't go there!*

Why is "Please sign a nondisclosure" such a turn-off to an investor? Because it screams out, "I'm stuck on my idea." We all have a finite amount of energy for anything. If you want a nondisclosure, that means you've spent way too much of your energy obsessing about the idea. It suggests you probably haven't thought enough about the team, which is what an investor is really interested in. It implies you haven't given much thought to your customers, or to the market. You've got stuck here: Nobody in the whole world has ever had a notion like mine. Which, plain and simple, tells me you probably haven't done your homework.

I'll say something like this: "Listen, if you think this is so unique, consider my 1:8:20 rule: *For every entrepreneur with an idea in Austin, there are eight in Boston with the same idea, and twenty in the garages of Palo Alto* (let alone the rest of Silicon Valley)."

My point is, ideas are far from scarce. They're a dime a dozen. *They're mere commodities.*

Nine times out of ten, even a cursory perusal of the Internet will prove this is so. Think you have a unique idea? C'mon, get off your rear end and do a simple Internet search, and just see what happens. Like the Waveset team during their own "Web-roaching" sessions, you'll probably find several companies that have already taken a given idea to market. Which suggests, by default, that many others are working on it. As Mike Turner himself says, "The Internet itself quickly debunks the myth that ideas are scarce. Ten years ago, you'd be sitting here in Austin with an idea, and there would be ten people thinking the same thought, but without an interconnected network there was no way you'd know it. You'd think you were just off doing your own unique thing.

"Now, with the Internet, all you have to do is a search on a concept—such as 'database firewall,' 'application firewall,' 'sensory input,' or whatever—and poof! Ten companies are doing it. Before, it would take five years to find this out. Today it's almost instantaneous."

Once entrepreneurs are disabused of the "great unique idea" notion, most of them are actually relieved. Here they've spent all this time believing the uniqueness of their idea was the most important prerequisite to success. Now, they're free. Free to go out and pursue an idea they'd be really, really great at. Free to tackle a concept they'd abandoned, believing it was not sufficiently "unique." What's more, once you get it that your idea does not have to be unique, you no longer have to keep it a secret.

Getting to market first? Big deal.

If you imagine you have a one-of-a-kind idea, it only follows that you're convinced you'll get the solution to market before anyone else. I see this all the time. People tout their "first mover" status as a huge competitive advantage. All I can say is, anyone who's gone to business school and makes this claim deserves a tuition refund.

Getting to market first doesn't mean anything. Don't get me wrong—time to market is critical, especially in the fast-paced high-tech markets. But "time to market" is not synonymous with "first to market." If first-to-market is your only real advantage, this book just paid for itself; I've saved you several years of time you might have wasted pursuing an idea that's probably not all that great. First-to-market is an unsustainable advantage. Remember when Netscape's browser was out long before Microsoft Explorer? What browser are you using right now? In addition, many an entrepreneur has woken up, only to discover he's built an unsustainable expense structure in service to the "first mover" advantage. I could go on. The point is, the examples are legion that "creating a new category" does not necessarily spell success.

As a matter of fact, there aren't many companies I can think of that *did* succeed after creating such a category. I can, though, think of plenty of businesses that entered an existing category and proceeded to stomp all those roaches to smithereens. How? By executing to *dominate*, not define, a market space.

Think there's no competition? You're naïve.

The third myth pertaining to the "good ideas are scarce" fallacy is the one labeled "I have no competition." This is another claim I hear from many a hopeful entrepreneur. As my colleague John Doggett, a fellow professor at the University of Texas business school, says in his characteristically blunt fashion, "This is complete and utter BS.

Every product has competition, even if it's just 'I want to keep my money.' "

John is right. Even if you haven't been able to locate competing companies and products, I assure you: *Competition exists.* Like John says, you have intense competition from people wanting to hang on to their money. In fact, this is probably the biggest competition out there. You also have competition in the form of plain old inertia. People's resistance to change is deep in their bones; this is a universal human trait.

Another form of competition? The do-it-yourself movement—a proclivity that's rife within today's big companies. People think (wrongly, most of the time) that they can save big bucks building their own software solutions rather than buying them. For example, when the Waveset team thoroughly surveyed their proposed customer base (during their market validation, the topic of our second kick), they discovered that the greatest competition came from "people using manual labor and development tools to patch together a solution," recalls Kevin Cunningham. "There were a few software vendors in the space, but they hadn't made huge inroads that we could see."

Still, the team experienced some paranoia about those competing software vendors. To some extent, I told them, their paranoia was a good, healthy thing. But I encouraged them not to obsess about it too much. Why? Because *the existence of competition suggests that the idea itself is competitive.* Competition functions as its own form of market validation.

Where did all the confusion come from with respect to competition? Mostly, I have to admit, from the venture community itself. Venture investors are completely schizoid on this issue. On the one hand, they want to see some competition—because, again, that helps validate the market. At the same time, they don't want to see *too much.* We don't want you taking on Microsoft, for example, with some wonderful new PC operating system (an extreme example, but you get the picture). With venture investors as bipolar as they are, no wonder entrepreneurs themselves have gotten a little off-base with respect to competition. The main thing to remember is this: *When you're tempted to say "I have no competition," find some.*

Because competition, rather than being a bad thing, serves in whatever form as an important corollary—an existing solution to the problem you've identified. And, as you're about to find out, a corollary is one of the prime characteristics of a compelling business proposition.

"Okay, so what *is* a solid business concept?"

I knew you'd be asking that. Let's look at what we've seen so far. We've seen that focusing on the idea *per se* leads you, as an entrepreneur, into a number of traps. You start thinking your idea has to be unique. You believe it has to have first-to-market potential. You start to delude yourself that there's no competition.

A much more productive approach is to think of your business in terms of the overall *value proposition:* Are the elements in place to proceed with a new venture? Is there a reasonable likelihood of success? Typically, five things characterize a viable business, each of which we'll explore in the sections to follow:

- It represents a new approach to existing business processes, ideally by applying technology in a new way.
- Real, existing corollaries exist in the marketplace, today.
- Today's market for the solution is large, representing revenues of at least $1 billion a year.
- Equally large ancillary markets, either vertically or horizontally aligned to the space, also exist.
- Most important of all, the startup team possesses good execution skills in the chosen space.

You need a new approach to existing business processes.

Throughout the 1960s and '70s, the manufacturing industry suffered from "boom and bust" inventory cycles. Manufacturers would build their widgets, stockpile them, and wait for customers to order. Inevitably, they had either overbuilt—and then would have to lay off workers—or they had underbuilt and would have to pay overtime to catch up.

Software programs for performing core business operations—such as manufacturing resource planning (MRP) and then enterprise resource planning (ERP)—vastly smoothed out these inventory cycles. For the first time, people could predict demand more accurately. They could streamline fundamental business processes. Now, with the Internet, manufacturers can make MRP, ERP, inventory control, and other information systems available not just internally but to partners and customers.

Nobody is inventing—or even reinventing—the basic processes of inventory control, resource planning, and others. *All these processes have existed in some form or another since the dawn of the manufacturing age.* Without the software, people would be performing the same operations, just slower. Without the Internet, the same information would be shared with partners, just not as efficiently.

Which perfectly illustrates my point: The vast majority of successful technology businesses start by applying new technology to an existing business process. From the outset, Waveset knew that people were already working out how the Internet could be used to share data with partners and other outsiders. The startup then determined how new technology—technology it would create—could make the process easier, faster, and more efficient. Another AV Labs company, Newgistics, took another existing, fundamental business process—"reverse logistics," or product returns—and figured out how consumers could more easily return goods purchased via catalogs or over the Internet. (You'll hear a lot more about Newgistics later on.)

Like Waveset and Newgistics, most successful companies are ones that discover how technology can be applied to ease an existing pain in the marketplace—how a new use of technology can improve the operation of current business processes.

You need existing corollaries in the marketplace.

Inevitably, any problem that truly needs solving will have corollaries—alternatives to your solution—in the market, right now. If there's a real problem, people are already trying to deal with it, somehow. When they don't have technology they can use, they're using manual solutions. Or they're piecing together systems. They might be assigning special departments to the task. Or maybe they're using consulting services. Or—and this is sometimes the stiffest competition of all—they're trying to ignore the problem, in the hopes that it will simply go away. (It's that nasty old inertia problem again.) As we all know, human nature is such that people will often put up with a great deal of pain—both in the workplace and outside of it.

As an illustration of this concept, consider eBay, the giant online auction site. The problem? How to sell no-longer-needed stuff to other people. A corollary? The garage sale. When eBay came along, people had been using garage sales for years to solve the problem—so the eBay idea was not unique. The eBay founders simply took the fundamental process of the garage sale, added elements of the auction (another existing business process), and figured out a way to move the transactions onto the Internet. In effect, eBay expanded the local garage sale to encompass the entire globe.

Similarly, Waveset discovered a massive corollary at work in large enterprises. These giant businesses were developing, in-house, methods for opening up a company's internal applications—supply chains, demand forecasts, and so on—to the outside world. The very pervasiveness of these attempts clued the Waveset team into the fact that they were onto something big. *A strong corollary proves there is a pain in the market.*

Are you unable to locate a corollary to your solution? Then that means there's no pain around the problem. My advice? Find something else to do.

You need a market size of at least $1 billion.

If you've given much thought to starting a business, you probably already have some vague idea that you need a "big market." Well, how big? And why is a large market important?

First of all, most venture investors require that a high-tech startup demonstrate it has a potential domestic market of at least $1 billion.[1] In other words, there is the potential that solving a particular problem can yield $1 billion in annual revenue. The problem is now addressed by competing vendors, by patched-together in-house solutions, through consulting services, by ignoring the pain, or whatever. All the existing corollaries added together today should equal $1 billion in revenue annually.

Why this figure? Because to be successful, a technology company should be able to see its way to hitting at least $100 million a year with its first product. That requires capturing 10% of a billion-dollar market. Now 10% is a tough goal, to be sure. But it's also one your company should show it can achieve, given the existence of a $1 billion market. (Of course, a $2 billion market is even better; then, you only have to show you can capture 5% market share.) The Waveset team, for example, discovered that the financial services market alone—Waveset's primary market—represented a $1 billion opportunity for an online access management security solution; 10% of this market could yield the new company its required $100 million in annual revenue. An aggressive goal? Yes. Achievable? You bet.

---

1. At AV Labs, we use a "bottoms-up" market analysis to help determine a market's size and the percentage penetration a startup can reasonably expect to capture. This analysis, which validates the market using comprehensive interviews with hundreds of prospective customers, is described in detail in the next kick.

You need ancillary markets.

You've probably also heard you can't build a company on one market alone. You need more than one market to really forge a winning business. What does this mean? And how can you find those other markets? Here's a way to think this through in a smart way.

In addition to the $100 million in revenue targeted with your first release—a release aimed at your first market—you need several *ancillary* markets. Each of these should also be able to produce $100 million in revenue. As I've said, Waveset decided its first release would target finance institutions as the first market. Once it had captured 10% of that market, it would provide a similar solution to the ancillary manufacturing and transportation markets. While the biggest pain resided in financial services, these ancillary markets also had piercing pain around the problem. They would be fairly easy to capture—particularly after Waveset had established its financial services beachhead. What did all of this add up to? Significant market headroom for future growth. (The "heat map" graphic in the second kick visually illustrates the concept of ancillary markets.)

Ancillary markets can be vertical or horizontal. Waveset's are vertical, meaning that Waveset will be taking the same solution into different types of businesses. With a horizontal strategy, a company targets all types of businesses with a particular solution, then supplements the solution with new product lines over time; a simple example would be an accounting solution sold across several vertical markets that adds inventory control, financial modeling, and so on. My main point is, *each ancillary market, whether vertical or horizontal, should be shown to have revenue potential of at least $1 billion.* The existence of these markets, whether ultimately pursued or not, gives the company viable market options and further mitigates risk.

Okay. Let's say you have an idea, and you've determined it represents a new approach to an existing business process. So far, so good. Then you find real, existing corollaries in the marketplace, today. Great. You figure out the primary market's a big one—$1 billion a year big. Plus, you have equally large ancillary markets aligned to the space, either vertically or horizontally.

Even when these features of a viable business concept are in place, your startup might still be a no-go. Unless, that is, your team embodies the most important characteristic of all: execution intelligence.

You need execution intelligence: This is where the rubber meets the road.

At AV Labs, we see huge numbers of business ideas every month. How often do we dole out the cash? Not very. With our first fund, we ignited just over twenty startups—a tiny fraction of the thousands of proposals we'd received. Were the entrepreneurs we passed on simply a bunch of morons? Absolutely not. In fact, most of them were highly intelligent. They were technically astute. Most of their ideas seemed to hold some promise. Without exception, all of them believed they could make a business thrive.

What did the majority of these entrepreneurs lack? By now, I'm sure you know. They'd been obsessing about the *idea*—not the *team*. Because they'd spent so much time developing the idea, they hadn't developed the one thing that almost always differentiates a successful company: execution intelligence.

Execution intelligence is a *must-have* for a winning business. AV Labs, like other investment firms working in today's economy, is in the people-flow business. We maintain a razor-sharp focus on the team: its knowledge of the space, its chemistry, its experience, its ability to work well together. That's what gets a new startup through the hard times. That's what enables it to execute. That's why we make it a top priority to help our teams build out their execution intelligence.

Most people don't really think of the team as an integral part of a new business concept. But it is. Why? Because twenty people will often have the same great idea for a business. Again, the *idea* is not the key. The *idea* is not what wins. What does? The ability to compose a team that can *execute*. That's why I devote the rest of this chapter to an exploration of execution intelligence—the ability of a particular group of people, in a particular place and time, to make a company thrive.

An execution intelligence benchmark—
six critical success factors.

Do you and your team have execution intelligence? Evaluate yourselves against these three most important characteristics—all of which I'll explore further in the sections to follow:

- *Domain knowledge.* Are you experienced in the market space where you will compete?
- *Fast-growth scar tissue.* Without it, you can't deal with the ups and downs of rapid growth.
- *Experience in hyper-competitive markets.* At some point, a large, well-financed competitor will loom up overnight and bellow loudly. Can you deal with that?

In addition, these elements round out the picture, and we'll take a closer look at them as well:

- *Risk management skills.* Massive shifts in strategy or product lines are inevitable. Are you nimble? Can you cope?
- *A comprehensive experience profile.* Taken together, your team members must have the marketing, technical, sales, and executive expertise it takes to grow and run a company.
- *Leadership know-how.* Your corps of employees will expand faster than you can imagine. Can you recruit, retain, and effectively manage these people?

The Waveset team possessed all six attributes. Will your team have all these characteristics? Probably not—especially not in the beginning. Most teams don't. What I present here is an ideal. Nonetheless, you'd be wise to evaluate yourself and your team against this benchmark. When you see you lack a particular characteristic, *get somebody on the team who has it.* Pronto. Every time you make a new management hire, keep what you need in mind. Think "execution intelligence" every time you recruit an advisor or board member who will help steer the company.[2]

When you do so, you'll prove you're able to recognize team deficiencies—and to remedy those deficiencies. This in itself is a characteristic of execution intelligence.

1. Domain knowledge—been there, know that.

Around the same time Mark and Mike and I did our twelve-ounce curls at Louie's 106, all four of the Waveset co-founders had a similar conversation with John Thornton. John is a general partner at Austin Ventures. He is one of the most astute investors I know. His insight and intelligence, not to mention his track record, are indispensable to Austin's current generation of startups.

The day he talked with Mark, Mike, Bill, and Kevin, John made a particularly shrewd observation. Mark recalls it quite vividly. "We were describing the various areas we were thinking about," he says. "We thought we wanted a real challenge, something brand-new, something far away from what we'd already done. So we'd sort of been avoiding the one idea that had a lot of relevance to the team's background and experience.

"When we first mentioned what turned out to be our final concept, John just looked at us for a minute, then pounded his hand on

2. Advisors and board members are crucial elements of the team. As you're about to see, the Waveset team wisely supplemented their own experience with key advisors who'd built companies from the ground up; we'll take an even closer look at the role of advisors and board members in the fifth kick.

DELL COMPUTER CORPORATION: THE EPITOME OF EXECUTION INTELLIGENCE

If anybody illustrates the truth that ideas are commodities, it's Dell. Here's a company that had the "great idea" of selling something as ubiquitous as paper clips. As you can guess, it was hardly this idea that served as a breakthrough. What did? Execution to dominate. Read on . . .

Ideas are a commodity. Execution is scarce.

Nobody embodies this fundamental business principle more fully than Michael Dell. As much as any Fortune 500 company in operation today, the company he founded in 1983 vividly illustrates the fact that when it comes to starting and running a successful business, execution counts for far more than a unique idea.

Michael Dell originally began Dell Computers based on a simple concept: Sell high-performance PC computer systems directly to buyers, avoiding the middleman. "The direct model is based on direct selling," he has said, "not using a reseller or the retail channel—and it's not new. Mainframes and minicomputers were originally sold directly, but [manufacturers] used the retail channel or resellers to sell to their lower-volume customers. We, however, sold—and continue to sell—directly to all our customers."[3]

So, the difference was not that Dell had the idea to sell direct. That, after all, wasn't new. What was new was the way Dell creatively implemented the old idea—the way he combined an existing sales model (direct sales) with an existing computer market to create a

------

3. All quotes from *Direct from Dell,* by Michael Dell, pp. 206–7, 222.

revolutionary way to sell computers. All of this in a low-margin, highly competitive, commodity-oriented space.

While Dell was first to pursue the notion in a major way, this first-to-market advantage had little or nothing to do with the company's success. Within a year or two of being in business, the landscape was littered with competitors aiming to dominate Dell's space. What made the difference? Why did Dell triumph and most of these competitors fail? One thing: *execution.*

Early on, Michael Dell recognized the elements of execution intelligence that were needed to supplement his own—and wasted no time recruiting experienced business executives to advise him and help lead the company. Lee Walker, a former venture capitalist and management executive, signed on as president of the company; a strong early advisor was George Kozmetsky, co-founder of Teledyne and former dean of the University of Texas school of business.

From those early beginnings to the present day, Michael Dell has executed relentlessly, based on his belief that "the key is not so much on a great idea or patent as it is on the execution and implementation of a great strategy.

"Look at Wal-Mart or Coke," Dell continues. "You can understand their strategy—it's really not that complicated. But it's genius! It's completely comprehensible, yet few companies can really replicate their success.

"Why? It's all about knowledge and execution."

A major aspect of that execution has been, for Michael Dell, a continuous focus on meeting customers' real needs. At the company's weekly Customer Advocate meetings held in the early days of Dell Computer, he recalls, "salespeople served as 'advocates' for their customers who had issues with Dell by sharing the issues with a larger group of employees from many different functions within the company. Actions were assigned on the spot to correct any processes that might be affecting customer satisfaction. . . . We began to realize that customers were less focused on what the industry calls 'big things'—such as product features or hot technology—probably because those needs had been largely satisfied. We were fascinated to learn how the 'little things' became 'big things' to the people who really mattered."

Insights such as these are what have enabled Dell to execute on his overriding goal: to provide "an extraordinary customer experience." This, after all, is the ultimate test of execution intelligence for the entrepreneur—and it's a test Michael Dell has passed time and time again.

the table as he said, 'With your experience and credibility, you're actually thinking about *not* doing this? You're missing the picture!' That's when we started to get it."

What did John help them see that day? This: Their prior experience—rather than being an argument *against* the idea—made pursuing it a no-brainer. Mike and Mark had worked together at Tivoli Systems, with Mike having been there almost from the start. Tivoli is a large Austin-based company (now a division of IBM) that provides powerful software used by information technology (IT) organizations to manage the computers and equipment in companies' internal networks. Bill and Kevin were also longtime Tivoli employees; both were directors, while Mike and Mark were VPs.

At Tivoli, all four of them got an intense education in the special problems of today's IT groups—the very organizations they would later target with the Waveset solution. "We know these people intimately," says Mark. "We understand their challenges, we're familiar with their budget constraints, and we know how badly they need to open up their IT systems to customers and partners. We're also very aware of the kinds of security and scalability problems that will arise when systems now used by, say, 25,000 internal users suddenly are accessed by twenty-five or thirty million outsiders. Our experience at Tivoli showed us what works and what doesn't work in the smaller environments. That's helping us figure out how to tackle the much more intense problems of large-scale external access."

Similarly, at Tivoli they became intimately aware of the "legacy" systems operating in today's enterprise. These mainframe applications—and other systems from the '70s and '80s—represent such an enormous investment by Fortune 500 companies that "they will, basically, never go away," Mark says. "We know we have to craft a solution that takes these legacy systems into account, or we'll never be accepted. And you can only know this if you've lived and breathed the reality of these companies.

"Essentially," he continues, "we're using our 'old economy' knowledge and experience base and applying it to a 'new economy' situation, attacking the same problems companies have had internally and solving those problems in an Internet age. And we're doing this in ways that make financial sense to our customers."

2. High-growth scar tissue—moving and changing at jet speed.

"Sure," you say, "I've worked in a startup before." Well, many people have by now. That doesn't necessarily mean they all have this characteristic of execution intelligence. Here's the question you have to ask yourself: No matter how hard you worked, no matter how many hours a week you put in, were you *driving* the changes, or riding the waves? If you weren't driving the company, the next question is this: Should you really be starting a new business? Think so? Well, maybe—but at the absolute minimum, realize that you have to bring someone on board who *has* driven growth at a startup company. Otherwise your team will flounder. And believe me, it won't be a pretty sight.

Consider the Waveset team. While he was at Tivoli, Mike Turner helped steer the company from zero revenue to more than $1 billion—all in only eight years' time. The most critical period, he recalls, was when "we shot from about $25 million to a billion-plus within three years."

This kind of growth stresses every system, mental and physical alike, in an organization. You sweat through vicious challenges like reprioritizing the budget overnight. As Tivoli VPs, Mike and Mark acquired plenty of experience meeting that challenge head-on. What's more, they helped build Tivoli's startup team to a workforce of more than 4,000. "Most important," says Mike, "we learned how to communicate to the troops fast—very fast. When IBM came in, we learned just how fast we'd been moving. With them, the sign-offs and approvals for a 'request for announcement' would take longer than it had taken Tivoli to build a whole new product."

The Waveset entrepreneurs refer to their tenure at Tivoli as a "popcorn popper" they lived through: "We were on top of the popcorn," says Kevin Cunningham, "and it stressed our skills and abilities to the max." Waveset is, of course, just at the beginning of this process of incredibly rapid expansion. As it occurs, this team will know how to handle it.

3. Experience in hyper-competitive markets— slaying the dragons.

When it comes to dealing with competition, execution intelligence is not forged from facing any old competitor. You need to have been up against people who wanted to kill you. This is not about the cola wars, where Coca-Cola and Pepsi fight it out over one or two points of share. No. This is about a day-to-day reality of technology start-ups: Eventually, a competitor will come along whose profit in one quarter is bigger than your annual revenue.

How do you know if you can handle that? Check your helmet: Are there dings in it? Do you have scars on your back from the loads you had to carry? And again—were you driving the troops through these competitive battles, or riding along behind?

At Tivoli, the Waveset team got dings in their helmets. At around the same time it was founded in 1989, Tivoli encountered a mammoth competitor in OpenVision. This West Coast startup had $30 million in initial financing (no small potatoes today—but a downright staggering sum at the time). Tivoli, by contrast, had $4 million. OpenVision's senior leadership came from Oracle with "a very impressive management team," recalls Mark McClain, "along with a fierce determination to dominate the same enterprise management market we were going after. They acquired multiple companies in an attempt to build a huge company overnight."

Tivoli was first to market, followed closely by the far-better-financed OpenVision. Throughout, as Mark puts it, Tivoli "stuck to our knitting. We decided to build product from scratch rather than acquiring and integrating pieces. It was a fundamental difference in strategy." The Tivoli strategy was the one that paid off, while Open-Vision faltered. In the process, the future Waveset team acquired valuable insight. "Acquisitions are hard in technology companies," Mark says. "Most of the time, putting companies together takes so much time that nobody who does this ever gets to market."

Later on, a second, even more threatening competitor loomed up. The future Waveset founders received yet another valuable lesson: A worthy opponent can radically accelerate a company's progress. Such was the case when Computer Associates, a behemoth of the computer services industry, decided to enter and capture Tivoli's market space. The indomitable Frank Moss, Tivoli's CEO, "turned our fear of CA into positive energy," recalls Mike Turner. "CA became a force that galvanized the entire company with a fierce will to do battle. We were David, they were Goliath, and we played that to our advantage in the business media and the marketplace. People started seeing us as the good guys who were going to democratize the industry."

It worked. So fired up was Tivoli to beat CA, so motivated was the team to crush this beast, that in short order, they dramatically boosted revenues and expanded the customer base. Mike and his colleagues witnessed Frank Moss turn an intensely feared competitor into an incredibly effective motivation tool. They learned how valuable competition can be for focusing the team around a common goal. It's a lesson that will stand them in good stead when Waveset encounters its own Goliaths.

4. Risk management—rolling with the punches.

From the start, the Waveset team knew they'd have to anticipate market trends. They were also aware that sudden, unexpected shifts can blindside even a well-run company. Where had they learned these things? You guessed it—at Tivoli.

The Tivoli solution was, essentially, a comprehensive "framework." It integrated and tied together all the tools used to oversee individual components—computers, servers, communications tools, network devices, what have you—across a company's network. This, says Kevin Cunningham, was what "caught fire in the marketplace and made the most sense for our customers.

"Then," Kevin continues, "industry analysts suddenly started saying these frameworks were too cumbersome. They said people should just buy 'point' products—solutions for solving specific network problems, however small. This brought on a shift in the market that threatened Tivoli's market share. For a long time, it was difficult to overcome. In the end, we embarked on a strategy that would enable the framework to deliver a greater solution than all the point products together could provide. We believed this would be our salvation in response to a market that had turned Tivoli out of favor."

As I write, the verdict remains out on whether Tivoli's new strategy will enable it to prevail. From Waveset's point of view, what's important is this: The shift taught the team that in a constantly changing, hard-to-read market, "what we believe to be true right now might be totally wrong in three or six months," as Mike Turner puts it. "We look for trends and try to anticipate what might happen. For example, one development we all see coming is that software will be delivered as a service. Nobody knows when this will be pervasive, but we're pretty sure it's coming. So we're building our product so that eventually, it can be offered as a service. We want to make sure we're never in a position where if the market goes someplace fast, we can't adapt."

To that end, the Waveset team is "constantly probing issues around customers' pain," says Mark McClain. In the beginning, the team performed an incredibly thorough market validation, moving several times through the process you'll learn about in the second kick. They discovered (somewhat unexpectedly) that internal customers—people in IT departments—were a higher priority than they'd thought. They also found that the financial services market had the most scorching pain—hence the greatest need for Waveset's solution. Once they had targeted this market, they began to "insist that everybody in the company talk to prospects and customers every day," says Mark. "It's hard, and it's time-consuming, but this daily contact is the only way to anticipate market forces and stay aware of what our customers really need." It is precisely this discipline that will enable *your* company to manage the inevitable risks of a rapidly changing marketplace. Remember: In business, nimbleness is all. The business you build will never end up being the one you started.

5. Experience profile—all the required capabilities.

Marketing know-how. Product development expertise. Sales leadership. If you're thinking about a startup, you'll need all of these in abundance. Consider Waveset. CEO Mike Turner had managed the huge Enterprise Business Unit at Tivoli. Mark McClain, Waveset's president, had headed up Tivoli's Worldwide Marketing group. Kevin Cunningham and Bill Kennedy had served at Tivoli as directors of product marketing and product development, respectively, enabling them to step into VP of marketing and VP of development roles at Waveset. Besides their tenures at Tivoli, all four had held a wide variety of marketing, development, and executive roles at other fast-growth companies. Between them, in fact, they had close to seventy years of experience in the software industry.

Within a few months of founding Waveset, the co-founders recruited Mary Morgan to head up sales. Mary was an experienced sales executive with a solid management background at BMC Software, a Houston-based enterprise management powerhouse, and at other companies. Not only did she round out the team, but because she was not from Tivoli, she added a fresh perspective—along with a substantial additional network of contacts and prospects.

The Waveset team also did something else that is crucial for any startup: They signed on key advisors whose experience supplemented their own. "We'd been through the wringer, we knew what the risks were, and we were experienced with leading organizations," says Mark McClain. "But we also knew we hadn't built a successful company from scratch. That's where our advisors would come in."

The Waveset team recruited Bill Wood and John Thornton, both highly experienced venture investors with strong track records leading startup companies. "They bring incredible value," says Mark. "They'll say things like, 'I've seen this before,' and know how to steer us through a particular situation. They provide an added measure of the experience we need to succeed."

6. Leadership know-how—building and keeping a strong corps of employees.

Waveset perfectly illustrates how valuable a startup's leaders are for recruiting and retaining new employees. "Other companies have a lot of infighting," says Mike Turner. "We have incredible loyalty to each other, loyalty that comes from our experiences working together for so long. That lets us focus on outside issues, not on internal empire-building. People see that when they come here to interview."

As a result, Waveset has "yet to spend a dime on recruiting." Not only that, but with a strong focus on culture and company values, they have managed to retain all their employees (a bit of a rarity hereabouts). "We spent as much time on culture and values in the first two or three months as on anything else," Mike says. "As a result, we encourage innovation, stress integrity, and reward employees when they reach key milestones. Our people know what the goals are, and we give them whatever they need to succeed in reaching those goals."

Which is yet another clear example of the execution intelligence of this killer team.

If you're just getting started, it's doubtful your team will possess Waveset's abundance of execution intelligence. The good news? You can develop it. How? Home in on a business concept that uses your market understanding and past experience. Do what you can to anticipate and plan for the inevitable risks—including competitive risks. Hire managers whose expertise supplements your own. Then recruit experienced executives and advisors who bring even more know-how to the table. Finally, do whatever it takes to build and retain a great team.

*

Let's assume you have a viable business proposition. Let's imagine you've assembled a team with execution intelligence. Then what? Time to take a look at something else: the market. Your single most critical task as a startup is market validation. To find out how to proceed, get ready for your second kick . . .

FIRST KICK: TAKEAWAYS

✳ Have a good idea? Big deal—good ideas are everywhere.

Ideas are commodities. It's *execution intelligence*—not a unique idea—that ignites a successful business.

✳ First to market? So what?

The "first mover advantage" is way overrated. If it's all you've got, the advantage is not sustainable.

✳ Yes, Virginia, there *is* a competitor. Probably more than one.

If you haven't identified the competition, that means you haven't analyzed the market adequately. Either that, or the solution isn't that great to start with.

✳ What's a viable business proposition (as opposed to "a great idea")?

- Represents a new approach to existing business processes.
- Has real, existing corollaries in the marketplace today.
- Has a primary market that can produce $1 billion-plus of revenue.
- Has equally large ancillary markets to sustain growth over time.
- Is undertaken by a team possessing execution intelligence in the space.

✳ Execution intelligence—what is it, anyway?

- *Domain knowledge.* Experience in the market space equals special insight into customers' unique problems.
- *Fast-growth scar tissue.* Growth is hard. The more you've experienced it, the more effective you'll be.
- *Experience in hyper-competitive markets.* Appreciate the competition. Know how to handle it.
- *Risk management.* Those who can anticipate market trends can adapt more easily to market changes.

- *Comprehensive experience profile.* Marketing. Sales. Product development. You need those skills in spades. You also need solid advisors.

- *Leadership know-how.* Who can hire, motivate, and retain strong employees? Great leaders.

✳ How many startup teams have execution intelligence?

Not many—not at first, anyway. But they can acquire it. That's why this is so important: *Keep execution intelligence in mind when you build the management team and bring on advisors and board members.*

YOU DON'T KNOW YOUR CUSTOMER AS WELL AS YOU THINK YOU DO

It was 11:30 at night. I'd been working since 4 P.M. with several team members of the startup company Ineto, helping them with a cornerstone early-stage activity: market validation. They'd been at it since that morning, hunched around a fluorescent-lit conference table in their tiny office suite. The table was strewn with papers—charts and graphs, scribbled notes, questionnaires. As stark evidence of a marathon brainstorming session, the cramped room's two trash bins overflowed with fast-food wrappers. The wall-sized whiteboard was filled with so much colored ink that it resembled some bizarre postmodernist painting.

I looked across the table at Mike Betzer, the thirty-nine-year-old Iowan who'd left a secure, cushy job as MCI's VP of information technology to start Ineto. I wondered if he might be regretting that decision right about now. I also figured he wanted to kill me. Fatigue and frustration etched Mike's normally good-natured face. I was the guy who had put him and his team through all this. And right now, for Mike, this whole market validation thing just wasn't making much sense.

Most entrepreneurs want to build it *now.* Don't. Validate the market first.

I can't tell you how many entrepreneurs I've seen fight tooth and nail for that last nickel of valuation, then go out and totally screw up their first product. How? By building the product without first validating the market. Listen up. There is no better way to get your product wrong. And if you get the product wrong, you're dead. At the very least, you're forced to go back to your investors for more money. When you do, you lose the valuation you fought so hard for. *Nothing dilutes a founding team's share more viciously than hitting the market with the wrong product.*

Instead, here's what you need to do: Use that critical first batch of dollars to validate the market, *then* put the engineers to work. That way, the product is what customers actually want. How do you know? Because you asked them.

Mike Betzer proved this to himself, as you're about to see. When Mike started the validation process, he flat-out resented it. By the time it was done, he'd become its biggest advocate. Now, any time I have entrepreneurs who get all glum when they learn they have to do market validation, I send them straight to Mike. He convinces them fast: "Build it now" is a lousy notion. Before you build it, *validate the market.*

Let's walk through how Mike got there. When I met him three months before that night in the conference room, he was champing at the bit to start building the Ineto offering—a Web-based service that would give companies better ways to manage and streamline their customer interactions. Did I blame Mike for his sense of urgency? Not at all. In fact, I understood it. Mike knew there were real, documented needs in the marketplace. A then-recent Gartner Group report said companies badly wanted to integrate e-mail, chat, and other customer communication channels with voice. Why? Because online customers demanded the same level of service they were accustomed to in the offline world. Customers wanted convenient ways to contact companies via phone, e-mail, or the Web. And they expected their requests to be answered quickly, by a knowledgeable representative.

Mike knew that for many mid-sized companies, providing this service in-house would be downright impossible. They simply couldn't afford the complex hardware and software systems involved, nor the extensive integration efforts. They needed a service like Ineto's. With Ineto, companies could route and prioritize customer requests across telephone, e-mail, and Internet channels. They could also connect customers with the right representatives, quickly and easily.

Mike had pioneered a similar solution for internal use at MCI. There, he'd spent thirteen years forging a reputation as the resident guru of customer communications. Ineto's other two co-founders, Mike's MCI colleagues Alasdhair Campbell and Stephen Michael, had years of experience in telecommunications and telephony. Based on their MCI experience, the Ineto team knew they could create a subscription-based solution many different companies could use. They could give companies far more sophisticated customer communication capabilities than they could ever afford on their own. Several investment funds were intrigued. Plus, Mike had lined up four killer engineers who were raring to start coding.

So what did Mike want to do? You got it. Race on ahead: Create the solution fast, sign up what he predicted would be hordes of business customers, IPO quickly, run a thriving company.

Sounds pretty good, right? Wrong.

Whoa. Stop right there.

Mike had fallen for a very common illusion: *I know my customer.* After all, thirteen years at MCI had prepared him for this startup venture. He *was sure he knew* what companies needed, and he knew how to provide it. The last thing he wanted to do was spend time validating what he already knew. He was annoyed. Until, that is, that night in the conference room. That night, the chaotic mound of raw research data assumed a recognizable pattern—finally.

For Ineto, this was the "Aha!" moment. Suddenly it was clear: Of all the customers the team had interviewed, of all the companies they had researched, those with the reddest-hot pain—those who needed Ineto the most—tended to have three major characteristics. I erased the whiteboard and wrote these characteristics down:

1. *Technology companies* had articulated the worst pain.
2. These companies tended to be *smaller,* with less than $500 million in revenues.
3. When it came to customer interaction, *growth rate* was the (until then, missing) factor that correlated most strongly with the first two characteristics.

The first two criteria were no big surprise; vertical markets and company size tend to delineate many target markets. The third determinant, though, was unexpected. *And it never could have been found without all that frustrating market validation work.*

"That's it," Mike said. His face changed, excitement replacing the worry and exhaustion. For the first time, he grasped the value of what the team had been doing. For the first time, he understood Ineto's true market: high-growth technology companies that were struggling with their growth and unsure about future growth patterns. These businesses' customer communications were expanding exponentially. To manage the process efficiently, they fiercely needed subscription services like Ineto's. *Now the Ineto team had a real sense of their customer—for the first time.*

For Ineto, this moment marked the end of Stage 1 in the three-stage acceleration process that AV Labs prescribes for market validation. The process features actual, person-to-person interviews with (typically) a hundred or more customers and market influencers. In a moment, we will explore it in detail. But first, a glimpse into what makes market validation so frustrating for so many startups. What makes entrepreneurs believe they can dispense with the process? And why is "I know my customer" such a dangerous fantasy?

Where does "I know my customer" come from?

Human nature, for one thing. We all tend to extrapolate big truths from a few data points. In Mike's case, he was assuming that because a customer communication service had been a big hit internally at MCI, it would be lapped up by thousands of other businesses. Plus, funding groups had been extremely positive. He'd even gotten a nod from former executives at MCI, two or three of whom were considering investing in the new venture. Colleagues and friends were equally enthusiastic. Surely, he figured, businesses would soon be all over the Ineto service.

Experience and feedback aren't the only factors that might tempt you away from market validation. All too often, so might an abundance of cool green cash. Even today, after multiple market corrections, you can raise money. No wonder you might want to take the money and run. After all, it's pretty dull spending months on market validation when you have millions in the bank. Competition is fierce. Getting to market is a must-do. So you might be overwhelmed with a desire to hit it hard and run like hell.

If you forgo market validation, though, you'll be adopting the "ready, fire, aim" approach to building a business. And you'll pay— the hard way.

"Ready, fire, aim": the money pit for startups.

Ineto's funding was contingent on early customer validation, so they really didn't have a choice but to do this work. Most entrepreneurs *do* have a choice. If you're like a lot of them, here's how you might proceed:

- Use your capital to build a team, rent office space, and get to work on product design and marketing.
- $10 million (in very round numbers!) later, try to go to market with the solution you've built.
- Because the product doesn't really fit the market, take the feedback from some subset of dissatisfied customers, then go back and build it again.
- Another $10 million or so—and another year or two—down the road, finally get it right. Maybe.

Clearly, the "ready, fire, aim" approach does not work. Take it, and you delay delivering a product customers really want. You risk losing early customers while you try to "get it right." You jeopardize the company's reputation and credibility. Worst of all, you throw a lot of money right down the toilet: When you have to go back to investors again and again, they end up owning more and more of the company. Eventually, you risk losing the business altogether.

I've already said this, but it's worth repeating: *"Ready, fire, aim" is the single biggest source of dilution for early-stage companies.* What *really* preserves equity is to get the product right the first time.

How? By conducting rigorous up-front validation that gives you insight into customers and their needs. This is the key startup activity we require at AV Labs. It is also the primary reason our startup companies go on to receive substantial subsequent financing, establish excellent boards of directors, recruit great teams, and achieve a strong early impact in their targeted markets. You can create similar results for your own company—but only if you take the time to validate the market.

Validating the market: Ready, aim, fire.

If startup entrepreneurs have one thing in common, it's this: They think the business plan is the be-all and end-all for getting funded. One of our later kicks will delve into this fallacy in greater detail. For now, suffice it to say that *once the market has been validated, most of the business plan writes itself.*

This is just one reason it's so important to thoroughly validate the market as your absolute first order of business. Before writing the business plan. Before filling out a team. Before going after major funding. *Definitely* before designing a product.

What does complete market validation cost? Done right, three months of time. This is a *minuscule* investment compared with spending millions of dollars and a year or more to build a product without a real market. Consider, too, these benefits:

- *You get the product right the first time.* As the product rolls out, you have a much better chance of hitting the right customers with the right features. Compared with products built without market validation, yours will be close to version 2 or 3—except it's the very first release.
- *A beta community emerges.* Many AV Labs startups recruit their first group of beta customers during market validation. These customers become indispensable for helping the companies design solutions that will meet the market's actual needs.
- *You identify a wide potential customer community.* Sales has a ready-made contact list for targeting prospects. You know who has the sharpest need for the product. You also know which markets are likely to produce additional customers.
- *You can more easily raise "smart" investment capital.* Mike Betzer says it best: "I wanted first-rate investors who would add value on our board. The knowledge we'd gained from market validation made it easy to line these guys up; when

they had an issue, I could draw from actual customer feedback and experience. They were impressed."

- *You use capital more efficiently.* No-brainer time: Isn't it more efficient to spend less than $1 million *(much* less, usually) validating the market up front, than to validate it product release by product release, to the tune of up to $10 million per release?
- *You clarify your competition.* Market validation makes formal competitive analysis easier by orders of magnitude. Customers will *tell* you who the competition is: What, if anything, already addresses the problem? How do these solutions fail? Who else is working on it? How are customers currently piecing together a semi-solution themselves?

Market validation à la AV Labs.

What's the goal of market validation? Simple—to find the initial target market. If you're a typical first-time entrepreneur, you might not even be clear about what "target market" means. You may envision the market as "everyone I can think of," Fortune 500 companies and startups alike. After all, if you have a great solution to a thorny problem, who *doesn't* need it?

Here, though, is the rub: *A company cannot sell to everybody.* Not for many, many years—and never, unless the product is a commodity like paper clips or PCs. Certainly, no technology startup can target "everybody." Not if it hopes to proceed with any focus or success.

What, then, is a target market? *A target market is a limited, discrete subset of companies or individuals whose pain is so great without the product that they will readily buy it.* For them, the proposed solution is an absolute "must-have." Once you have identified these customers, you can use their feedback and input to design a product that will *sell.*

At AV Labs, our companies validate the market using three stages of analysis. I refer to these stages, collectively, as the *Pyramid of Influence.* Entrepreneurs set forth to ascend the pyramid only after they've laid critical groundwork using secondary research.

Figure 1 illustrates the process.

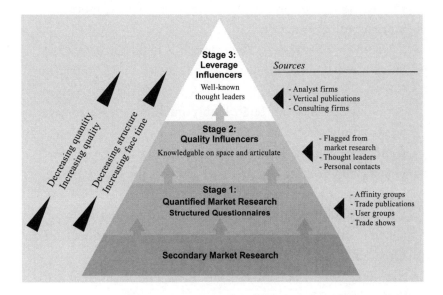

Figure 1. Market validation: the Pyramid of Influence

As the figure suggests, key validation activities include:

- *Identifying research contacts.* At each successive stage, you identify contacts by drawing both from results so far and from outside sources. Take Ineto, for instance. Secondary research showed the team that the transportation, communication, manufacturing, technology, financial services, insurance, retail trade, and wholesale trade industries might need the Ineto service. Ineto targeted these industries in Stage 1.
- *Obtaining progressively more useful research.* As you climb the pyramid, the team contacts fewer and fewer individuals. At the same time, you obtain information that's richer and

more informative. A Stage 2 *quality influencer,* for example, provides data that is five times more valuable than a single Stage 1 interview. By the time Ineto reached Stage 2, the team had discovered that high-growth companies in manufacturing, technology, and finance needed the product most acutely; narrowing the research to these contacts yielded more and more useful information.

- *Structuring the research.* The research is highly structured in Stage 1, which relies primarily on quantitative questionnaires for the data points. By the time you reach the top, you're obtaining feedback through highly qualitative, face-to-face presentations and relationships.
- *Contacting hundreds of people.* Depending on the market, you usually contact hundreds of individuals. For example, Cody Menard—co-founder of Covasoft, which provides an e-business transaction management solution—and his team talked to more than 300 people during market validation. (The fifth kick describes Covasoft in depth.)
- *Repeating the levels.* Finally, and most important, *it is not unusual for a team to start over several times before completing the process.* If Stage 2 research disproves all the initial hypotheses, for example, the entire pyramid must be scaled anew—starting with secondary market research. WebQA, an AV Labs company, started over three times. In the end, WebQA found that its idea simply didn't pan out in the market—a discovery that cost the team a fraction of what they would have spent to discover the same thing *without* market validation.

Lay the groundwork with secondary research: Is the idea viable?

Before AV Labs seed-funds a startup, a team must prove it has found substantial pain around a particular problem. Not only that, it also has to prove there's a likely market for a proposed solution (although at this point, no one knows what the precise market will be). How can this be accomplished? Through high-level *secondary research*— research covering market sizing, the direction of market trends, growth of these markets, and other outside, objective indicators of how large the opportunity is.

As we have seen, Mike Betzer had ample opportunity to perform secondary research while pioneering the call center solution within MCI. Tactics like these are also useful:

- Research competitors and potential customers using the Internet.
- Read the industry press, including such periodicals as *Information Week* and *Red Herring,* for a sense of current business and technology trends. It's also useful to read vertically focused periodicals in the specific industry being targeted. Both Mike Betzer and Covasoft's Cody Menard found *Computerworld,* with its emphasis on information technology issues, helpful; Mike also consulted *Call Center Magazine.*
- Acquire reports from respected analyst groups, such as Forrester Research, Gartner Group, Giga, International Data Corporation (IDC), Meta Group, and others.

Remember: *This high-level secondary research does not qualify as market validation.* It merely sets the stage for your much more concentrated primary research effort. If you're smart, you won't even *think* about building a product after secondary research alone—even if you can find investors willing to dole out the bucks at this point. By now you know it's a sure-fire way to suck yourself into the quicksand of "ready, fire, aim." Take the secondary research merely as a starting point. Then continue on with . . .

Market validation Stage 1: Explore the pain.

Here you perform quantifiable market research to discover your customers' pain. This involves progressing through these steps, explored in the following sections:

1. Construct hypotheses about the prospective market.
2. Gather data to prove or disprove your hypotheses.
3. Isolate the most searing pain points, using what I call the "heat map."

Develop hypotheses: Where's the market?

Kick off the process with at least three hypotheses that address these critical questions: Who needs the product most? What does this market look like? The Ineto team started here:

- The product is critical for companies growing at 50% a year or faster; ten to twenty people communicate with customers.
- Distributed call centers totaling more than 100 people in Fortune 500 companies have the greatest need for the product.
- Need is most acute in high-growth companies having at least $10 million in Internet-based transactions a year.

As you can see, well-formulated market hypotheses are specific. They home in on characteristics like company size, growth rate, sales models, and so on. During market validation, you test each of them against actual data culled from the market.

Important point: *A hypothesis almost never holds up.* Growth, for instance, might not turn out to be a key factor, while number of people communicating with customers might be. Moreover—and inevitably—your research will yield market features you haven't even thought of yet. As Peter Simon, head of the Boston-based consulting firm Simon Management, puts it, "You know you're getting close to the right answer when you've radically modified where you started."

Gather data: What's the pain?

For your company to fly, you have to uncover customer pain that is absolutely tormenting. Ross Garber, co-founder of Vignette Corporation, often suggests asking this: Is the company selling aspirin, or is it selling vitamins? Is the proposed solution a must-have, like aspirin? Or is it simply something people would *like* to have, like vitamins? As someone who sparked a successful startup to help businesses build and manage their Internet sites, Ross knows that to have a valid market, the answer *has* to be aspirin. That is what you seek to discover during Stage 1. Here, you interview the target market to find out exactly where the greatest pain is. *Who has the worst headache?* Why? Exactly what solution will make these people's lives easier?

Here's how you can find out: by interviewing at least 100 potential customers, using a questionnaire that enables you to quantify the results. Your goal at this stage is not to present the proposed solution but *to understand these customers and develop a sense of their pain.* Indeed, it is vital that your team not even mention the solution at this stage of the game. All you want is for the customers to tell you about their pain.

Ineto discovered two critical things in the Stage 1 interviews:

- *For some customers, the product would be a vitamin.* These well-established firms had stable growth curves and steady year-round customer interaction volume. They didn't express much pain around their current customer communication methods.
- *For others, the product would be aspirin.* This is the "Aha!" moment I described in the beginning of this chapter—the scalding pain of high-growth companies. For them, the Ineto product would address a distinct pain: the expense of integrating products, combined with unpredictable or seasonal fluctuations in customer interaction volume. Some of the companies reporting this pain were big online retailers, who tend to have exponential growth and increased holiday season interactions.

Typically, you obtain your Stage 1 interview contacts via mailing lists from industry trade magazines or trade groups. Interviewees should include the full spectrum of people who may come in contact with your product—those who will use it, buy it, recommend it, pay for it, technically review it, and so on. All these groups have requirements. Your task? Find out what those requirements are.

Make everyone do the work—including you.

It's way too easy for an entrepreneur to get smug when that big check clears. "Hmm," you'll be tempted to think, "I can hire a couple of people to do this. Either that or assign one or two of my (least favorite) team members." To that, I say: Don't even think about it. *You* have to do this work, *right along with everybody on your team.*

I reiterate: That's *everybody*—from founder to receptionist, engineers to marketers. At AV Labs, we require that the team itself conduct at least half of the interviews personally. All day every day, for weeks on end, the entire company talks on the telephone with potential customers. As they do, three fundamentally amazing things start to happen:

- *Engineers develop a customer-focused perspective.* First of all, they realize how hard it is to get through to people in the first place, much less find people who want the product. They quickly forsake the "if you build it, they will come" mind-set when they discover it takes ten phone calls for every single interview they actually get to conduct. Mike Betzer says the engineers on his team were "shocked when it sometimes took two full days on the phone to obtain one interview." Imagine, then, what it takes to get people to shell out money to buy a product. Most important, the engineers begin to connect on a gut level with how the product might affect people's day-to-day lives, giving them a customer-centered point of view that engineers tend to lack otherwise. (Which is not to say engineers enjoy this process; if you want to see them get a quick anxiety attack, tell them they have to get on the phone and do customer interviews.)

- *Everyone learns about the sales process.* This exercise reveals how harrowing and tedious sales can be. Say, for example, that the product relates to human resources; if you say you want to talk to somebody in HR, your initial contact will say, more often than not, "Who in HR?" You may be astonished by the sheer complexity of finding the right person. You will definitely develop a newfound appreciation for the difficulty of making a sale.

- *The team becomes evangelically focused on the customer.* Because everyone participates in the research effort, each team member begins to connect with customers in a new and powerful way. They learn more about customer environments than they'd ever imagined. This connection deepens over time as the company culture becomes ever more customer-oriented. Mike Betzer has expressed amazement, for example, that his engineers now ask for solid market data when he requests feature changes.

Use professionals to keep the data valid.

At AV Labs, we normally require teams to use a professional market research firm to help with Stage 1 market validation. These consultants provide several critical services. They help construct the questionnaire and sift the raw data. They also conduct the other half of the interviews (with the team conducting half). Throughout, they work closely with the team. An example of this type of firm is Simon Management, which has helped usher several AV Labs companies through this process.

Why should you collaborate with outside professionals on this vital effort? Because a research firm is objective—and your team, inevitably, is *not.* Human nature being what it is, the team will always be inclined to plant ideas. While you intensely *need* to know the truth at this point, you often *don't want* to know. Who wants to hear it, for example, when a customer says they're really not bothered by a problem? Unlike you, an objective outside consultant is trained simply to report what the data indicates.

What's more, this collaboration helps make your team itself more objective. Time and time again, I have watched as professional market researchers put the brakes on two particularly unproductive interview tactics:

- *Leading the witness.* You may be inclined to ask questions in such a way that you're more likely to get the answers you want. You might start questions with "Don't you hate when . . ." or "Wouldn't you like it better if . . ."—lead-ins guaranteed to elicit responses that are not objective.
- *Selling the solution.* Again, you *must not* talk to customers about the solution at this stage. You are after one thing, and one thing only: a clear view of customer experiences and environments, requirements for performing a particular task, and the source of customers' most biting pain.

Not only will research professionals help ensure that your team asks questions correctly and objectively, but—not surprisingly—the team itself will often get into the act. Once, Mike Betzer got ribbed by his team for trying to sell the product during a Stage 1 interview. They told him he was "off-survey" and made him drop that interview from his compiled data.

Says Mike himself of the Ineto team's experience with the consultants, "They kept us honest. Because they forced us to approach the interviews objectively, we found out a lot of our assumptions just weren't valid from the customer's perspective. Ineto finished the interviews committed to only building what the customers said they needed. We couldn't have gotten there without the outside expertise."

The heat map: Where is the most excruciating pain?

As the final exercise in Stage 1, your team constructs what we call the *heat map*. This graphic representation is indispensable for helping you zero in on the target market, locating the market within a combination of three variables. Ineto's Stage 1 heat map is shown in Figure 2.

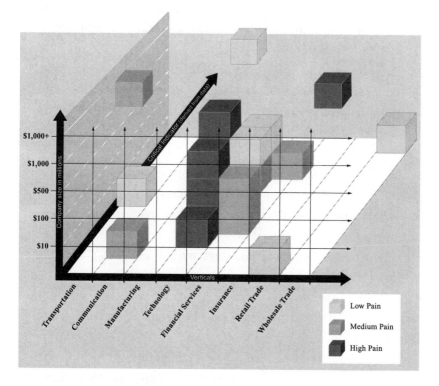

Figure 2. The heat map: finding the market's hot spots.

By literally drawing this Rubik's-cube graphic, you're able to visually represent the precise location in the market of the greatest pain. This gives you a more focused target market, which is the basis for further exploration in Stage 2.

Note these characteristics of the heat map:

- The horizontal axis represents some major aspect of the hypothetical market. Here, we see the prospective vertical markets
researched by the Ineto team.
- The vertical axis indicates another major feature of the market—in this case, company size, which dramatically affected
customers' desire for the Ineto solution.
- The depth (diagonal) axis represents some critical indicator
derived from the raw data. This was the breakthrough for
Ineto, which discovered that its critical market determinant—
and major differentiator—was growth rate.
- Color (or, in this case, shading) indicates the degree of pain
intensity as cubes are drawn along the three axes. This gave
Ineto the precise markets it needed to approach in subsequent
validation stages.

As Figure 2 shows, Ineto's "hot spots" centered, primarily,
around high-growth technology companies with revenues of $500
million or less. Financial services companies experienced some pain,
but not as much. Because they expressed the most blistering pain,
high-growth technology companies would be Ineto's first target
market. Financial services, with somewhat less pain but with a strong
need for the solution, would serve as a good *ancillary* market. Iso-
lated clusters of pain in the heat map highlight other ancillary markets.

To construct the heat map, you take the raw data from the Stage
1 interviews, beat your head against the wall, and tease out which set
of axes yield the reddest-hot clumps of pain. Here's where the
research professionals can come in extremely handy, though even
with them, it can take many days, sometimes even weeks. But—as
the Ineto team discovered that night in the conference room—the
result is a "Eureka!" moment. Suddenly, everything falls into place.
You have succeeded in clarifying a possible target market.

"Without this process," says Mike, "we would have missed the fact that high growth was the critical determinant of need. We would have gone after mainly big, established corporations instead—and we wouldn't have been nearly as successful." As an added bonus, the high-growth companies were similar to Ineto itself; finding them enabled the company to start building a very compatible customer community.

Once you have clarified your target market, your team proceeds to Stage 2.

Market validation Stage 2: Envision the solution.

As you embark upon this stage, your team has narrowed your hypotheses down to one. Stage 2 is more qualitative than Stage 1. It involves some face-to-face meetings. Your objective? To test the hypothesis against a set of *quality influencers.* Stage 2 contacts are pragmatic and articulate. Most important, they either experience the pain firsthand, or they understand that pain.

Who are the Stage 2 quality influencers? Most are people who, in their Stage 1 interviews, expressed especially distressing pain, a high degree of interest in a possible solution, and a willingness to be contacted again. In Ineto's case, quality influencers tended to be senior managers of customer support and sales. These contacts were unsure how much growth they would be experiencing in twelve to twenty-four months. The Ineto service made sense: It could save them significant time and money, while also enabling them to improve customer satisfaction.

You can consult the heat map's "hot spots" to identify additional customer contacts. You might be amazed by what happens. Even when you call "hot spot" contacts you haven't spoken to before, they may want a solution so desperately that they'll ask for a demo— right now. I've seen this happen many times. Speakers, writers, analysts, and other thought leaders within the market space make good Stage 2 candidates as well.

Conventional wisdom might suggest that so-called "early adopters," or people with a particular yen for bleeding-edge technology, might be the best contacts for Stage 2 research. In our experience, this is not the case. What *is* most important? That the customers interviewed have experience with the pain and the ability to articulate it.

Blanket the quality influencers.
To prepare for interviewing your Stage 2 contacts, take the market data from Stage 1. Then, using what you've learned, create:

- *A first-pass presentation.* The presentation outlines the pain you will address, the market segment with the most biting pain, and—at a very high level—how your solution can solve this pain. In Mike Betzer's presentation, for example, he described the high-growth company's inherent inability to accurately predict growth with respect to customer interactions. He also showed how Ineto would align its pay-per-use service with these companies' business models.
- *A prototype of the solution.* Screens illustrate the user experience and provide a high-level demo of basic functionality. Covasoft cobbled together an even more detailed Stage 2 prototype in response to anxious requests by prospective customers.

In Stage 2, your team hits every one of the pre-identified quality influencers with the presentation and prototype. All the while, you carefully record their feedback. Be prepared: Initially, the influencers will inevitably respond less than favorably to all or part of your proposal. What does that mean? Simply that your team must go back, tweak to reflect the feedback, and iterate through the process again. Because 85% of the Ineto customers had cared only about voice interactions, Mike's initial presentation focused much more on voice than on e-mail, chat, and other electronic interactions. In response to feedback from Stage 2 thought leaders, he pumped up the volume on the non-voice side of things. The object is to achieve consensus among *all* the influencers—customers and thought leaders alike— that a proposed solution addresses the market's pain.

Result: a laser-sharp customer focus.
Stage 2 results are absolutely indispensable, in three key respects:

- *Product features.* You may be surprised by Stage 2 product-related results. If you're typical, you have considered solving the pain as a baseline—*of course* your product will do *that.* What you may not realize is this: when customers are tormented by their pain, a simple, quick solution is *all* they want. They're not really interested in bells and whistles. Mike, for example, was "anxious to nail the features that would make the service years ahead of its competition." What he discovered in Stage 2 was that in Ineto's case, customers wanted "calls and e-mails to be delivered to the customer-care agents—no fuss, no frills, just deliver it." You'll discover what Mike did: People don't need a 747 to go to the grocery store.
- *Core customers.* The customers whom Cody Menard and the Covasoft team interviewed in Stage 2 morphed into beta sites for testing the first Covasoft release. The Ineto team built the company's Customer Advisory Board, a group of customers nationwide who agreed to provide input on product directions through several Ineto releases. The key thing to remember is this: The quality influencers of Stage 2 tend to stick with your startup. They will act as partners who help keep you close to the customer as the years go by.
- *A fine-tuned presentation and prototype.* Stage 2 feedback enables your team to sharpen these critical artifacts to the point where, when the "heavy hitters" of Stage 3 are approached, these leverage influencers quickly understand

what you are doing—and are more than willing to lend their stamp of approval.

Which brings us to the third and final stage of the process.

Market validation Stage 3: Establish credibility.

By the time a startup enters Stage 3, it is about 90% "there" in terms of being ready to set sail as a viable venture. You use Stage 3 to forge that final 10%. Here, your team creates a base of influence for building credibility.

Who are the leverage influencers contacted—most often, face to face—in Stage 3? Some will be the thought leaders interviewed in Stage 2. Others will be representatives of well-known analyst firms, such as Aberdeen Group, Forrester Research, Gartner Group, Giga, IDC, and Meta Group, who work in the market space. Still others will be editors of vertical publications that sell into the market. Others will be consulting firms such as Accenture, EDS, KPMG, or Pricewaterhouse Coopers, whose clients may be in a position to implement the proposed solution.

As you visit these people with your fine-tuned company presentation and solution prototype, here's what you aim to do: *Get them excited.* Excited about your company, about the product, and about your startup's prospects. Believe me, they will have plenty of feedback, some positive and some not so positive. As you receive this feedback, you continue to hone the presentation until it expresses your solution's advantages with absolute clarity and conviction.

Again, the process can take several iterations. But it is well worth it, for three key reasons:

- *Visibility in analyst reports and publications.* Industry analysts get paid to spot new trends and promising companies. They're more than happy to spread the word about any new company whose vision (and knowledge of the market) impresses them.

AMAZON.COM: "CUSTOMER-DRIVEN" TO THE *N*TH DEGREE.

When it comes to market validation—repeated, ongoing market validation—Amazon is as good as it gets. Since its launch in 1995, Amazon has taken "getting to know the customer" to a new level. They've made a science of it. In the process, this company has helped ignite the e-commerce revolution and redefined retail.

Amazon got its start when founder and CEO Jeff Bezos, who previously managed a hedge fund for D.E. Shaw in New York, recognized a tremendous opportunity in Internet retailing. He also recognized the importance of understanding the customer. According to Bezos, "70 percent of an online company's resources should fuel the customer experience, while the remaining 30 percent should be used to communicate the benefits of the customer experience."[4]

Bezos knew the Internet was too slow. The Internet was such a pain to use, in fact, that Amazon would have to deliver overwhelming value to compensate customers for the wait. This helps explain why, from the time Amazon was launched, it has dedicated itself to uncovering and addressing *customers' pain*. As a result, Amazon is recognized as being responsible for many of the innovative aspects of online shopping that are now taken for granted by Internet retailers—among them one-click shopping, product recommendations, personalized site greetings, and customer-tracking systems.

What sets Amazon apart? Its ability to come up with novel ways to deal with customers and leapfrog the competition. How? Accord-

---

4. Dennis Bloomquist, "Caring for E-Customers," *Business Finance,* July 2000.

ing to Bezos, "We ask customers what they want." The company encourages e-mail feedback. It sorts through purchase histories to learn customer preferences. It conducts live focus groups. It acquires companies that own valuable customer data. Most important, it tries to collect information in ways that avoid imposing on customers.

Amazon uses the data it collects to personalize buyers' online experience. The site recommends books based on a customer's previous purchases. It also greets customers by name and maintains a "wish list" of desired products and services that others can refer to for gift-giving. From the get-go, Amazon has listened to customer feedback and modified the site to better meet customer needs. Over the years, it has implemented a variety of features to enhance the customer experience: easy-to-use browsing, interactive searchable product catalogs, editorial and customer reviews, one-click ordering, secure credit-card payment, remote access, timely order fulfillment, and a fair return policy.

Amazon articulated this customer-centric focus in a recent annual report: "We believe that our ability to establish and maintain long-term relationships with our customers and to encourage repeat visits and purchases depends, in part, on the strength of our customer service operations. We seek to achieve frequent communication with and feedback from our customers to continually improve the Amazon.com experience."

All this helps explain why Amazon.com is not losing customers to its competitors. In fact, according to Bezos, more than 60% of Amazon's sales are repeat business.[5] With Amazon as good as it is, why would customers bother to sign up elsewhere? It is Amazon's constant focus on customers that has enabled the company to revolutionize the way retail sales are conducted using the Internet.

---

5. Eryn Brown, "7 Selling to Customers," *Fortune*, May 1999.

So are the editors of publications. Early in its life, Ineto was named one of *Red Herring*'s "Top Ten to Watch" for 2001. When Mike went to *Red Herring*, he took as fodder the analyst validations he had obtained in Stage 3.

- *Revenue possibilities.* Consulting firms love to introduce new technology solutions that make a real difference in their client environments. They also like to be first on the trigger with this.

- *Easier financing.* You can incorporate positive analyst feedback into the presentation you use to obtain major financing from top-tier investors. When it comes to raising money, a well-placed, positive quote from a well-known analyst gives you an enormous advantage. Witness Lane15, an AV Labs company that is building software to manage the new Infini-Band computer network environment. During market validation, Lane15 received positive mentions from analyst firms Aberdeen and IDC, both of which validated the market pain and the benefit of Lane15's products. These analyst validations figured into Austin Ventures' decision to invest in the company. (You'll learn more about Lane15 in the sixth kick.)

Indeed, by the end of Stage 3, you will be thoroughly prepared to confront even the most rigorous investors. Your company's case is no longer hypothetical—it is proven. Your market is precisely targeted. Customers are already on board as advocates, partners, and advisors. Major industry influencers are in the loop and excited. And not only is funding now more accessible, but your team can proceed with the confidence that it is addressing the market's actual needs.

Mike, once again, says it best: "The market validation process was more powerful than I expected, from the first customer survey on. At first I thought it was just another hoop I had to jump through. I asked myself, 'Is this for real, or is Rob Adams just always wanting to do this process no matter what?' I found out it's for real. As a result of all this work, we have the right target market for Ineto and a great board of directors. Already, our market valuation is many times what it would have been without the process."

No longer is Mike possessed by the illusion *I know my customer.* In fact, he now knows that despite the work his company has done, despite his deep understanding of Ineto's market space, you can *never* know your customer.

Think you know your customer now? *Not a chance.*

As University of Texas business professor John Doggett likes to say, "Customers are nasty critters." They change daily—particularly in today's fast-moving business environment. True, market validation gives you a clear window into the target market. You also come to understand your customers and their environments. But this is only a snapshot. Believe me: The picture is constantly evolving, along with your customers' ever-changing needs.

That's why it is imperative to develop effective, ongoing strategies for assessing customers and their needs. Otherwise, you lose your edge—and you lose it fast. Mike Betzer knew this. Soon after the Ineto team validated the market, they assembled the Customer Advisory Board. They are committed to staying in constant touch with users of the solution—from beta through all the product releases. From its inception, your company must be similarly committed. You must build a culture that values strong, ongoing relationships with customers.

"The Customer Advisory Board came in frequently prior to our first release," says Mike. "Every time, we updated the research we had started during the Stage 1 interview phase. They had to indicate what they liked and what they didn't like, in great detail. We got to know them, again and again.

"We intend to keep doing this as long as Ineto is a company," he continues. "Our #1 commitment is this: Build what the customers want, and build only what they want."

Building what the customers want. That brings us to our next kick: strategies for creating a product—fast—that addresses customer pain. To discover more about these strategies, turn the page and read on . . .

SECOND KICK: TAKEAWAYS

✴ Think you know your customer? Stop right there.
This is an illusion—and it can be deadly. It leads to . . .

✴ "Ready, fire, aim"—a sure-fire way to bite the dust. Don't go there.
This is what happens when you start a business without validating the market: product delays. Missing the mark with customers. Heavy dilution for founders and investors.

✴ "Ready, aim, fire." It can happen only with market validation.
- The product is right the first time. The right audience gets the right solution.
- A beta community emerges. These customers have red-hot pain and want the solution *now.* They're enthusiastic. They'll help drive the product forward. They'll stick with you.
- A wider potential customer community materializes. These customers need what you've got—and you can go after them.
- It's easier to raise "smart" investment capital. It's also easier to recruit great employees, advisors, and board members. That's because the business has been developed and fine-tuned with a solid foundation in the market.
- Capital is used more efficiently. With the right product the first time, you can dispense with costly rebuilds.
- You know the competition. The customers will tell you all about it.

✴ Ascending the market-validation pyramid, step by step:
What are you looking for? *Pain.* Wicked, brutal, vicious, hideous pain—the pain that makes people want to fix it *now.*

- *Lay the groundwork.* Verify there's pain around the problem you've found, along with a likely market. Use secondary research—the

Internet, analyst reports, the industry press—to discover market data, the market size, and the direction of market trends.

- *Stage 1: Explore the pain.* Use questionnaires to do quantified market research—which uncovers the target market.
  - Generate several hypotheses about target markets.
  - Perform customer interviews to locate the greatest pain.
  - Create a "heat map" that visually represents where the worst pain lies.
- *Stage 2: Envision the solution.* Test the target market (found in Stage 1) against a set of quality influencers. Develop and sharpen a presentation and product prototype.
- *Stage 3: Establish credibility.* Get leverage influencers (thought leaders, analysts, consultants, and editors) excited about your company, product, and prospects.

Think you know your customer *now?* Nope.

All you have is a one-time snapshot. Never stop focusing on the customer! Implement effective, ongoing strategies for assessing customers and their needs. Validate the market again and again. Either that, or lose your edge—the first step to becoming dead meat.

DON'T WAIT TO SHIP A KILLER PRODUCT—GET TO MARKET FAST

When AV Labs got started, we looked like the classic startup. We occupied what we called the "Club House"—less than 1,000 square feet of musty, green-carpeted open space with grasscloth wallpaper that somehow ran horizontally around the room. The Club House was tucked into a ground-floor corner of the old Norwood Towers office building in downtown Austin. I remember staring out the window one misty fall afternoon, late in the day, while Phil Siegel and I put the finishing touches on our strategy for an impending conference call.

Phil was a Venture Fellow at the Labs. He'd been working pretty much nonstop for the past three months, and he had black circles under his eyes to prove it. Now we were about to find out if all that hard work was going to pay off. We were calling Phil's contact at R.R. Donnelley & Sons—the giant catalog printing and shipping company—to sell them on a partnership with Phil's startup, Newgistics. As Phil dialed the number and pressed the telephone speaker button, my heart skipped a beat. This was an incredibly audacious move. Donnelley was a mega-corporation. Newgistics was tiny, completely unknown outside the confines of AV Labs. For Newgistics to succeed, it needed Donnelley as a key partner. There are times when you have to be audacious, and this was one of those times.

By the end of that conference call, we felt like masters of our universe. Donnelley had given a thumbs-up to our goal: an alliance with Newgistics. Plus, they'd insisted on investing in the new company. Talk about a stretch—an investment had been the furthest thing from our minds. All we'd hoped for was a buy-in to the business strategy, a "maybe" on the partnership, the willingness to talk further. Now, Newgistics had a major partner *and* a big investor. Phil suddenly looked about ten years younger.

In retrospect, though, it's not all that surprising. Why? Because if anything, we were overprepared for the pitch to Donnelley. Phil had thoroughly validated the market. He had conceived a partner-focused business strategy that would take a solution to market fast. He was persuasive on the role Donnelley and other partners would play. More important, he saw from their point of view how a Newgistics alliance could bring them added revenue. What was left? Articulating this solid business case and convincing Donnelley to partner up. Recruiting the giant as an investor was an unexpected bonus.

How did Phil get to the point where he was able to pull this off? It didn't happen overnight. In fact, Phil started out thinking Newgistics had to do it all—by itself—to be successful. He was possessed of an illusion that's all too common in the startup world: *I have to ship the killer product.* It's a myth that is capable of sinking even the most promising new business.

In this chapter, we'll walk through how Phil jettisoned this fallacy. We'll see how he developed, instead, a well-thought-out product strategy that enabled Newgistics to achieve one of a startup's primary goals: *to get to market fast with a product that solves customer pain.* (Remember: not so fast that it happens before market validation. I don't mean to contradict what I advocated in the second kick: Getting to market fast only makes sense when you're targeting a validated market.) There are two viable approaches to this task, and we'll explore them both:

- *Partnering or buying, versus making*—the Newgistics strategy.
- *Delivering a minimally acceptable feature set*—an approach used effectively by Salion, another AV Labs company.

Before either Newgistics or Salion was able to forge their successful strategies, they had to revise their thinking—radically. Both believed they had to ship the killer product. And both had to learn a critical lesson: If failing to validate the market is the worst source of dilution for a founding team, shipping a killer product is the biggest source of out-and-out failure.

Want to boil the ocean? Careful . . .

Get ready—when you do market validation, you'll be bowled over by the sheer complexity of the customer pain. As an outgrowth of that discovery, you'll be amazed by how complex the remedy needs to be. Try not to be too shocked, though. Instead, keep this in mind: A good opportunity is *by definition* complex. It is in this complexity that real opportunity lies. What's more, truly validating a market gives you intelligence nobody else has about the size and scope of a problem. Inevitably, the problem is bigger and deeper than anyone could have predicted.

What will you be tempted to do? Set out to address the problem *in its entirety.* I call this "boiling the ocean." Your thinking will go something like this: If customers need this complex solution, then as red-blooded entrepreneurs, we'll deliver it. And we will get the resources we need to do so, within our own company. Otherwise there is no way to properly address this pain!

Freeze. Back up. Get off that path. Unless, that is, you're dying to assume crippling development costs and delay your time to market. If you ship a killer product, you'll do both—at a time when your capital is most expensive, and when time to market is everything. Ship a killer product, and you'll kill your company.

In a moment, we will examine the time-to-market and development-cost consequences of the killer-product fallacy. First, let's look at the complex solutions envisioned by Newgistics and Salion—solutions that are no more complex than your own will likely be.

Envisioning a complex solution—Newgistics' experience.

Phil Siegel had an awesome background. During more than a decade at Boston Consulting Group, a premier global management consulting group, he had acquired a deep understanding of consumer and retail businesses. By the time he joined AV Labs, Phil was itching to identify a startup opportunity. He would steer the new business through market validation, develop a business model, and serve as interim CEO until a permanent chief executive could be recruited.

Phil's idea for Newgistics grew out of a conversation with his wife, Lauren, a dedicated Internet and catalog shopper who relished the convenience of online buying. She'd just ordered a blouse from a well-known Internet retailer, and it didn't fit. Now she'd have to e-mail the site, pack and ship the suit, and wait until the merchant received it before getting credit toward another order. Why, Lauren lamented, did returning or exchanging these goods have to be so inconvenient? Why wasn't there a way to do it as easily as with a bricks-and-mortar retailer? Phil had a hunch that millions of online and catalog shoppers would second her concern. He resolved to start a company that would streamline the complex product return process—not just for the end consumer but for online and catalog retail merchants as well.

Phil initially envisioned a sophisticated hosted website linking consumers to the e-tailers and catalogers. The site would be driven by software crafted to reflect each merchant's return policies and procedures. The result? A convenient online venue where consumers could communicate with the merchants, understand the policies, and set up returns.

Then Phil validated the market. Quickly he found out (surprise, surprise) that the website alone—however sophisticated, however cutting-edge—wouldn't cut the mustard. The problem was much more complex than he'd assumed. A viable, competitive solution would have to account for that complexity. Specifically, this solution would have to address the savage pain of two major market segments:

- *End consumers,* who ordered via the Internet or catalogs, wanted faster, more convenient, physically local ways to return goods. They also wanted to receive instant credit—just as they did when returning goods to a bricks-and-mortar retail store.
- *E-merchants and catalogers* wanted to offer customers faster, more cost-effective returns, along with instant credit. In addition—and this is a point Phil had not considered—these merchants had ferocious pain around the warehousing and disposal of returned merchandise.

Market validation gave Phil deeper and deeper insight into these problems. In the process, he began to grasp what a complete offering would entail. In addition to the website and software he'd envisioned early on, Newgistics would have to provide neighborhood return locations; a shipping and delivery system; and warehouses where the returned merchandise could be sorted for resale, distributed to charity, or destroyed. In short, Newgistics would enter what is known as the "reverse logistics" business—an existing multibillion-dollar industry with companies specializing in everything from pickup to delivery, sorting to shipping, consolidating to liquidating.

Where was the compelling niche for Newgistics? In packaging and delivering these services to new categories—e-retailers and catalogers—that needed them desperately. No one inside the reverse logistics industry was serving these customers. What's more, while various competitors provided needed components individually, nobody offered a complete, integrated solution. This was what the market required. And this, Phil vowed, was exactly what Newgistics would provide.

Daunting? Yep.

Doing it all? Save yourself some time. Throw your $$ on a bonfire.

As he wrapped up the Newgistics market validation, Phil Siegel was possessed by all-or-nothing "killer product" thinking. Go there, and you'll be lured into the belief that your startup has to create all the elements of a complete solution—all by yourself. Take Phil, for example. Phil seriously evaluated what it would take to deliver this solution. And he found out fast: *Solving a compelling customer pain often requires resources a startup will never have.*

The neighborhood return sites alone would set Newgistics back anywhere from $75–100 million. Shipping and delivery infrastructure, $50–100 million. Warehouses, $25–50 million. And the website and other software? $5–10 million. Could Phil acquire that much financing? No. Could you? Absolutely not. And even if you could, taking the money would be utterly shortsighted. If you're to have any hope of getting to market fast with something that fixes customers' pain, you have to come up with a different strategy.

Another complex problem: Salion's experience.

Salion, another AV Labs portfolio company, faced a dilemma similar to Phil's. Like Newgistics, Salion set out to address extremely complex problems in the marketplace. Like Newgistics, it came face-to-face with the enormous drawbacks of the killer-product approach. And it, too, was forced to adopt a different strategy.

Salion arose from a collaboration between AV Labs and the strategy consulting firm McKinsey & Co. The Labs and McKinsey set out to find an infrastructure-related opportunity in the world of business-to-business exchanges. B2B exchanges use the Internet to connect buyers and suppliers of goods and services. Several leading companies already had a strong foothold in the space. But we were convinced, as McKinsey senior partner Bruce Roberson puts it, that there remained "some problem customers would pay to have solved." In the beginning, we believed the problem involved the speed of hooking up a company to an exchange. We figured the startup would create technology to help businesses connect more efficiently.

Wrong. During market validation, we talked to more than 250 companies doing business across B2B exchanges. We also took several trips up the market validation pyramid, testing and discarding several hypotheses. Where, in the end, did we find the most vexing pain? With B2B suppliers. Many solutions eased *buyers'* pain in the e-commerce world—search engines, reverse auctions, process optimization, comparison shopping, and more. But nothing really existed to help *suppliers.* Thanks to this discrepancy, B2B exchanges represented a losing proposition for the suppliers. They were getting the profit squeezed out of them. They were desperate for a way to equalize the equation.

How could we address this bitter pain? With a complex, multi-faceted solution that would:

- Enable suppliers to bid efficiently with multiple buyers.
- Provide information from other suppliers about a particular buyer.
- Offer a process for reusing market knowledge.
- Provide a range of other capabilities, including workflow collaboration tools and network security.

If that sounds complex, consider the huge diversity of the Salion customer base. One large supplier community sold their goods and services via proposals. Others sold via catalogs. Both groups occupied a variety of industries, including manufacturing, resale, wholesale supply, and more. All of them needed the Salion solution, and they needed it badly.

What would happen if Salion went after all these markets in the first release? What if it tried to deliver all the functionality these people needed? Simple. Getting to market would take two or three years. Not a possibility—not for the successful company, at least.

Doing it all? Instead, tell the competition:
"Here, take my market."

How should you see fast time to market? As an absolute must. From a competitive standpoint, it is risky indeed to take more than a year on the first release. Remember, too, that a product spec is linked to *current* market needs. The markets are always changing. The longer your development cycle, the bigger the chance your product will fail to gibe with what the market needs *right then.*

Had Salion set forth to deliver an all-encompassing solution, the startup would have been dead meat in no time. Once again: A killer product does just that. It kills the company.

Killer product? Forget it. Zero in on customer pain.

How can you keep yourself out of killer-product traps? First, understand your customer. How? Validate the market. Newgistics and Salion are crystal-clear examples of how validating the market creates a shift from product-focused to solution-centered thinking. Think of it this way: *When you start a company, you're not delivering a product. You're addressing a pain point.*

Here, though, is the rub: *There is never enough money or time to fully address the customer pain uncovered during market validation.* How, then, can you deliver a needed solution—quickly? Adopt either of these approaches, one of which can usually be found at the core of all successful technology startups:

- *Integrate others' products and/or services through a value-added approach.* Here, you integrate others' offerings in a way that brands your company as the solution. The stronger the partners, the louder you trumpet their involvement. Newgistics pursued this strategy quite successfully, as we're about to see.
- *For the first release, ship the minimum functionality to prove there's a market.* If you have a software company, you can take Salion's approach: Deliver the solution's core components, achieve market traction, then enhance functionality through a customer-driven *circular* development process (as opposed to the usual serial process). The keys? There are two: First, limit the first release enough to achieve time to market; and second, address enough top pain points that the target audience will buy in.

When you take either of these two product paths, you'll reap a huge set of advantages:

- *Continued market validation.* Getting to market quickly— with a product that sells—is the final step in market validation. It's simple: When people open their wallets and part with their money, you have *proof* that the business is worth continuing.
- *Less capital expenditure and market risk.* The solution addresses a real, validated market need. It strikes while market requirements are current. What's more, an efficient amount of money has been spent getting to market—thereby preserving your valuation.
- *The ability to hire a stronger management team.* Market validation and a fast entry strategy are magnets for top-flight board members, CEOs, VPs, and other executives. Once Phil Siegel had the Newgistics strategy in place, he was able to hire a logistics heavyweight—Gabe Gabriel—as CEO. Similarly,

Salion hired an e-commerce industry veteran, CEO Rick Hahn. You cannot attract seasoned executives like these without a solid market foundation.

- *The ability to raise more capital, at better rates.* Nothing piques the interest of quality investors like a shipped product, market acceptance, and serious partners. Your valuation will be optimal as well—which, as you'll see in the next kick, minimizes dilution for the founders and investors.

- *Credibility with customers.* Anyone who has started and run a business can testify: The earliest customers are the best customers. When people get what they need—right now—to solve a nasty pain, they're loyal. They evangelize to their friends and colleagues. They line up for future releases. What's more, they're strong customer references—crucial for any successful product launch.

Fill the gaps: partner, partner, partner.

Let's go back for a moment to Newgistics' returns solution. As Phil Siegel learned through market validation, this solution would have to provide several key elements: neighborhood return locations, shipping and delivery systems, warehouses, and software. He also found out—quickly—that the company didn't have the money to create a complete, integrated solution. It also didn't have the time. Not, that is, if Newgistics tried to do it all by itself.

"Our epiphany," Phil recalls, "was that we would bring all these pieces together by partnering with other companies that could supply them. Our value was in the software and the packaging of services. Our partners would contribute everything else. Newgistics, of course, would establish the brand and manage the process."

Recruit partners. Use this four-part process.

Okay, so you've uncovered intense pain in the marketplace around a problem. You've also seen how complex your solution will have to be. You understand your customers, you understand their pain, and you know what it'll take to achieve a competitive advantage. If you've read this far, you also know that *you can't achieve success trying to bring a complete solution to market by yourself.*

Quite possibly, your competitive edge will depend, like Newgistics', on partnering with the right people. How on earth, you may ask, can this be done? How can a mite-sized startup partner successfully with a slew of large, established companies? At AV Labs, we've developed the following partnering process. Our companies use it all the time to establish vital partner relationships. Try it for yourself—you'll be astonished at how effective it is.

1. What can you build—and what must others contribute?

No way could Newgistics buy a fleet of trucks, build Newgistics-owned-and-operated returns centers around the country, and construct warehouses. Instead, Phil focused Newgistics around what it *could* realistically create: software used in the return locations to process returns, extend instant credit, and log the returns into merchant systems. A hosted website would function as the online focal point for the return activities. Using software it had created, Newgistics would brand and broker the transaction and manage the process. The software component could easily be built and deployed in less than a year, and for less than $10 million. As for other, more expensive components of its reverse logistics solution, Newgistics would rely on partners who already had these elements in place.

2. Who can deliver the needed components or services?

There are three different types of partners: those who provide key solution components; strategic partners who contribute marketing assistance, an investment, or crucial introductions; and investors, who lend credibility and critical access to other players, potential partners, and industry contacts. Who to go after? That depends on the nature of your business and the market space. Do you need, say, credibility with the Fortune 500? A particular vertical market to which a strategic partner might provide access? Visibility through a name-brand alliance? Investment dollars? An elegant technical or operational solution?

In Newgistics' early stages, the latter was most critical. For its neighborhood return drop-off points, Newgistics evaluated packing and mailing businesses, supermarkets, drugstores, and more. For warehousing and processing, it identified USF Processors, a division of USFreightways, as a perfect partner—not only for its services, but also for its relationships with a number of large retailers. Ideal for shipping and delivery would be R.R. Donnelley Logistics, a division of R.R. Donnelley & Sons; the division's extensive nationwide shipping network supplemented Donnelley's thriving catalog printing business, which itself could give access to leading catalogers.

3. What's in it for your partners?

As we saw at the beginning of this chapter, Phil did his homework before he approached R.R. Donnelley about partnering with Newgistics. One of the things he did was to figure out how Donnelley and the other partners could expect to make money through the partnership.

The grocery stores and mail centers used as return drop points would enjoy more traffic—particularly when consumers began to recognize the convenience of one-stop returns. R.R. Donnelley would expand its trucking business and acquire an extra product (the return service) to sell its catalog printing customers. As for USFreightways, the warehousing giant would achieve fast, relatively painless access to a new market, in addition to incremental business for its warehousing operations.

"The key here," says Phil, "was to tailor the whole proposal to make sure everybody got what they wanted. We wanted money, credibility, and customers. The partners wanted more traffic, a new product line, an avenue for cracking a new market segment. We had all this lined out before we approached the partners."

4. Pitch to partners as though they were customers.

Here, you start with the well-honed pitch developed during Stage 3 of market validation. What do you add? Information that tells partners how they fit. Let your partners know how they can help solve a fierce customer pain. And show them how they can raise their own revenues in the process.

We've seen how well this process worked for Phil. Remember what happened when he approached R.R. Donnelley about a partnership? He landed a big investment as well. The same thing happened when Newgistics went to USFreightways. A partner-focused strategy paid off big for this new company, which reeled in not only two critical partners but two strong strategic investors.

The Solution Map: the total picture.

What will your new business look like after you complete the partnering process? It will resemble the Solution Map shown in Figure 3.

As the figure suggests, if you partner wisely you'll be creating your own DNA. You'll be choosing your own parents. Every time you bring in another advisor, investor, partner, or customer, that relationship yields a whole new set of advisors, investors, partners, and customers. Your startup is enriched with an ever-growing network of relationships:

- Investors provide more than just financing. They contribute key industry contacts, potential customers, advice, and more.
- Advisors extend your reach through contacts, domain expertise, and entrée to new customers.
- A solution partner puts in place some crucial aspect of the total solution. In Newgistics' case, R.R. Donnelley con-

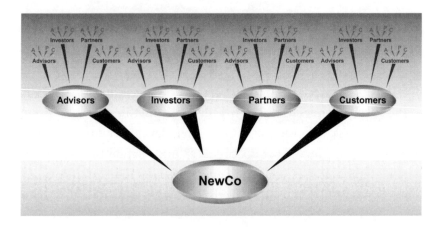

Figure 3. Solution Map: Assembling a complete product through
advisors, investors, partners, and customers.

tributes shipping and delivery through its trucking network;
USFreightways, warehousing and sorting capabilities; and the
neighborhood return locations, physical sites where consumers can return goods and receive instant credit.
- Strategic partners (who may also serve as investors) add another
  important dimension. Donnelley, for example, offers a wide
  network of major catalog merchants, such as Lillian Vernon.
- Your company is the glue that binds all these components
  together. Newgistics, for instance, provides software and a
  hosted website for managing the entire return logistics
  process, with partners contributing other elements of the
  complete solution.

When customers look at Newgistics, what do they see? They see
what Newgistics delivers to market: an elegantly orchestrated
process that vastly simplifies the return of merchandise for the end
consumer, for e-merchants, and for catalogers. To a customer, this
solution is what "Newgistics" is.

From the startup's own perspective, though, Newgistics is something else. It is really more of a value-added solution than anything

else. "We identified a better mousetrap," Phil Siegel says, "then used others to help build it. Lots of other companies are providing just the software, but we're doing that *and* orchestrating the entire process. With Newgistics, people don't have to implement their own processes—they can simply use ours, which works very well. Without the partnerships, there is no way we could have pulled this off."

Prove the market. Deliver a minimally accepted feature set.

For companies like Newgistics, partnerships are the key to hitting the market fast. Companies whose core value is software take a different, equally valid approach. Salion fits this category. If you do too, here's what you need to do: For the first release, deliver a *minimally acceptable set* of features and functionality that will be accepted by a sizeable group of customers. This will prove your market. It will help you establish a beachhead for a future product line. *It will give you a toehold*—even a small one at this stage—*in a market that has blistering pain around the problem.*

The results? One, you lasso a base of established customers who are likely to adopt later releases and serve as references. Two, you prove that you can get to market quickly, with a product the market accepts. And three, you show you have market expertise—which makes it much easier to raise financing for moving forward.

The benefits, then, are *huge*. Still, if you're like a lot of entrepreneurs, you may be inclined to balk. And in a way, your reluctance is understandable. Why? Because at first glance, the approach seems counterintuitive, for two reasons:

- Market validation uncovers *hundreds* of features customers require—and you're naturally inclined to deliver them all. Salion, for example, found its customers needed (for starters) a buyer-information clearinghouse, tools for leveraging work on proposals already completed, and better ways to develop proposals. Surely (or so the thinking went) all this functionality would be required in any product Salion brought to market.

- Because (thanks to market validation) you know what a complete, total solution should look like, delivering only part of it seems to make your product "incomplete" by definition.

Both these perceptions are by-products of the killer-product fallacy. As we have seen, adhering to this illusion costs far too much—money-wise and time-wise. Far better, as Salion CEO Rick Hahn puts it, to "get out there with something valuable ASAP. A little bit of value quickly is much better than more value later."

How did Rick navigate Salion toward its rapid product debut? With a set of tactics, explored in the sections to follow, that are designed to accomplish two critical tasks—solve a pain, and reach the market fast:

- For the first release, target the minimally acceptable set of features for a substantial market.
- Recruit alpha customers early—even as early as the idea phase.
- Limit product functionality to a well-defined subset of the most important features.
- Use marketing to clearly communicate your ultimate product vision, versus the reality of the first release.

Identify a subset of the market.

Which customers need a solution most? *Who has the reddest-hot pain*—and hence the greatest willingness to fix it with something new? The heat map described in the second kick is an excellent source of this information. In graphic form, the heat map shows you whom to target in the first release. A well-defined, focused customer base makes it easier to communicate with customers through all phases of the release. That keeps your team on track to provide the features customers need the most.

Take Salion, for instance. Which of Salion's B2B supplier customers had the most brutal pain? Those who sold via proposals, as opposed to catalogs. Manufacturers—designers and makers of custom and semi-custom products built to buyers' specs—indicated the fiercest pain of all. Salion determined that its initial release would home in on these manufacturer customers.

Recruit early alpha customers.

As you learned during the last kick, you know you're on to a real opportunity when Stage 2 customer contacts *beg* for your solution. Recall, for example, that Mike Betzer of Ineto recruited his Customer Advisory Board at this stage—customers with severe pain, who agreed to help steer Ineto's customer communications service. I recommend that you sign up some of these customers yourself. They will serve as sounding boards throughout the development process. They will keep your team focused on the pain—and on solving that pain.

How did early alpha customers figure into Salion's process? They were crucial, according to CEO Rick Hahn. "Even at the idea phase," he recalls, "we recruited our most enthusiastic B2B suppliers to partner with us as alpha customers. We said, 'Let us build this and quickly develop early functionality, while you provide feedback to keep us on track.' We knew how valuable their participation would be. For that reason, we promised them all additional functionality as it was delivered—with eighteen months of product at reduced rates." Not only did the Salion alpha community accelerate progress on the first release, but they also helped steer the product in "directions guaranteed to solve real pain in the market," says Rick.

Focus your product's functionality.

As I've said, it's inevitable your team will want to deliver *all* the features customers want—particularly when you're all fired up by successful market validation. The problem is, there will be literally *hundreds* of these features—far too many to provide in the first release if you're also to meet time-to-market demands. What, then, are you to do? Figure out the *minimal* functionality that addresses the *highest* pain point across the *broadest* swath of the market.

For Salion's manufacturing supplier customers, the thorniest pain involved finding requests for proposals (RFPs), the lifeblood for new business. They wanted a speedier, more accurate proposal-development process. They also needed ways to track and store proposal-related intelligence for reuse and analysis. In response, the first release of the Salion product contained:

- A search engine for finding RFPs.
- Tools for plotting interdependency timelines, tracking due dates, and internally collaborating to develop a proposal.
- A proposal-information repository in database form, enabling the suppliers to determine what was winning business and what was losing it.

As Rick says, "This release solved our supplier customers' single biggest problem. Typically, they submit a hundred proposals for every five they win. With Salion, they can determine which ones to spend the most time on, so that they can win a higher percentage of business. Our goal is to help customers transition from low-margin business to high-margin business. By focusing and targeting the early release, and by using alpha customers to help, we got a great start toward creating a product for general availability."

Use marketing to define the future of the solution.

As Geoffrey Moore points out in his landmark book *Crossing the Chasm*, there is "a gap between the marketing promise made to the customer—the compelling value proposition—and the ability of the shipped product to fulfill that promise." Never is this more true

MICROSOFT: THE RELEASE THAT'S "GOOD ENOUGH"

It's not just the startup that can profit from an early partial release. Nobody has perfected this strategy quite like Microsoft. Again and again, this giant of the industry has hit the market with product debuts containing the bare minimum set of features needed by the market. What then occurs is a perfect lesson for any company that thinks it must release a "killer product" to be accepted.

Microsoft's critics (competitors?) often complain, sometimes bitterly, about the lack of comprehensive features in early versions of Microsoft products. This was especially true of Microsoft's early attempts at the Windows operating system. Pundits would rail for hours on end about how Windows wouldn't work well on every single PC made, with every network protocol, with every peripheral, or with each and every third-party software utility. Microsoft understood this clearly—and astutely improved the product, release by release.

In their book *Gates: How Microsoft's Mogul Reinvented an Industry—and Made Himself the Richest Man in America,* Stephen Manes and Paul Andrews describe the market response to Windows 3.0: ". . . after all these years, Windows was still not perfect, still not as technically sophisticated as OS/2, *but it was good enough.* It had a great game of solitaire. You could customize your desktop and display colors and icons for hours on end. And once and for all . . . programmers were rid of the 640K barrier."[6]

The key phrase is this: With the 3.0 release, Windows was "good

---

6. All material from Manes and Andrews, pp. 389–90.

enough"—good enough to work on the most widely used machines, with the most popular peripherals, and with the network protocols and third-party software from companies most friendly to Microsoft. Windows contained features important to both programmers (breaking the 640K memory barrier) and end users (solitaire—seemingly trivial, but perhaps the most widely used application in the world?). With each iteration of Windows, Microsoft co-opted more machines, more peripherals, more protocols, and more third-party software utilities.

The end result? Today, Windows has became a robust, dominant platform for both business users and consumers. It really *is* most things to most people. And each step was meticulously calculated by Microsoft, one release at a time.

than with your startup's first release. At this point, your value proposition extends well beyond what is possible or prudent for your product debut.

How can you close the gap? By marketing your solution based on the overall value proposition, rather than what is or is not available currently. Don't get me wrong: The current reality *must be clearly articulated*—but at the same time, show your customers the path to the ultimate vision. In doing so, you accomplish a great deal toward moving your business forward. Customers see precisely how your "partial" release is but a *building block* for the wider functionality to come.[7] Not only do they perceive the product's room for growth, but they understand your company's potential to address their pain completely and effectively.

This approach is illustrated in Figure 4.

---

7. Or what Moore calls the "potential product," which he says "represents the product's room for growth as more and more ancillary products come on the market and as customer-specific enhancements to the system are made."

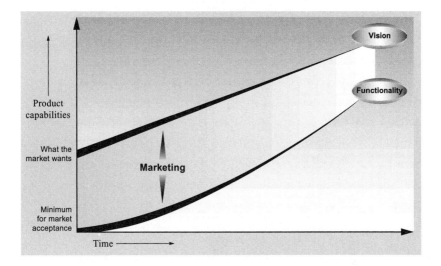

Figure 4. Selling the vision, articulating the reality.

To carry out this strategy:

- Release a product containing the minimum functionality required for market acceptance.
- Clearly articulate what is product and what is vision.
- Release by release, enhance the product—always in response to customer input—until the gap between the product (real, existing functionality) and the value proposition (a vision to deliver all that the market wants) narrows over time.

Rick Hahn developed a presentation for current and potential Salion customers, in which he outlined Salion's ultimate supplier-oriented solution. Customers were able to see a clear path from the current release to this larger solution. Similarly, Newgistics placed the company's return logistics product—named ReturnValet—within a much wider landscape of future Newgistics products. Each of the products will use the same basic components of the Return-

Valet product—the solution's DNA, if you will—and combine these elements in new and innovative ways. Together, the Newgistics products will provide a complete logistics solution.

Like all successful companies, Newgistics and Salion came to realize that customers want solutions for their pain, not "killer products." Today's customers have complex, extremely irksome business issues. If your startup understands these customers and addresses their pain, you will be well accepted. If, on the other hand, you focus on "shipping a killer product," you will dramatically *increase* your company's risk.

Increasing risk is the *opposite* of what you want to do in an infant company. You want to *decrease* the risk—which raises the valuation of your startup. You want to optimize your capital structure. What's that all about? Find out, in our next kick . . .

THIRD KICK: TAKEAWAYS

✳ Can you boil the ocean? No. So don't try it.

There is *no way* to solve every aspect of customers' pain—not in the first release, and not using your company's own resources. A "killer product" will kill one thing: your company.

- It delays time to market.
- It costs more than a startup (any company, for that matter) can afford.

✳ How to proceed? Partner up. Or ship a subset of the features customers require.

- Integrate other companies' products and/or services into your offering—while branding your company as the ultimate solution provider.
- For release #1, ship the minimally acceptable set of features customers need.
- If some feature of your product is available elsewhere, *license it*—don't build it yourself.

✳ You can't beat these results:

- Fast time to market. Beat competitors to the punch—and complete the final step in market validation (people opening their wallets and parting with their dollars).
- Less capital for getting there. That minimizes dilution for yourself, your employees, and your investors.
- Seasoned executives for the management team.
- Additional capital at more attractive valuations.
- Credibility with current and future customers.

✳ Get great partners with a four-step process.

1. Map out a complete solution to your customers' pain. What can you provide? What's needed from others?

2. Identify who's ideal for delivering the needed goods or services.
3. Answer this: How will the alliance benefit *them?*
4. Go after the partner just as zealously as you'd go after a key customer.

✷ Here's how to use the "minimally accepted feature set" strategy.

- Pinpoint: Who has the most acute pain and, hence, the greatest incentive to adopt something new?
- Recruit alpha and beta customers *early.* Listen to them. Incorporate their suggestions. Use them to get to market faster, with the features they see as most critical.
- Use marketing to close the gap between your total value proposition (the *ultimate* vision) and what's available *now.* That gets customers on your path to the future.

FOURTH KICK

YOU DON'T NEED THE BIG BUCKS RIGHT OUT OF THE GATE

Whenever I think of Mediaprise, I think of the Starbucks in Westlake. The team and I met many times at the popular west Austin coffee shop, getting to know each other and batting around ideas for their fledgling business. The sessions would start sometime after work, with me naïvely hoping we'd wind it up in an hour or two. Then we'd get deep into company strategy. Around 10 or 11 o'clock, I'd go home with a caffeine buzz.

Our fourth or fifth Starbucks meeting was pretty monumental. By now we knew each other well. What's more, their company was on track as a potential investment for the Labs.

"This is looking very intriguing," I told them. "I'd like to get you in front of the whole team."

"Awesome," said co-founder Anurag Kumar, an intense, soft-spoken thirty-nine-year-old whose voice retains the cadence of his native India. "All we're going to need is about $10 million to get off the ground."

I froze. Was my sudden distraction from all the caffeine surging through my brain, or from what I'd just heard? I wasn't sure. All I knew was, in that split second I went from being excited about the deal to thinking it might not work.

Ten million dollars? *Not.*

If you're like Anurag and his co-founders, you have fallen prey to a startup myth that's incredibly widespread—and totally ludicrous: *I must raise a lot of money quickly to be successful.* My advice? Lose this notion, and lose it fast. You need a new, radically different view of what your financing should look like—in your company's earliest stages and throughout its life. You're about to acquire this new view—and find out just how critical it is to your success.

Why do so many entrepreneurs believe they have to get their hands on the big bucks to launch a business? In a lot of ways, it seems self-evident. Consider Mediaprise, for instance.

The Mediaprise idea sprang from the experiences of Anurag Kumar. Anurag spent many years at IBM, heading up a Customer Relationship Management group. While he was there, more and more businesses were starting to offer products over the Internet. Gradually Anurag began noticing a problem: Businesses were delivering limited, outdated product information to their channel partners and e-tail sites. The possibilities were intriguing. What if there was a better, easier way? What if they could give their outlets product information that was rich, up-to-date, and brand- and content-intensive? What if they could disseminate promotional material, graphics, streaming audio and video, and 3-D models in a consistent manner? These capabilities, Anurag reasoned, would enable them to entice more business customers to buy. They could raise consumer confidence. What's more, they could protect and enhance their image and marketing programs in distribution and retail channels.

Anurag was convinced he might be on to something big. He teamed up with Mohan Warrior, an engineer from Motorola and an old school friend from India, and Steve Keys, an executive colleague at IBM. Together, the team performed secondary market research to determine whether a company could be built around Anurag's idea. Before long, they'd identified a gargantuan market—one consisting of hundreds of manufacturers. Most of these businesses, they predicted, would need the Mediaprise solution for building out their exchanges and e-commerce sites.

How could the new company capture this market? The team believed it would take a complete product and a solid delivery structure. Only then, they thought, would Mediaprise have credibility. Only then would it be able to sell the manufacturers on this unique new concept. What would it cost to get there? A bundle. A *great big* bundle, in fact—enough for people, physical infrastructure, software licenses, and more. The $10 million would make a good start. That much, they figured, would last long enough to build a product and make a splash in the market.

This was a cockeyed notion. We set them straight, and fast. In the end, the team chose not to pursue multimillion-dollar financing—at least not early on. They did the math. They realized how much it would *really* take to build a complete product and get it to market. Far better, they decided, to increase their valuation in the short term. That way, they could raise the needed money within a year's time— *and* have meaningful ownership left over for themselves.

In this chapter, you'll see how the team worked with us to forge a path very different from the "quick money" approach. You'll explore how you can devise just such a path for yourself. How do you begin? With a small seed round, followed by subsequent larger rounds of financing. Throughout, you obtain funding in a way that heightens your company's valuation while reducing its risk. All the while, you maximize ownership for the founding team and existing investors.

As the Mediaprise team designed this alternative approach to funding, they learned a valuable lesson, one you're about to learn as well: With respect to financing, the key to success is to raise the *right amount* of capital at the *right stage* of development.

What's it all about? Market risk.

Why is it so critical to take a careful step-by-step approach to raising money? Why should you raise funds only as your company valuation rises (also known as "capitalizing the company," or simply "capitalization")? Here's why: because of the incredible risk inherent in today's fast-changing markets. Prior to the early 1990s or so, engineering itself was the main risk. Today, with most development technology stable and reliable, the technical risk is no longer that high. What *is* high? *Market risk.* The risk you're off on the market. The risk you'll launch a product and point it in the wrong place. The risk you'll have to regroup and raise even more money—probably having to do it several times.

Which is precisely why most of today's companies fail: They are unable to get the *right product* to the *right market* with a *reasonable* amount of money. The lesson? If you're going to raise large amounts of money, do it only as you reduce (or *mitigate)* the risk. (At the end of this book, you'll find an appendix titled "Capitalization Primer," an overview of the key concepts explored in this chapter—risk mitigation, valuation, and so on. Readers who are unfamiliar with financing issues will want to consult it.)

Investors are constantly assessing market risk. The higher they perceive a company's risk to be, the less likely they are to hand over the cash. Mitigating market risk, then, is one of your essential tasks as an entrepreneur. The best approach? To proceed with the three activities we've explored so far:

- Put together a team with solid execution intelligence.
- Validate the market.
- Forge a strategy for getting a product out there quickly. Nothing proves you're right and mitigates risk faster than customers opening their wallets and parting with their money.

Together, these tasks reduce the key risks of your early-stage venture. What's more, they make it far more likely that you can get the financing you need—along with the ability to move forward and capture the market.

Get big $$ fast, and dive headfirst into quicksand.

Where did the "quick money" illusion come from, anyway? And why is it so dangerous?

I can assure you, Anurag Kumar and the other Mediaprise cofounders were hardly atypical. I would wager you might also think *you* need megabucks fast to get your business started. After all, consider the sky-high expense of labor alone. Labor consumes the lion's share of the typical startup's budget. Add office space, computer and networking equipment, benefits, travel, and more—and what do you get? The idea that creating a new technology product requires huge sums indeed.

Up until the Nasdaq correction in the spring of 2000, it was easy to obtain multimillion-dollar funding to start an entrepreneurial venture. Many people have failed to realize: *Even since the correction, and even during ongoing times of softness in the market, investors continue to put money into technology startups.* This is not likely to change. Why? For as long as technology spawns new markets—and that will occur for many years to come, despite inevitable economic ups and downs—the right management teams with the right ideas will continue to raise financing.

The problem lies in raising *too much* money, too fast. What tends to happen? A self-destructive cycle that spins round and round:

- The company becomes *output-oriented,* a term coined by AV Labs Venture Fellow Phil Siegel, as opposed to *execution-oriented.* And the results are disastrous.
- The company is heavily diluted as it raises more and more

money, hoping to get closer and closer to being successful. Then it simply engages in more output-oriented behaviors and repeats the cycle.

The following sections explore each of these calamities. As you're about to see, falling into the output-oriented snare creates ever more pressure to produce more output-oriented results. Don't give in to this cycle—or your company will soon be circling the drain.

Output mania: Spend, spend, spend.

What will the average human being do when given a lot of money? You got it—spend. That's human nature. And overfunded startups do it all the time. If you're in one of these companies, you spend lots of time spending your money. You spend on *things* you can point to as evidence of progress—on *outputs*. Case in point? Infrastructure. You might spend three days negotiating 10% off the price of a copier, or a week picking out and pricing ergonomically correct office furniture—then check off the boxes and call this progress. Another common output? Team-building events. One Austin startup paid for the entire team to spend a long weekend in Cozumel, Mexico, then proudly trumpeted this fact in a recruitment brochure. (I have nothing against team-building outings—they're necessary. But come on: Cozumel? Get real!)

Paradoxically, even market research can be output-oriented. You might simply conduct research, then fail to interpret the results. I've seen it many times. An output-oriented company will say, "I've conducted a hundred customer interviews in thirty days." The execution-oriented company will say, "Here are the conclusions I've reached, based on market validation." Output-oriented research is little more than *make-work*. In contrast, execution-oriented research yields changes in perspective and affects the way a company proceeds to increase its value. Similarly, "I had ten customer meetings last month" is an *output;* "I signed up two beta customers" is evidence of *execution*. The difference? One, while laudable, does nothing to advance the business model. The other represents *tangible progress toward proving that model.*

Needless to say, there are a million output-oriented activities out there. These outputs—whether they be things, events, parties, expensive deals, or whatever—are not necessarily bad in themselves. When do they become problems? *When you mistake them for actual business progress.*

As an example, consider drkoop.com, the Austin-based company that built the well-known health website. Drkoop.com was founded in 1997. The original goal was to give consumers a secure way to store medical records on the Internet. This would enable people to interact more easily with physicians, hospitals, and other health-care providers. Before long, the company realized it was positioned to become a leading source of general health-related information. So it quickly changed its strategy to focus on building the drkoop.com site. The site was launched in mid-1998. By that fall, it had become the most heavily trafficked health site on the Internet.

In the manner of those frenzied times, drkoop.com rushed to an initial public offering. A mere one year after site launch, it raised $84.4 million in an IPO. This enormous financing event, more than anything else, was what ultimately undermined the company. Why? Because it spurred the management team *to spend all the company's money*—and then some—in ways that did little *to actually advance the business.* The IPO set in motion a self-destructive *tsunami* of output mania.

Greg Bashaw, one of my MBA students at the University of Texas, visited the drkoop.com premises with a group of fellow students in early 2000. I often send students on these expeditions to get a bird's-eye view of the inner workings of Austin's businesses. "We were amazed by the opulent office space," Greg recalled after the visit. "The cubicles were furnished with real wood desks, and everybody had a Herman Miller Aeron chair—which cost about $700 each!—and top-of-the-line computer equipment." Then, Greg and his companions queried an executive in an expensively furnished conference room. They began to realize that the only thing driving the company's (at that time) sky-high valuation was *traffic* to the content-rich site. In other words, the stock price—and hence the valuation—was based on the number of *eyeballs* attracted to drkoop.com. "When we asked him how they were turning those eyeballs into revenue," says Greg, "he couldn't answer. He just kept repeating the website traffic numbers."

The company spent a huge amount of its IPO proceeds not just on office space and furniture but on a range of other *outputs*—company meals, onsite massages, and the like—that, while nice, were hardly the stuff of a startup attempting to optimize its capital structure. The company also inked huge deals with AOL and Go Network in an attempt to beef up traffic to the site. All the while, drkoop.com did little to advance its original vision of building a medical records portal—and even less to validate whether there was really a market for such a portal. While drkoop.com was successfully attracting site visitors, it was not creating ways to build customer loyalty, retain customers, or generate revenue. Despite the outputs (great traffic numbers, expensive office space, employee perks), *it had not accomplished the core task of any business:* to execute against a viable revenue model. Had the company not received the $84.4 million so soon—or had it used those funds to validate a market and develop a workable revenue model—it might well be thriving today.

Dilution: slashing your ownership.

When you go out to get money from investors, they will acquire a percentage of the company and set its value *based on the risk of the investment.* By definition, the earlier your financing, the greater the risk: Early on, you have yet to produce or market a product, so your pre-investment (or "pre-money") valuation is typically in the single-digit millions. At this point, risk is sky-high. Valuation, rock-bottom.

Take Mediaprise. What if the team had been able to raise the $10 million they thought they needed? They would have been left with an unappetizingly tiny slice of the pie going forward. Let's imagine, for example, that investors had assigned a pre-money valuation of $5 million (a generous valuation at this stage). Post-investment, Mediaprise would have had a valuation of $15 million ($5 million pre-money, plus the $10 million from investors). What would the investors have walked away with? Ten-fifteenths—a whopping 67%—of the company.

Most quality investors want to see the founding team owning much more at this stage. Why? Because the consequences of early, heavy dilution are absolutely *heinous:*

- Employees are not as motivated. Today's technology startups draw people based on the perceived likelihood of a payoff (or a "liquidity event," which transforms shares into cash). The bigger the slice owned by the company's employees, the more lucrative the payoff for them.
- Next round, investors will be less interested. Savvy investors know that when employees own most of the stock, a company is *hungrier.* It's more *energetic.* And it is also *more determined* to make sure later investors enjoy a smaller piece of the pie— thereby preserving ownership for employees and existing investors.

When you go after huge sums of cash that dilute your ownership early on, then *you're making a huge mistake.* Now let's take a look at a saner, more reasonable way to proceed.

Be logical. Optimize your capitalization.

How can you avoid the pitfalls of too much financing, too soon? By *optimizing your capitalization.* This means raising *less,* not more, capital in the early stages, when money is most expensive. After you get this early funding, you aim to hit clearly defined milestones that *raise valuation*—and *mitigate risk* for follow-on investors in the next (and more substantial) financing rounds.

All our AV Labs portfolio companies use this approach—because it works. Our companies have received follow-on financing from top-tier investment firms and *Fortune*-class strategic investors. Their follow-on–round valuations tend to be much higher than those of most other companies at similar stages. What's more, their founders' dilution is lower. What does that mean? The entrepreneurs and their teams get to own more of the companies as they proceed to gain a foothold in the market.

Raise your company's valuation and reduce your risk— with value inflection points.

Value inflection points are carefully planned *execution milestones.* They accomplish two things: They mitigate risk, and they increase valuation. AV Labs considers it imperative that our entrepreneurs clearly define their seed-round value inflection points. We draw up a list of mutually agreed-upon points before we ink a deal. Then we review the team's progress monthly, helping to steer the company through the seed phase in an organized, execution-oriented way. The goal? To increase the business value—which *lowers the risk* and makes the startup *more attractive* for Series A investors.

This process is good for more than just the seed period. It works at *every* financing stage—from seed round to Series A, B, or C, through the IPO and secondary offering. As you employ a value inflection–based approach for your own company, keep the following in mind:

- To continue to optimize the capital structure, you should raise subsequent financing only after you hit the current round's value inflection points.
- Map out *in advance* what a round's milestones are. Use your

capital to execute against them. With Mediaprise, we established early on that before the company would seek Series A financing, it would first validate the market, then develop a profitable business model, next identify the target vertical markets, and finally design a product.

- With value inflection points, valuation rises to a level where even a large next-round investment produces minimum dilution for founders, employees, and existing investors. Mediaprise raised $10 million at Series A; because the team had optimized their capital structure with their seed round, dilution was managed effectively.

- For every financing round, raise *only what you need to get through the next set of value inflection points with a comfortable margin of cash.* Which means, again, that you must define these value inflection points in advance.

- Always, focus on executing the next set of value inflection points—*not* on "becoming profitable." Remember this: Continually hitting value inflection points is *precisely* what drives a company to profitablility. You're breaking up a large, complex task into manageable parts. It's the only way any such task can be accomplished.

- If you consistently execute against planned value inflection points, you will always be in a position to attain follow-on financing.

Is infrastructure a value inflection point? Never.

No company—at any stage of its development—should *ever* view infrastructure-related outputs as value inflection points. This is particularly critical for the early-stage startup. "Even from the beginning," says Anurag Kumar of Mediaprise, "our mind-set was that we would not invest heavily in infrastructure, office, and overhead. It just wasn't that important. We wanted to create a comfortable, exciting environment with an attractive look and feel, but that was as far as we were willing to go infrastructure-wise."

At AV Labs, we are *adamant* that our startup teams not zero in on infrastructure. So much so, in fact, that we often handle these items for them. Tommy Deavenport, the Lab's VP of finance and operations, spearheads this effort. "It's not that the companies can't do these things without our help," Tommy says. "The object is, we want them accomplished as efficiently as possible. An inexperienced entrepreneur could waste a lot of time and money—and we want to make sure that doesn't happen."

When helping teams find office space, for example, Tommy gives them a solid feel for the market, so they'll understand terms and pricing before working with a broker. "We have pre-negotiated ready-to-go arrangements with equipment vendors, real estate companies, accountants, legal firms, marketing firms, and more," Tommy says. "We don't have preferred suppliers, but word travels fast amongst our companies as to who provides the best services. Putting deals in place with these providers saves the entrepreneurs a lot of time." If you don't have an AV Labs to handle infrastructure for you, just make sure you take care of these issues quickly—and with a minimum of cost and effort. Then, your team can turn their full attention toward tackling value inflection points. That's what brings value to the business. That's what moves you forward.

Seed-round value inflection points: the Big Two.
What qualifies as a value inflection point during the seed round? Essentially, *any effort that helps prove the concept.* In other words, any activity that demonstrates a viable market, proves the business model, or otherwise makes success more likely. Each seed-round value inflection point advances valuation. Combined, they raise it enough to obtain a Series A round at preferred valuations.

What *must* you do during the seed round? Two things: Validate the market, and develop a profitable business model. These two milestones mitigate your risk more than anything else. They are *absolutely required* for next-round financing. To really nail it, you will determine a number of other important value inflection points as well—milestones that will depend on your company and its business.

Validate the market: #1 seed-round must-do.
By now, you already know this. *Market validation is*—hands down—*the most important early-stage milestone.* AV Labs requires it of all our companies. "We spent our first three months solely on market validation," recalls Anurag Kumar, who adds that, initially, the team was "shocked that the validation project would be so time-consuming and produce the dramatic results that it did."

As always, validating the market proved the Mediaprise concept. The results? It raised the startup's valuation and mitigated the risk. In the process, it also uncovered a new, critically important requirement. As the team had expected, their manufacturer customers had profound pain around distributing "rich media"—streaming audio and video, 3-D models, and the like—to resale partners. In addition, though, Mediaprise would have to provide more comprehensive brand-advancing services. Managing the relationship between manufacturers and their resale partners would solve an acute pain in the market. So would offering a reliable way to share brand information.

Develop a profitable business model: #2 seed-round must-do.
Given you've proven a market for your product, *is demand sufficient to generate profits?* The answer had better be "yes"—and you'd better be able to show how you'll get there early on. As we worked with the Mediaprise team to fine-tune their business model, we encouraged them to identify a *single, limited* vertical market to focus on during the Series A round. Why? Because limiting the market would enable them to prove the value proposition within one market before spreading the solution across the entire marketplace. They would be using capital *more efficiently.* The team would be *more focused.* Last but not least, the concept would prove out *far more rapidly.* Mediaprise identified consumer appliance manufacturers as an ideal vertical

target for the Series A period. The company went on to close early customers in this category. In addition, the Mediaprise team worked to ensure consistent messages and to accelerate its plan of execution.

In short, the team developed the business model to a point where they knew which markets they would target, and in what order. They designed product, sales, and marketing models for each of these targets. They fleshed out, based on markets, how the company's revenue and expense lines ramped. They determined how much capital they needed to reach cash-flow breakeven. They based all these projections on market validation results, on customer contacts, and on how their financials compared to companies with similar business models. Co-founder Steve Keys says the business model produced during the seed round was "sharp and on target. It clearly delineated the business strategy from a customer-focused point of view." What did that do? Again: It helped mitigate risk and increase valuation for the Series A round.

Other value inflection points—seed round and beyond.

If you're smart, you'll hold fast to a value-inflection-point strategy through *all* your funding rounds (including an IPO—which, as you'll see, you should really view as "just another financing round," rather than an "exit strategy"). Run your company this way, and you'll stay focused on *business model execution*—not on infrastructure and other extraneous outputs. The results? A steady rise in your company's value. Along with a corresponding reduction in risk.

I reiterate: The specific value inflection points defined for a particular round depends on your company, its stage of development, and its business. Here, though, are some common milestones:

Recruit senior executives and key advisors.
During the seed round, flesh out your senior management and acquire key advisors. This validates that people are willing to bet their reputations and careers on the opportunity. Quite often, you

VIGNETTE CORPORATION: SANE CAPITALIZATION—FOR AN INSANELY BIG PAYOFF

When Ross Garber and Neil Webber founded Vignette Corporation in late 1995, they adopted a money-raising philosophy that would help them manage valuation in sane, reasonable increments as Vignette grew. Read on . . .

At the start, a friend offered to invest big bucks. Ross and Neil said no. "The valuation we could get was just not that good," recalls Neil. "We would have suffered. The risk was really high."

No wonder, because Ross and Neil aimed to do no less than carve out a brand-new market. Soon, they predicted, businesses worldwide would want to go online. Maybe Vignette could provide the tools and applications to help make that happen. With a view toward building a "market-driven company"—a view that persists to this day—the entrepreneurs funded themselves for four months of "cold-calling every website we could think of," Neil says. "We talked to them about their problems and figured out what the opportunity was to build a broad platform to meet their needs."

Armed with a business model and plenty of enthusiastic potential customers, Ross and Neil received seed funding in February 1996, from Austin Ventures and Sigma Partners. "It was enough to last us four or five months, maybe six if we were lucky," says Neil. That was fine with them, though, because the Vignette co-founders had adopted a money-raising philosophy they hoped would enable them to manage valuation in sane, reasonable increments as the company grew. It's a philosophy that has stood Vignette in very good stead—not only through the seed phase and three rounds of venture financing, but through a successful IPO in early 1999.

What is this philosophy? Neil says it best: "Every time you hit a value inflection point, such as quitting your job, developing a business model, calling a set of customers, or whatever, you achieve a stair-step increase in valuation and corresponding reduction in risk."

Vignette's seed goals were simple: to start building a high-quality engineering team, and to design a product "shell," with a storefront and screens, they could take to customers to demonstrate what the Vignette solution would do. By mid-1996, valuation had risen—and risk decreased—enough to obtain Series A financing for completing a 1.0 release and landing five or six big-name customers. Then, by mid-1997, "the customer acceptance risk had been taken out of the equation," Neil recalls. A Series B financing round provided enough money to "finish building out the entire company, launch big in the public-relations arena, and develop a nationwide sales force."

So successful was Vignette's execution of these milestones that by the fall of 1998, it had been named "Best Private Company in America" by *Red Herring*. Plans were made to go public. When the markets (temporarily) fell apart due to the Asian financial crisis, the IPO was shelved in favor of one last "mezzanine" round of venture capital to take the company through another year of aggressive expansion. Then, with the markets back stronger than anyone had expected by early 1999, the company completed its successful IPO.

Vignette remains a strong, viable business. And this, according to Neil, is due largely to a constant focus on the market and a commitment to the value inflection-based approach to capitalization. Hitting value inflection points matters much more, he says, than dilution. "Entrepreneurs get uptight about how much of their company they're selling," he says. "True, you want to manage dilution—but increasing the value of the company is the most important thing. Many people said our mezzanine round was too dilutive. But ultimately, we used that money to increase the value of the company. It more than paid for itself."

will find it equally vital in subsequent rounds—particularly when your business expands into new areas. Finding a CEO was one of Mediaprise's key early value inflection points. Anurag Kumar, who had served in the role up to that time, recognized the importance of having an experienced, seasoned CEO to drive the company toward deeper market penetration.

Recall from the second kick how as Ineto moved through its own seed, Series A, and Series B rounds, it needed a corps of strong advisors. Ineto wanted to provide an Internet-based service for managing customer communications, so for its advisors, Ineto drafted several former senior executives from MCI. All of them agreed to contribute their well-honed insight into call center technology and telecommunications. They also agreed to invest in the company and serve on its board of directors. Advisors such as these function as crucial partners for senior management.

Hire quality managers and individual contributors.

Building the team is an ongoing effort. Mediaprise hired directors of marketing, professional services, technology, and infrastructure during the seed round. It also brought on board a small technical team to continue designing and prototyping a product, along with two product marketers to help define product-specific marketing strategies. The engineering, sales, and marketing teams continued to expand during the Series A and subsequent rounds.

How many employees should you hire during a given funding period? No one can predict with total certainty. You should, however, establish up-front which technical and business roles will likely need to be filled, and when. In a tight job market, it can take months to fill a senior engineer's position—and even longer to hire experienced senior managers, product marketing managers, and marketing communications people. Develop a quarter-by-quarter hiring plan. And remember: *The team* is what enables you to execute on your business model—thereby raising valuation and minimizing the risk. Investors know that. They will be watching your team like hawks.

Prototype and develop the product.
Depending on the company and its product, your seed-round prototype might be a high-level demonstration of proposed functionality. Or it might be a more fleshed-out, minimally functional release. Your goal is this: *to prove the concept,* which requires creating a prototype in some form. Early on, Mediaprise built a very high-level prototype consisting primarily of screen mock-ups. They used it for conceptual-level selling. The prototype was *indispensable* for meeting both with prospective customers and with investors.

Neil Webber, a co-founder of Vignette Corporation—one of Austin's prominent technology successes—recalls that during Vignette's seed round, he and his colleagues created "a shell, or a storefront with screens, that would suffice as a demo to customers of what we would do." Once this was accomplished, Vignette developed a working product that attracted paying customers. In short order, it acquired the loyal customer base that quickly made Vignette a leading provider of e-business software and services.

In the early stages, the prototype helps generate sales. As you move beyond the prototype stage, the product takes on fuller functionality. What determines this functionality at any given point? *The requirements of the market.* During the Mediaprise Series A period, the product was fleshed out to prove the technology's scalability. Because it was a hosted platform, *proof* was required that multiple customers could be served from the platform simultaneously. Similarly, Newgistics (the company with the returns logistics process described in our third kick) had to establish its *process* for some subset of a huge nationwide customer base. During the Series A round, Newgistics chose to roll out the solution in the Dallas/Ft. Worth area. As for Vignette, it elected to have a complete version 1.0 produced and on the market during that round.

*Sign on brand-name customers—and gain continued
market acceptance.*
When high-profile customers sign on your dotted line, that's a significant value inflection point. Why? Because—and I've said it
before, but it's worth repeating—*When customers open their wallets,
you have the ultimate market validation.* If your product is only in
prototype stage, you can obtain letters of intent, which are letters
stating that the customer intends to adopt the solution. Mediaprise
obtained letters of intent from a major manufacturer and a major dis-
tributor during the seed round—a strong validation point when time
came to raise the next round. At the seed stage, customers will often
sign on as "alpha" or "beta" customers, agreeing to field-test the
evolving product. These agreements are significant—particularly
when they generate revenue. Later on, your customer roster will
include businesses that purchase entire product lines.

For its Series A round, Mediaprise set out to capture up to five
large, high-visibility manufacturer customers. Each of these paying,
subscribing customers would bring in $400,000 per year in revenue,
for a Series A first-year revenue goal of $2 million. Vignette's Series A
objective was to sign up to ten big-name customers. As these examples suggest, your company will have its own unique customer-
related goals at each stage. Your overriding objective? Line up *enough*
customers to minimize the "customer traction" risk. Which requires,
of course, that you remain a lean, mean validating machine—one with
a constant awareness of customers' changing needs.

Establish partnerships.
As we saw during the third kick, major partners might be required
for you to execute your business model successfully. Each partner
provides some key solution component. Consider the reverse logistics startup Newgistics, which needed retail, distribution, and warehousing partners to serve its e-merchant and cataloger customers. By
landing these partners during the seed phase, Newgistics chalked up

a huge win valuation-wise. The partners made it possible for Newgistics to offer *a complete solution*—and to do so quickly. For an even stronger validation point, the partners also invested in the company.

Depending on your company, other kinds of partnerships might be value inflection points as well. We're all aware, for example, of the ubiquitous press releases that flood today's hyperactive marketplace. A large percentage of these releases announce industry partnerships. Most times, the agreements involve pacts to sell each other's products or some other collaborative business arrangement. Depending on the industry, the partnerships might actually be meaningful revenue-wise. Or they might, as Vignette co-founder Neil Webber puts it, be "simply a matter of dotting the I's and crossing the T's"— showing the industry, and the market, that one is a "player." Establishing (and, of course, announcing) these partnerships is a value inflection point for Series A and subsequent rounds.

Line up investors.

Recuiting investors is an extremely critical value inflection point—at any stage. You should aim for a good mix of investors. Each will (typically) play one of the following roles:

- *Lead investor.* A round is "led" by one major investor—most often, a venture capital firm—that invests the majority of the new money. Obtaining a term sheet from the next round's lead investor is a crucial milestone. It establishes valuation— and, equally important, makes it easier to line up other investors. Austin Ventures led Mediaprise's Series A round based on the company's execution of its seed-round value inflection points.

- *Strategic investor(s).* This type of investor is both a business partner and a major source of financing. These investors add credibility, which raises value. You will recall that Newgistics, the return logistics startup, received Series A financing from both of its corporate business partners, R.R. Donnelley and USFreightways. Another portfolio company, Lane15 Software, established partnerships and received strategic financing from Compaq, Dell, and Intel. Lane15 is creating software for managing the new InfiniBand computer network environment, an industry development spearheaded by these strategic investors and other powerhouse hardware companies. (You'll get to know Lane15 a lot better a bit later on in this book.)

- *Other investors.* Any time you land a quality lead or strategic investor, you're paving the way for similar commitments from additional investors. On the basis of Austin Ventures' agreement to lead the Series A round, Mediaprise attracted an additional investment from AV Labs, and new investors Access Venture Partners and the West Coast firm meVC. Each of these investors brought its own unique value to the table. MeVC, for instance, specializes in the Mediaprise market niche and was able to hook the company up with potential customers and key analysts.

Important! Follow the "comfortable margin" rule.

When it comes to cash, there are four main rules we give our companies:

Rule number one, never run out of cash.
Rule number two, never run out of cash.
Rule number three, never run out of cash.
Rule number four, when in doubt see the first three rules.

This is critical. *Always* determine how much your team needs to accomplish a round's value inflection points, then add a reasonable margin to that figure. How much? That depends on the industry, your business model, your team's experience, and other company-specific factors. What does the margin accomplish? It gives you flexibility. It enables your team to deal with the inevitable unforeseen challenges that beset any growing company. It helps ensure you won't get caught short.

Don't pooh-pooh the comfortable margin, and *don't make it too small*. If you're forced to go out and raise capital before achieving a round's value inflection points, you're in trouble. The valuation has not risen enough—nor the risk been mitigated enough—to warrant a step up in valuation. You're sunk.

A related point. Not only does it cost *more money* than you think to accomplish a set of value inflection points, but *it also takes twice as long to raise capital.* The tougher the economic environment, the more true this becomes. If you think you need three months to raise a financing round, apply the "2X formula" and give yourself six.

What's the IPO? Just another financing round.

If you're like most people, you see the IPO as the be-all and end-all, the end point, the pot of gold at the end of the rainbow. Get smart. *See it differently.* View the IPO as merely the next financing round. When you have an IPO, that says your company has mitigated its risk, validated its market, and proven its business model enough to be able to raise money in the public markets.

Don't get me wrong. I'm not saying an IPO is not important. We all know otherwise. In fact, the event is in itself a significant value inflection point. "The IPO is incredibly important in terms of branding and validating the company," says Charles Sansbury, senior VP of corporate development at Vignette, "especially from the point of view of customers who worry about vendor viability. They now know for sure there's plenty of money on the balance sheet."

At IPO time, all the principles we've explored in this chapter continue to apply. You must earmark all the money you raise for a well-defined, planned-out set of value inflection points. You must continue building value and advancing the business model. Vignette, for example, wisely used a portion of its IPO proceeds to—among other things—develop relationships with channel partners. These partners now deliver millions of dollars in OEM sales.

Jump aboard the virtuous circle of time to market.

A company is a continuous work in progress. What happens when you choose to pursue an optimized capitalization strategy? What do you accomplish when you take only the money that's needed to hit a set of value inflection points, then work toward those milestones? Your business acquires significant momentum toward building value and reducing risk. Which leads to *more funding,* which increases the momentum even more for hitting new value inflection points, which helps build *more value* and *reduces the risk* even further.

Figure 5 illustrates this process. I call it the "virtuous circle of time to market," because the key driver is always market validation (the most "virtuous" value inflection point of all). What is the best form of market validation? *Selling your product.*

The virtuous circle stands in sharp contrast to the value-decreasing cycle of *output*-oriented behavior sparked when a company obtains a lot of money quickly. In the virtuous circle, each trip around the circle—from the seed round to Series A to Series B and so on, through an IPO and secondary offering—is marked by the execution of key value inflection points. As the figure shows, for most businesses these milestones involve continuing market validation. Staff expansion. Business model validation. Product evolution. Market penetration. Partnerships. The addition of executives

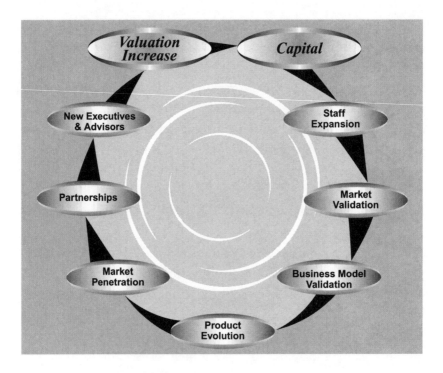

Figure 5. Virtuous circle of time to market.

and advisors. These accomplishments are the core drivers of any business.

This self-perpetuating dynamic ensures that the company will hit existing and new markets with the right product. That it will remain responsive to customers' real needs. And that more and more customers will "vote with their money" to produce profitability as time goes by. Which is, of course, the *ultimate* risk mitigation.

"Getting a small seed round in the beginning was perfect for Mediaprise," says Anurag Kumar. "Given where we were at that point, we couldn't have gotten a good pre-money valuation. A bigger investment would have brutally diluted our ownership. This way, we kept a larger percentage of the company. Best of all, we focused the company on achieving clear milestones that raised the valuation before we obtained follow-on financing. We will continue to subscribe to this capitalization strategy as we proceed to grow Mediaprise. It's by far the best approach for the team, for our investors, and for the business."

✳

Speaking of investors, we've talked a little bit about what they're looking for when they evaluate a company. Let's dive into that issue a little more deeply. What *do* investors want, anyway? The next kick will tell you . . .

FOURTH KICK: TAKEAWAYS

✴ **$10 million right out of the gate? Lose that thought.**
When it comes to financing, here's the rule: Raise what's needed to move to the next stage of development. That goes double for the early-stage company.

✴ **Why not raise megabucks right away? Two reasons:**
- You'll probably spend too much on *outputs:* infrastructure, big events, expensive deals, and the like. Think this is tangible evidence of progress? Think again. *Output-oriented activities add no real value.*
- You'll dilute ownership for the founding team and investors—in a serious way, and with deadly consequences.

✴ **Be "execution-oriented" when it comes to raising money. How? Think *value inflection points.*
- These execution milestones reduce risk.
- They increase company valuation.
- You should carefully plan them in advance.
- Hit *all* of them before you raise more cash.
- Then, raise enough to accomplish your next set of value inflection points.

✴ *Must-do* **early-stage value inflection points—the Big Two:**
- Market validation, market validation, market validation.
- Proof that you have a profitable business model.

✴ **Additional value inflection points for the seed stage and beyond.**
- Key senior executives and great advisors.
- High-quality managers and employees.

- Product prototype and development.
- Brand-name customers—and ever-expanding market acceptance.
- Major partners.
- Smart, connected investors.

✳ Don't forget the "comfortable margin" rule.

Figure out how much you need to get through the next set of value inflection points. Then add a comfortable margin. Plus, if you think it will take three months to raise financing, give yourself six. Remember: *Never run out of cash.*

✳ What's an IPO?

No, it's not a pot at the end of the rainbow. Think of the IPO this way: as just another round of financing.

✳ Sane, prudent financing: the virtuous circle of time to market.

Each trip around the financing circle is marked by the execution of key value inflection points. Stay on the circle—and stay on track.

INVESTORS FUND GREAT TEAMS—NOT BUSINESS PLANS

With its great breakfast menu, La Madeleine in the Westlake neighborhood is an office-away-from-the-office for much of the Austin high-tech community. On any weekday morning, the French-style café is packed with entrepreneurs, venture people, consultants, and other local players. Since La Madeleine is right on my way to the office and is so good for staying plugged-in, I like to meet people there for early breakfasts. That gives us plenty of time to eat, take care of business, and catch up on the Austin startup scene before heading off to start the "real" workday.

One La Madeleine breakfast I particularly remember is the one I had a while back with Jens Tellefsen. Jens and his startup team had given a presentation at AV Labs the afternoon before. They were impressive. In fact, the minute they were out of the office, we knew we'd found the right deal in a space we were targeting. We were excited by this company and its team. Now, I had a chance to informally share our decision with the thirty-five-year-old Swede.

"Jens," I said as we unloaded our trays and sat down. "You guys were great—it's a go."

"Excellent!" Jens replied. "You know, we knew the presentation went well, but we were a bit worried about one or two sections of the business plan. We never discussed it in the meeting. So I guess it was clear enough, eh?"

"Jens—let me tell you how we evaluate these deals," I said. "We never focus on the plan. Once we evaluate the market space and the team, we wait to see the presentation."

I was relieved by Jens' reaction. "You're kidding!" he chuckled, seemingly not a bit put out that we hadn't gone deep on his forty-odd-page business plan. "We spent months on that thing. Oh well, I suppose it doesn't matter much at this point."

"It really doesn't," I told him. "In fact, don't even think about the business plan again—not anytime soon, at least."

"Gladly," he laughed. Then Jens and I covered some details of what would be in the term sheet. Later, as I wound through the hills west of downtown and into the city, I pondered the fact that people learn important business lessons in all kinds of places. Over breakfast at La Madeleine, Jens Tellefsen picked up some very handy insights about the business plan. In this chapter, you'll learn the same things he did:

- The business plan is *not* the be-all and end-all for getting funded.
- Sometimes investors don't even *read* business plans.
- What are the critical criteria? Your team and your market space.

Here, we'll solve a mystery that has befuddled many an entrepreneur: *What do investors really want, anyway?* What *does* help recruit prospective backers, if not the business plan? How can you put together a team that, like Jens', is likely to get you funded? How can you pinpoint a market with real potential? And what's the best way to articulate all this for investors?

First, let's back up and look at the business plan. Let's see just how crazy it is to toil over this document—especially when you make it #1 on your to-do list.

"Huh? Stop writing my business plan?" That's right. Cork it.

Did "Write a business plan!" come down from a mountaintop, carved on a stone tablet? I don't think so. But that's what people tend to believe, and it's really no wonder. Check it out for yourself: Perform a cursory search of the Amazon.com database, for a starter. You'll get a list of more than 600 books on business plans. Look under software, and you'll get more than ten business-plan software packages. Plus, there are nearly seventy business plan–related products from an Internet-based firm that sells management products and services. There's even a video: *How to Really Create a Successful Business Plan.* (I really promise—that's the actual title.)

It kills me to think of all the entrepreneurs—not just high-tech startup wannabes, but people dreaming of corner retail stores, or restaurants, or other businesses—combing through all these offerings, trying to decide which one is best. It must be incredibly confusing. Things get even more confusing when they dive into the nuts and bolts of writing and assembling their business plans. Nine times out of ten, they have no clue what they're doing—even if they're following the dotted lines in whatever how-to book or video or whatever. Nine times out of ten, they're wasting their time.

Don't get me wrong. Is it *bad* that all the business-plan assistance is available? Not at all. At some point, most entrepreneurs—though not all of them, by any means—*do* write business plans. Indeed, even the AV Labs website encourages startups seeking funding to introduce themselves with "a business plan and/or executive summary."

Writing a business plan, then, is not the problem. What is? Viewing the business plan as your *primary* goal, right out of the gate. "Okay guys, we've quit our jobs. Now let's write a business plan and get us some money." That's what I'm talking about. (Sound familiar?) It's a very dangerous course. It you follow it, you're labeling yourself a victim of the myth that *investors fund business plans.* Here's how the thinking goes: Write a good plan and throw it over the transom to a venture firm. Worse yet, blindly e-mail it to venture firms around the country. The money is bound to follow. Use the correct format, and investors will salivate over the opportunity to dole out the cash. Make the plan detailed and thorough, and your chances go up even more.

If you subscribe to these beliefs, you could spend weeks or months burning the midnight oil, laboring over a document. *Before you really do much of anything else.*

The business plan's an output. Give it a rest.

Remember output mania? When you give in to output mania, you produce some tangible *thing*—an artifact, a claim, or whatever. But you do little to advance your business model. Write a business plan too soon, and you're engaging in output mania. The early business plan is a tragic waste of your resources—particularly when crafted at a time when you have little or no funding.

What should you be doing instead? Assembling a team. Defining and validating your market. Devising a profitable business model. These are *execution-oriented* projects. They advance the business model. And they're far more likely than a business plan to lure the investor's dollar. In a nutshell:

> Execution-oriented projects + no business plan =
> decent chance of getting funded.
> Business plan + output orientation = a snowball's chance.

This is what Jens learned when I told him we hadn't gone deep on his business plan. "I thought a detailed business plan was essential for raising money," he says. "Now I know that all the time we spent getting those details down on paper was probably not worthwhile. The investors were much more interested in meeting the team and evaluating our grasp of the market—not whether we had written a comprehensive business plan in our early stages."

Where should the business plan be on your agenda? Dead last.

Early-stage, execution-oriented projects lay the groundwork for your company. You must tackle them well before you even begin to *think* of writing a business plan. Indeed, once you've done these things, *the business plan writes itself.* Or—and this was what happened with Jens and his team—the business plan becomes totally irrelevant. Sometimes, you flat-out don't need a business plan at all. As Jens himself puts it, "We decided not to spend any time on a business plan as we approached investors for our subsequent Series A round. It just didn't seem to add any value."

That's right: No investor *ever* dove into a business plan from Jens and his team. Yet they received seed funding—money they used to validate the market, build the team, and develop a business model. What's more, they raised substantial follow-on funding for growing the business. And they did it *without a business plan.*

"Okay, so if a business plan isn't important, what is?" *The work.*

If you're obsessing over a business plan, I have one piece of advice: *Stop! Don't focus on the plan . . . do the work.* What work, you ask? The projects we've already explored in this book:

- Put together a great team—working colleagues, plus a cadre of rock-solid advisors and board members. What are you after? *Execution intelligence.*
- As thoroughly you can with the resources you have, *validate the market.*
- Define a solution that solves some of your customers' most vicious pain, and devise a strategy for *getting to market fast*— either by partnering with established businesses or by designing a minimally accepted feature set with the first release.

- Figure out how much money you need—and define the *value inflection points* you'll hit with that sum.

While I've already talked about these activities, they bear further examination here. Why? Because for investors, they're what's critical. If you knock out these milestones, you'll be prepared to face even the most finicky investors confidently. *Even if you haven't produced a complete business plan,* you will be ready for your first and most important sales job: convincing investors to fund the company.

Intimidated by the funding pitch? Think of it as a sales call.

As you'll see later, the core artifacts you'll need to get funding will often be a hard-hitting PowerPoint presentation and an executive summary. If you're required to write a business plan, doing so will be straight-forward—so long as you've done "the work." If you have, then the business plan can be written in a week or less. *Not* weeks or months.

Now let's look at the funding presentation itself. It's often referred to as a "pitch." And no wonder, because it's very much like another well-known pitch—the corporate sales pitch. Your team is, after all, *selling itself* to a group of people—in this case, investors. You're convincing your audience to buy off on the notion that you and your ideas can evolve into a viable business. You and your ideas are, in effect, the product being sold.

Besides its objectives, other features of a funding pitch also resemble the corporate sales process:

- *You cater your message to the audience's needs.* Investors want to see proof that you've done "the work"—or, if you haven't, that your team recognizes the need to do it. This is just like the corporate sales pitch, where a sales rep matches product and company messages to a prospect's needs.
- *You clearly articulate features and benefits.* When you sell a product, you convince a customer that the product features

will produce clear-cut advantages—greater productivity, lower costs, and so on. In a similar vein, when you sell investors, you present features (the team, the market, the solution) and benefits (the projected payoff to investors).

- *Relationships rule.* As any good corporate salesperson knows, the relationship game is key. You play this game prior to making a spiel—via referrals, phone calls, materials sent ahead, and so on. In the same way, you build relationships prior to pitching investors. You ask yourself key questions: Who are the biggest influencers on my investor prospect? How do I get to those people, and how can they give me more credibility? Most often, as you'll see, trusted, well-respected advisors refer you to investors before any meetings take place. (In fact, very few plans are *ever* funded over the transom. Without the relationships, you can pretty much forget it.)

- *You supplement the pitch with collateral.* Here's where the business plan finally comes in. When you make a funding pitch, the plan functions exactly as a corporate brochure does in a corporate sales call. You use it as support. You leave it behind. It bolsters the points you've made in your spiel. But it seldom, if ever, initiates the relationship. And it is not what makes the sale. *Relying on a business plan to obtain funding is like sending a brochure to a corporate sales prospect, then sitting back and waiting for a check to arrive.* It doesn't work.

Later on, you'll find out more about the funding pitch. For now, remember this: If you have done "the work," what does the pitch involve? Crafting that work into clear, coherent *sales messages* for investors. And viewing these investors as your first and (at this stage, at least) most critically important customers.

Now, let's take a look at "the work" as it was accomplished by Jens' company, called allmystuff, and by another AV Labs company, Covasoft. How did this work help make these startups attractive investments?

Building your team: Round up A+ colleagues and advisors.

As allmystuff and Covasoft both illustrate, a solid team has to be one of your #1 priorities. Most definitely, you should assemble a team prior to writing a business plan. If at all possible, do so before approaching investors. When we first got wind of allmystuff, the team bios alone made us want to look seriously at the company. As for Covasoft, the team had not yet been completely recruited. But the members who were in place made a very compelling case that their experience, business concept, and market space warranted an investment. With Covasoft, one of the first things investors did was help them build the team.

Assemble all the right stuff at the right time—how allmystuff did it.

I've already said how impressed we were at AV Labs the day we met with Jens and his allmystuff co-founders. They were technically astute—and very experienced in the proposed e-business market space. Take a lesson from this: Before you present a business concept to investors, do whatever you can to build such a team. Your startup's most critical ingredient is *execution intelligence.*

The well-put-together allmystuff team did not come about by accident. Yours won't, either. "From the time I had the original idea, I actively sought to create a well-balanced group of smart, capable people who could do anything really well, and whose expertise complemented each other," recalls Jens, whose prior startup experience no doubt contributed to his team-building abilities. He looked for people with strong entrepreneurial backgrounds who would be "comfortable moving into ill-defined spaces and pursuing innovative business ideas." He sought out those who had worked on large business development initiatives, built sophisticated products, and crafted infrastructure solutions. Within a few months of the idea's inception, a core team of five people had coalesced.

Key team members had held management-level positions at either Trilogy Systems or pcOrder.com, two Austin-based e-business pioneers. Jens had spearheaded a Trilogy business unit to create, market, and sell a sales-compensation management solution; he would serve as CEO. As CTO, he brought on Scott Miller. Scott's experience in product management and development had been honed at pcOrder.com, which offered a site where customers could interactively configure and order PC systems. Similarly accomplished team members joined up to steer business and product development.

What did allmystuff set out to do? Essentially, their customers would be durable goods manufacturers and retailers. With the allmystuff solution, these businesses could give consumers product ownership information over the Internet. The big payoff? Increased post-sale (or "downstream") revenue. According to Jens, the people on the core team "could knock out the initial phase of the solution very quickly." They also had business and development skills for getting the solution to market. Jens and his executive team pounded home this fact in their presentation to us. It worked. As I have said, the team itself played a big role in our decision to invest.

Round out your skills set—how Covasoft did it.

Cody Menard is a perfect example of the "techie" who conceives a brilliant idea for a business. Cody was a longtime engineering manager and former director of BMC's Enterprise Resource Planning (ERP) group. Along the way, he noticed a problem in the burgeoning e-business world: Businesses needed better ways to manage their e-business transactions and environments.

Determined to form a company to provide e-business management solutions, he corralled BMC colleague Kim Evans. Kim's management experience in partner and client services made her a fit for leading these functions initially. Cody would spearhead development.

In addition to recruiting Kim, Cody wrote a business plan—using, incidentally, "a book on business plans that said you needed market information," he recalls. Even so, he lacked awareness of the market, marketing issues, and general business—which made it hard to envision, much less describe, a solid business strategy. Around that time, Cody approached the venture firm Trellis Partners. Trellis partner John Long, himself an electrical engineer by training, immediately saw value in the concept and market space. By the same token, John realized Cody needed a major business player on the team. In short order, he hooked him up with Gary Neill, an executive well-versed in startup finance and operations. Gary signed on as CEO.

Gary's business acumen complemented his own technical know-how to "an astonishing degree," Cody says. "Before Gary came on board, the pitch was 90 percent technical; afterward it was just 40 to 50 percent technical, with the rest devoted to business issues." Indeed, it was on the strength of this that AV Labs agreed to seed-fund and work with Covasoft. The stronger, better-rounded team also figured into our decision. Take a lesson from Cody himself: "If you're a techie with a great idea, you need a CEO who understands how to make the business and marketing case for you. Otherwise you don't have a chance."

Again, remember this: Your team and market space are decisive indicators of your company's future success. That's why, when you go for funding, one of these things might occur:

- If you have an outstanding team but a mediocre market space, investors may fund your team and guide you toward a more promising market. When they're confronted with an ideal mix of skills in one team, *few investors can pass it up.* It's simply too unique.
- If you have a well-defined, valid market but your team needs work, investors will often sign on to help build the team. This is what John Long of Trellis Partners did with Covasoft. Of course, you need one or two existing team members—people like Cody and Kim—who are strong in their respective areas.

Even with a great market space, what happens with a mediocre team? By and large, *investors will just say no.*[8]

Advisors and board members—supplement your knowledge and expertise.

When examining a startup team, investors will put your advisors and board of directors under a microscope. Why? Because *great advisors and directors are crucial,* for two reasons:

- *They lend legitimacy.* Are your advisors well-known investors? Experienced, highly regarded entrepreneurs? Technical gurus with special insight into the product and its evolution? Strategic partners? By definition, a great advisor "pre-qualifies" your company—otherwise, he or she would never sign on to participate. The more astute your advisors, the more attractive the opportunity. Advisors help establish the relationship that will *lead* to a "sale;" they introduce you to your investors ("customers") prior to the actual funding pitch, where *you* make the sale.
- *They provide guidance.* Good advisors can help steer everything from product directions to market segmentation. If you're smart, you'll recognize this. You'll gather up as much expert assistance as you can. In this case, investors are your market and customers (the people you'll be selling to). Great advisors can help you understand what these customers seek.

---

8. As an early-stage funder and accelerator, AV Labs tends to be more flexible in this regard than larger follow-on investors who make multimillion-dollar investments at higher valuations. We almost always help our companies strengthen their founding teams. We also provide experts from our ranks of seasoned Venture Fellows to serve in executive roles until permanent replacements can be found. Before our companies go for Series A financing, we require that all major executive roles be filled with permanent hires. This only heightens the likelihood of substantial funding—investors look very closely at the complete team and evaluate its execution intelligence.

Before Jens Tellefsen approached AV Labs, he spent a lot of time building a team of advisors. "I wanted to find the smartest people in Austin," he recalls. With a keen eye for who that might be, he spent time with such local industry stars as Ross Garber, co-founder of Vignette Corporation; Andy Palmer, co-founder and vice president of pcOrder and Bow Street, a company that helps corporate customers develop their e-business; and Paul Tobias, a partner at Wilson Sonsini Goodrich and Rosati, one of Austin's premier high-tech law firms.

Believe me, this early advisor roster played a big role in AV Labs' decision to work with allmystuff. Later on, when the company went for its Series A funding, follow-on investors were equally impressed. By then, allmystuff had taken on another advisor: Guy Hoffman, a venture partner at TL Ventures. "Guy helped a lot," Jens says. "He is sophisticated in terms of the questions and challenges of an e-commerce business. He's built a business himself and knows what it takes to run a company from an operations standpoint." As he worked with the allmystuff team, says Jens, Guy made a strong case for going after manufacturing and retail companies, as opposed to hosting a business-to-consumer site catering to the end consumer. As we will see in the following section, heeding this advice made a big difference for the company.

In a similar vein, Trellis Partners' John Long was an early and very influential advisor to Cody Menard and Covasoft. John has a reputation as an astute investor with solid market knowledge and insight.

Define your market space: What is the risk? What's the potential?

Investors will see your market space as absolutely essential. It all comes down, again, to market risk. The lower the risk, the more attractive the investment. How can you show investors that your company has a relatively lower market risk? With evidence that your team knows your market. That you understand who you'll target with the solution, and why. And that you're committed to *solving the customers' pain.*

What's the best way to minimize market risk? You've got it— *market validation.* Market validation is the key feature that will make your "product" (your company) attractive to your "customer" (investors). It's what will close the sale. I've said it before, but I'll say it again: AV Labs companies are required to thoroughly validate their markets. We fund and work with very early-stage firms, so we almost always take on companies that have yet to do market validation. Most, in fact, have merely performed high-level secondary research. Complete market validation becomes one of their first projects.

Why do we stress market validation so strongly? Among other reasons, because larger follow-on investors—the ones who'll sign on to put tens of millions of dollars into a company over its lifetime— want *proof* that it's been done. It must be in place for the investors to buy off on the company. And needless to say: You should do market validation well before you undertake a business plan.

Tapping into downstream revenues—how allmystuff did it.
Jens Tellefsen's initial concept for allmystuff arose from three basic principles:

- *Consumer pain.* Today's consumers are frustrated with aspects of product ownership. Keeping track of receipts—not to mention warranty information, owner's manuals, compatible parts and accessories, and other relevant information—is cumbersome, at best. At the same time, these sophisticated and demanding consumers expect hands-on service. They want one-click Internet purchases. And they demand other relevant ownership services as well. Most manufacturers and retailers simply don't offer such services.
- *Manufacturer and retailer pain.* These companies have almost no idea who their customers are. They are certainly not able to spark ongoing relationships throughout a product life cycle.

Only now are they starting to focus on how to engage with customers after the initial purchase, beyond the traditional avenues of customer support, sales, and delivery logistics.

- *Downstream revenue potential.* In many categories, businesses can make more money downstream—*after* the initial sale—than within the sale itself. Cross-selling, parts and accessories, extended service warranties, and upgrades are all opportunities for downstream revenue. How can companies capture this potential?

Prior to approaching AV Labs, the allmystuff team talked to a few potential customers. More important, they drew on their experience with the manufacturer and retailer markets. Jens recalls being "flabbergasted by how little these businesses knew about their customers and how little they did to engage with customers." Hence the insight that led to the allmystuff business concept—an insight that was sufficiently compelling for AV Labs to seed-fund the startup.

What was the major seed-round objective (value inflection point)? Dramatically expanded market validation. The team extensively surveyed consumers. They also talked to at least fifty manufacturers and retailers about their pain around post-sale customer interaction. What was the biggest opportunity? To enable these businesses to offer "consumer product ownership" pages on their respective websites. Originally, the company planned to host an allmystuff.com site, where consumers could track their own product information. This plan was shelved in response both to the market and to investors, who wanted allmystuff to leverage consumer traffic to manufacturers' and e-tailers' sites. Investors, in particular, felt the risk of a business-to-consumer model was too great in today's market (to say the least).

What did follow-on investors find so attractive about allmystuff? The team's extensive market validation, understanding of the market space, and customer-oriented focus. According to Guy Hoffman, who led the Series A investment, "the team gave me scripts and reports of research conducted directly with representatives of customer companies. I was able to validate that what they were telling me was what they had heard from their target audience, not from family or friends or business associates. This played a pivotal role in our decision to fund the company."

Refining the business idea—how Covasoft did it.

You've seen that Cody Menard learned (from potential investors, no less) that his technical know-how was great for building products but insufficient for starting and running a business. When this happened, Cody was "shocked," he recalls. "Coming from a totally technical perspective, it was amazing to me that investors spend more time on the market than on the technology. They said, 'You have to prove there's a market, that people will pay for this.' I had absolutely no idea how to go about doing that."

As we have already seen, bringing the business-oriented Gary Neill on board as CEO was a huge boon. By the time the team approached AV Labs, they had scoped part of the market through preliminary Internet research. They'd also obtained a seminal research report from industry analyst firm International Data Corporation. We were sufficiently sold on the concept's potential to seed-fund the company and help it land larger Series A financing. Immediately, of course, we steered the team to—you guessed it—market validation.

They interviewed several hundred customers. These conversations, says Cody, "greatly affected the development process and helped define the product direction. Some features we had thought were important became much less so. We altered the development schedule to address the hottest pain points first. What evolved was a commitment to focus on the features customers told us were most needed."

Covasoft identified an initial customer base from its market validation effort. It also pinpointed the target market for the first release. AV Labs worked with the team to refine (and refine, and refine again) their presentation to encompass the wealth of information they were obtaining. "Just between my pitch and the first one we did after Gary Neill came on board, there was a huge difference," Cody says. "By the time we revised the pitch over and over again to reflect our growing market understanding, it was 100 percent different. I would not have recognized my original business plan in the presentation we finally gave to obtain Series A financing."

What you need to focus on next: time to market and financing.

Again, the team and the market space are must-haves for attracting investment dollars. Once these two features are in place, you have a good chance of raising needed funds. At the same time, you should also—before approaching an investor, *certainly* prior to writing a business plan—articulate prudent time-to-market and capitalization strategies. These additional projects only help heighten investors' interest.[9]

Get to market—fast.

Investors—particularly large follow-on investors—want to see a workable strategy for getting to market quickly. The two most common strategies? As you saw in the third kick, you can either partner with established businesses, or provide minimally accepted feature sets for the first release.

By the time Jens and the allmystuff team went for Series A financing, they had designed a solution that would enable manufacturers and retailers to maximize downstream, or post-sale, revenue. As an

---

9. Once again, it is important to distinguish the seed investor, such as AV Labs, from the follow-on investment firm looking to provide multimillion-dollar financing. At AV Labs, we normally require that during this early phase, a company validate the market, develop a viable business model, and identify and recruit follow-on investors. Part of validation is to create a product prototype with enough detail to demonstrate how the finished product will function. Teams use, refine, and reuse this prototype while progressing through market validation. Throughout, we educate our teams in the value-inflection-point approach. They map out execution milestones for the seed round and—to up their chances of follow-on financing—define Series A value inflection points as well.

initial product, the team would deliver a "product ownership module," which would let companies give their consumers complete access to their own and related products. This initial offering would entice the end consumers to register their products. It would also, the team predicted, make consumers more likely to buy additional goods.

As its initial target market, allmystuff went after manufacturers and retailers of computers, computer peripherals, and consumer electronics. These market segments had expressed the most wicked pain. Eventually, the allmystuff target market will include makers of everything from household appliances to cars.

Limiting the market helped make allmystuff a compelling investment. So did deciding on an initial product offering that would fulfill a key part of the allmystuff vision. Allmystuff, investors felt, would be able to reach its target market quickly. It all added up to a decision to invest.

Optimized capitalization strategy.

As the allmystuff team went after their Series A financing, they defined clear value inflection points for the round. These execution milestones would build out the company. They would also prove that large numbers of manufacturing and retail customers would adopt the solution. The value inflection points included:

- Closing a number of name-brand accounts that would have the allmystuff solution up and running. During seed-round market validation interviews, Black & Decker emerged as a good prospect; Jens and his co-founders were able to meet with Black & Decker's VP of e-commerce. Other good prospects were 3Com, Casio, and Dell. All three inked deals with allmystuff shortly after the Series A round closed.
- Showing allmystuff could sell its enterprise software solution for significant dollars—amounts that would bring the company hundreds of thousands in yearly revenue per customer.

- Identifying a large untapped market (or ancillary market) the company could grow into.
- Completing the management team. Vice presidents of engineering, finance, and marketing would be hired.

When they outlined these value inflection points in their pitch to Series A investors, Jens and his team proved they knew how to propel the company forward and increase its valuation. If you are entering the high-tech arena with a new company, you must have this understanding. If you do—and if you also have a strong team and a viable market space—you will be downright irresistible to even the most demanding investor.

Okay, you do need a PowerPoint presentation— but keep it *brief*.

Let's assume you've done the work I've described on the preceding pages. You have a strong team—one that embodies attributes of execution intelligence. Top-notch management and advisors are on board, providing guidance and support. You've defined a viable market space for the proposed solution. You have a strategy for getting to market quickly. You've also defined key value inflection points for the upcoming round.

What's next? Articulating all this work, and all this knowledge, to investors. Conducting, in other words, the sales pitch that will convince investors to buy the company's potential. For this, I suggest that *the best way to proceed is to develop a twelve-slide PowerPoint presentation, a one- or two-page executive summary, and team and advisor bios.*

In a moment, we will take a closer look at these items. But first, keep in mind that before the pitch can even be given, you have to get a meeting with an investment group. How can you make that happen? There's one almost surefire way: *a good referral.*

Get referrals: It's all about relationships.

Very occasionally, investors will agree to meet with a team simply on the strength of an executive summary and/or business plan received "cold." I can guarantee, though, that this doesn't happen very often—just as corporate executives don't often meet with sales reps simply because they've received a product brochure. As a matter of fact, at AV Labs we meet with fewer than 10% of the companies that introduce themselves this way. The rest of the time, we meet with teams who've been referred to us.

"People told us never to send a business plan cold," Jens says, speaking of his team's preparation for raising their Series A money. "I had to find people who could introduce me to the investment firms." Jens developed what he calls a "pipeline of people" to accomplish this. He used the "guerilla tactic" of making sure at least one person— sometimes as many as three—told a particular firm about allmystuff. Only then would he send the allmystuff executive summary and bios.

John Thornton of Austin Ventures, for example, first made us aware of Jens Tellefsen and allmystuff. It was also through John— along with John Long of Trellis Partners—that we heard about Covasoft. We knew, based on the recommendations of John Thornton and John Long, that allmystuff and Covasoft would be interesting. These companies were, in effect, *pre-qualified* as investment prospects.

Why do investors make such excellent referrals for getting to see other investors? For the same reason a reputable customer's recommendation makes it easier for a sales rep to meet with a corporate prospect. Corporate customers can recognize the value of a particular solution. Investors are in business to recognize strong teams and viable business concepts. Like corporate executives who keep an eye on the bottom line, investors understand the risk of investing in a startup. They will refer only those companies with *manageable* risk. What's more, if they're willing to refer a team to other investors, it means they're willing to put their reputations behind the company. That only heightens the attractiveness of investing in the team.

AV LABS: ONE MODEL FOR THE EARLY-STAGE DEAL FLOW

At AV Labs, we're contacted by a flood of aspiring entrepreneurs every month. Sometimes we receive a complete twenty-five to thirty-page business plan. Sometimes we get a three- or four-page executive summary. Sometimes a team sends us a one-page overview. What happens then? How does one startup accelerator proceed to evaluate these submissions? Read on . . .

Michael Rovner, a partner at AV Labs, heads up a team of Venture Fellows tasked with evaluating all the business plans, executive summaries, and overviews we receive. At least two people read each plan. Some opportunities require "extra squinting" to understand their full potential, and having multiple readers helps ensure they get a fair shake. What do the evaluating teams look for? The "Big Three" ingredients: a great *team,* a viable *product concept,* and a big *market space.*

"The plan or summary you send a venture firm," says Michael, "should be seen as a ticket to the game. For us, it's an artifact designed to get you a meeting—no more, no less. As long as the team, the business concept, and the market space can be articulated in a few pages, it's probably more prudent to keep it to that. Why spend the time on a complete business plan when the action really happens at the meeting?

"If a team's first submission makes them interesting enough to meet with, that means they've gotten over the first hurdle. Even so, the chances of getting funded are only slightly higher. We've funded teams that didn't have business plans—but we've never funded anyone without a meeting.

"Part of our model is to reply quickly after someone sends us a plan. People who come here may not have an operating history; they just have people and a good idea. We want them to feel confident that we're attentive. Everyone in the Labs has raised money before, so we know what it feels like for a plan to languish with an investor. We're always quick to evaluate and respond.

"If you submit a plan on Monday, we'll have an answer by Friday afternoon. And if we want a meeting, we'll put space on the calendar for the following week. If there's not a fit, we'll suggest others to talk to.

"Prior to the meeting, I do a thorough reference check. It's a misconception to think we simply call the references a team provides. I almost *never* call the people listed as references, in fact. I want to get as far away from the references as I possibly can. Since the high-tech scene is pretty incestuous, you can easily find people who've worked with just about anybody. Everybody has strengths, and everybody has weaknesses. Part of working with a startup involves playing to strengths and managing weaknesses.

"As for the PowerPoint presentation, we try to take the mystery out of it as much as possible. It's not an intelligence test—we just want to hear as much about the idea and the team as we can in about twenty minutes, then spend the rest of the hour asking questions so we understand the opportunity even more. We expect the entire team to be there, because we're particularly interested in learning about them. We might ask them beforehand to send résumés, if we haven't already received them.

"Who attends a particular presentation will vary. We'll get people who understand the market space the team is addressing. As a team or idea becomes more interesting to us, we will devote more resources to the evaluation process. More AV Labs people will attend the meetings so we can get to a decision point even faster.

"What do we look for in the pitch? Essentially, the ability to articulate why this idea will work. We all have well-calibrated BS meters, and we want to know we're not being BS'ed. We want evidence that their pursuit can change if it needs to, because the market changes, and you have to change to be successful. Talk to anyone in our portfolio, and they'll tell you their original plan is not the one they're operating with today. So we want to feel the entrepreneur is bright but also flexible, able to roll with the punches."

Besides other investors, you can use several additional sources of referral to heighten investors' willingness to meet with you:

- Business leaders, such as CEOs of successful companies in an investor's existing portfolio.
- Investment bankers who analyze prospective ventures on a regular basis.
- People who have signed on to be service providers (such as law or accounting firms) or strategic partners of your company. Not only are strategic partners excellent referrals, but they often can point you toward specialized investors with a particular interest in the market space.
- Other entrepreneurs with whom the investor already works.

You *must* have one or two good referrals. "Referrals put you above the noise," as Jens puts it. "Investors get hundreds of plans, and referrals help you stand out. Plus, good referrals indicate how you network, whether you can figure out how to get into companies to sell your solution, and so on. If you can get to the right referrals using the right network, odds are you have some idea what you're doing."

And this, Jens adds, "is much more important than the business plan itself."

Hone the contents of your pitch.

Here is the pitching process as we do it at AV Labs. Our process is not atypical for the first visit with a venture firm. At the Labs, the typical pitch gets one hour. The centerpiece is a short, to-the-point Power-Point presentation of around twelve slides. It lasts about twenty minutes, leaving the rest of the time for questions and answers.

Here is an outline you can follow for preparing a presentation:

- *Company overview.* A quick, one-slide overview of the company and its position in the market.
- *Customer pain/problem.* Spread across multiple slides, this is the focus of the presentation. What customer problem are you solving? Why is it a problem? How severe is this problem (in other words, will the customer pay, right now, for a solution that will mitigate the pain)? What market segments have the most awful pain? How big is the market? How have you validated the customers' needs?
- *Solution.* What is the solution—and how is it unique? Typically, this can be covered in one slide.
- *Competition.* Who are your direct and indirect competitors? Are they venture-backed? Public? What are their solutions, their revenues, and other strengths and weaknesses? (In other words, what are the corollaries of the problem you've uncovered?)
- *Team.* Short bios concisely show why your team members are uniquely qualified for the roles they will fill. Include advisors and directors here.
- *Business model.* What is the revenue model (i.e., flat fee, transaction fee, licensing)? The marketing model? How will the company make money? How will the product be sold and distributed? What is the hiring ramp and customer adoption rate? How much capital are you raising now, and what milestones will you reach? Remember, investors see *lots* of plans—

so accelerate through the obvious, and don't go overboard on long-range financials. Sufficiently articulating the business model generally requires multiple slides.

- *Financials.* When does the company get to profitability? How much capital will it take to get there? When is cash-flow breakeven? What is the operating plan?

Again: When you've performed the hard work of analyzing the market, assembling a strong team, and forging strategies for getting to market while optimizing capital, putting together this PowerPoint presentation will be straightforward and very satisfying.

What are investors looking for in the pitch?

Throughout the pitch, and throughout the following question-and-answer period, your investor audience will be sizing you up. They want to see a clearly delineated market space. They want you to convince them that *real opportunity* exists. Most critical, though, will be their assessment of *your team.*

What does this mean, in practical terms? Three things, all of which I'll delve into in the following sections:

- Have as many team members participating as you can.
- Make sure everyone projects *energy, enthusiasm,* and *confidence.*
- Maximize the team's *malleability*—the ability to respond "on the fly" to unforeseen changes in the market. Only with flexibility can you change course when needed. And there is one sure way to help ensure your entire team has these characteristics: Have *everyone* participate in *market validation.*

Multiple team members showing their stuff.

When Jens and the allmystuff team gave their pitch at AV Labs—and when they later presented to potential Series A investors—*all five co-*

founding team members participated. Jens pitched the high-level business information, CTO Scott Miller the technical, and so on. Likewise, Cody Menard of Covasoft presented the technical aspects of the Covasoft solution, leaving business- and market-related issues to his partner, Gary Neill.

This was an *excellent* strategy. I recommend following it when you seek financing yourself. You'll be showing your investor audience that all the core competencies are in place. They'll be able to identify any potential deficiencies—so that later, they can help the team expand or suggest other needed changes. Finally, you want the investors to get a feel for your people. Investors need a sense of how well the team can work together toward your objectives. They also need to know they can collaborate successfully with your particular team. Sometimes, there simply won't be a match in the latter sense. If other factors are in place, though, the investors will become a good source of referral to other, more compatible investors.

Energy, enthusiasm, confidence.

Starting and running a company is not for wimps. It's brutal. It's utterly time-consuming. It's a strange, hectic, unpredictable existence, and it goes on for years. What does that mean? That you need a special type of energy to pull it off. Your investor audience will be watching like hawks for this energy.

"Everyone has a different concept of what starting a business is like," says Michael Rovner, a partner at AV Labs who is responsible for (among many other things) evaluating new deals. "We look for people who are highly motivated—people who are passionate about providing their solution to customers, people who really want to make a new company fly. We want people who are qualified and motivated, not just ambitious."

For the pitch, your team needs to be so calm and confident that it's *obvious* how much work you've done. Investors will be looking for depth of understanding beneath the high-level information.

They'll be evaluating your ability to summarize complex issues in an easily understood way.

"We spend most of our time looking at the team, business model, and product plan," says Michael. "Early-stage companies can waste time on unimportant details. What *is* important is that when our companies take their solutions to customers, the customers understand and respond enthusiastically. The question you should be asking yourselves is: Have we validated our market, business model, and technology plan?"

Most critically, investors will want to assess whether the team is able to respond to a sea of changes in the market—whether they have the malleability required to start and run a successful company.

Malleability.

Get ready. The Q&A period following your pitch is usually intense. *Very* intense. Here, investors dive beneath the surface. They look for a deeper, more detailed view of your company, your technology, and your team.

"We ask a lot of peripheral questions," as Michael Rovner puts it. "We might *not want answers*—we just want to evaluate the entrepreneurs' thought process." Investors want to see you're open to different ways of looking at things. They want *proof* that you can respond articulately to unexpected questions and observations. This reveals an essential quality: malleability.

"A long time ago," Jens remembers, "Rob told me that the ideas I had in the beginning would morph so much I wouldn't recognize them in a few months. He was right. You have to be comfortable not keeping your sacred cows."

How does this malleability play out? In a variety of ways. For Jens and the allmystuff team, it showed up in, among other things, their willingness to *evolve the team*. As they were meeting with potential Series A investors, they made it clear that they were "not here to have a particular role or title," Jens says. "We're here to build a great company, and we'll embrace the right people in any role whatever if that will bring us to the next level."

In addition, Jens and his team substantially refocused the company based on feedback they received while pitching to Series A investors. "What started during those meetings evolved into a major morphing. We started as a central portal where end consumers could go to stores and manage all their products, and changed into an enterprise solution provider for manufacturers and retailers," says Jens.

This is precisely the kind of malleability investors want to see in your pitch meeting. Mark my words, you'll be faced with questions and observations that are difficult and challenging. Your team will be forced to consider points of view you may not have contemplated before. Respond thoughtfully. Respond with *flexibility* and *openness*. If you do, you're much more likely to get a thumbs-up.

"Some people think they need to have all the answers," says Michael Rovner. "This is not accurate. You need to be willing to think about things. You have to be willing to be wrong. If you can't accept that you may have made a wrong choice, or that you haven't thought about something hard enough, you don't have what it takes to navigate a new company through a fast-changing market."

The business plan: Sometimes you do need it.

No. Investors *do not fund business plans.* They fund *opportunities*— opportunities for excellent teams to respond to real market needs. At the same time, there are times when you have to write a business plan. Some investors require it. Or, you may have a great team and a fantastic business concept, yet still be too raw, too young, and too new to the market to be able to get referrals. In that case, the only way you can get investors' attention is to write a business plan.

Even then, your business plan will be no more than a product brochure—a sales tool that expands on the concise, hard-hitting features-and-benefits spiel in your funding pitch. It will give investors a place to look for more in-depth information.[10] Before you even start writing your plan, *do the other work first.* Do that work, and writing a business plan will take no more than a week. If it takes much longer, get a clue: Your team may be focusing on the wrong things.

Have that team? Have that market space? Let's say you do, and let's say you're ready to go get financing. Whom should you approach? How can you distinguish a quality investor? And what's that relationship like, anyway? If these questions intrigue you, you're in the right place. You'll get some answers in the next kick . . .

---

10. The AV Labs website (www.avlabs.com) provides an outline you can use while producing a business plan. In addition, as I mentioned earlier in this chapter, there are many good sources of information on this topic.

FIFTH KICK: TAKEAWAYS

✴ **Think investors fund business plans? Think again.**
They fund *great teams* pursuing *a viable market space.*

✴ **What *is* a business plan, anyway?**
A fancy brochure. Certainly *not* the key to getting funded. A business plan simply fleshes out the points you make in the funding pitch. *The pitch* is where the action is.

✴ **What's more important than a business plan? *The work.***
- Putting together a great management team.
- Thoroughly validating the market.
- Defining a fast time-to-market strategy that meets customers' needs.
- Determining how much money you need to achieve a set of value inflection points.

✴ **A funding pitch is like a corporate sale. Treat it that way.**
- Match the messages (the company's features and benefits) to the needs of your investor audience.
- Get referrals. Remember: *Relationships are key.*
- Use collateral (such as a business plan) to supplement the spiel. The plan is a takeaway that supports your key points.

✴ **Do a pitch in about twelve slides and about twenty minutes. Investors want to see:**
- All team members showing their stuff.
- Energy, enthusiasm, and confidence.
- Openness to different ways of seeing things: Can you be nimble in the face of change?

INVESTORS WILL WAIT FOR QUALITY RETURNS—FROM QUALITY COMPANIES

When you hear "Texas," you may envision endless concrete expanses or tumbleweeds blowing down dusty dirt roads. The fact is, though, Austin has some of the most beautiful rolling hills in the country. Nothing personifies the central Texas hill-country attitude better than The Oasis, a rambling restaurant perched on a cliff overlooking Lake Travis. From its tree fort–like decks, The Oasis offers spectacular sunsets, views of sailboats on the lake, and a rolling green vista stretching westward for miles. They ring the bell every day at sundown so everybody can watch the show. Besides the view, they're famous for the margaritas (not that that's why we like to go there).

One spring evening, a group of us from AV Labs joined Alisa Nessler at The Oasis, so that Alisa could give us a brain-dump on her ideas for a startup. Alisa had come aboard as a Venture Fellow a couple months back. She'd been working hard on a business concept. We'd all pitched in here and there, rooting for her success while helping out however we could. The visit to The Oasis would give us a chance to get an update on where Alisa was in the process. Plus, none of us had any big objections to sitting on The Oasis' deck for an hour or two.

Alisa was in a pensive mood as she sipped her margarita. Before moving to Austin to join the Labs, she'd put in a stint as CEO of Seattle-based Appliant, which helps customers manage their website performance. Prior to that, she'd been CEO at the Austin network security startup Haystack Labs. She was eager to build another business from the ground up, and she believed the idea she'd been pursuing was becoming more and more promising. Now it was time to transform the idea into an AV Labs portfolio company.

"There's one issue," she said, eyeing a motorboat as it blasted across the lake. "I'm concerned there won't be a real revenue ramp for at least twenty-four months."

"Does the market opportunity compensate in later years?" I asked—even though I knew what the answer was.

"Yeah, I'm convinced it does," said Alisa. "But isn't that a long time for an investor to wait?"

"Not really," I replied. It was fun to see the relief on Alisa's face.

We covered a few other early-stage funding issues, then resumed our brainstorming about the concept, all the while enjoying a twilit view of the lake and hills. Later on, it occurred to me that Alisa had stumbled across a critical lesson: *Good investors are in it for the long haul.*

No matter what you believe about investors, quality ones do *not* consider twenty-four months a "long time." Give them the right opportunity, and they'll wait longer. What are they looking for? A company of *lasting value.* If you start such a company, you'll produce quality returns—no matter when the revenue comes in or the investors get out. What's more, your investors will serve as crucial players on the team. They'll contribute strategic contacts. They'll give you advice you simply can't get anywhere else. They'll grease the wheels for later investments. Chances are, they will continue investing themselves.

How can you make all that happen? *By finding the right investors.* You're about to discover how. I'll explore the different kinds of investors you can go after—not just the venture variety. You'll also get a foretaste of the kinds of value you should expect from your investors. First, though, it's worth taking a closer look at Alisa's misconception. Her notion about investors may have been misguided, but it was hardly unique.

The "vulture capitalist": Ooooh, *scary.*

Investors want their money back quickly. That's only one of the more benign ideas you probably have about investors (particularly venture investors). If you're like most of the entrepreneurs I run across, you see these guys as direct descendants of the Big Bad Wolf. You imagine they'll insist on a wretchedly low valuation, all the better to steal your company. They'll enthrone their own pet executives for no good reason—and kick you out in the process. They'll squash innovation, thwart creativity, and drive your company so hard it careens right into the ground. In short, they'll screw you any way they can. Who's afraid of the Big Bad VCs? Just about everybody.

Even if you don't see dripping fangs when you think "investor"—and Alisa didn't—you might still assume, as she did, that they demand quick returns. Where did all these ideas come from, anyway? I think they got their start in the late '90s. Back then, as I've already said, lots of startups went public well before they were ripe enough to do so. Their risk profiles didn't merit entering the public markets. Alan Greenspan touched on the insanity of it all when he used phrases like "irrational exuberance" to describe the Nasdaq of those times. Truly, it was lunacy. And many, many otherwise sane people participated—institutional investors, stock-buying individuals, and technology companies alike.

Volumes could be written, and no doubt will be, about what exactly happened during those years. For our purposes here, let's just say this: For a while, some investors *did* get their money back quickly. Very quickly, in fact—often in a year or two. Chasing a fast buck became the name of the game. Many investors hallucinated dollar signs everywhere. They entered markets they didn't really know.

They spread their management talent way too thin. They worked with teams they didn't necessarily connect with. Way overextended, they couldn't add much value. As more and more companies rushed to IPOs before it was prudent—and as more and more investors dove into markets they barely understood—huge numbers of people came to believe (understandably) that investors expected big returns. *Huge* returns. Virtually *overnight.* That only helped spawn other, even more negative preconceptions. Like this one: VCs are out to dilute your ownership.

Calm down. Get a grip. Realize this: Not until the economic hiccup of the '90s did investments produce those ultra-speedy returns. What's more, it's not likely to occur again any time soon. What do longtime business fundamentals tell us? Even with a viable firm, it can take *five to seven years* for venture funds to produce returns. That's even when portfolios are populated by high-growth companies. More and more people recognize this as the market exhibits more rational (if also painful, for many) behavior.

Don't get me wrong. There *are,* still, venture investors—and other kinds of investors as well—who continue to expect unrealistically quick returns. *Be wary of them.* Most often, these investors know zilch about the industries they're entering. They don't grasp their own responsibility to contribute beyond merely handing out money. They provide little if any support. They contribute virtually no solid business advice. And far too many entrepreneurs—sometimes out of desperation, more often out of sheer ignorance or an unwillingness to adhere to sound business principles—seek and receive funding from them.

Go that route, and you're simply getting "green" money.[11] You're doing *nothing* to increase the value of your company.

---

11. I call this money "green" because, in the United States at least, *all* money is green. Think of this kind of money as just any old money—as a commodity. You want *smart* money—money that adds to your company's value beyond the raw value of green money alone. If green money is the only kind you're able to raise, then take a hint: *Don't go there.*

What is the opposite of green money? *Smart* money, from quality investors. These investors are savvy about the industries they're putting money in. They anticipate the inevitable bumps in the road. They're committed to adding to your company's value over the long haul. They have a track record of success. If you want to build a quality company, you have to find smart money. Smart money is a huge value-add. Green money? A great big *value-subtract.*

Want smart money? Be bold. Pick your investors.

Why is a quality investor in the game? For one and only one purpose: to create value, which maximizes the return on investment. *Smart investors will do whatever is necessary to create value.* Sometimes, they *will* bring in a new CEO, if the founding CEO has outgrown his or her role. Sometimes they *will* refocus your business in new directions, if that's what is necessary.

Before you ink a deal with a quality investor, ask yourself: Are you irrevocably wedded to the status quo? Are you after a safe gig to perpetuate a lifestyle? "Yes" answers are fine. They don't mean you're bad, or wrong. But they do mean *you should not seek investment capital.*

Now, ask yourself this: Do you aim to create value? Do you want to make a lot of money for yourself and the team? If that's the case, a quality investor can help make it happen. These investors will be closely aligned with you around maximizing the payoff. And it is precisely this alignment of interests that will produce long-term success.[12]

---

12. Take, for example, the misconception that venture investment substantially dilutes the founders' ownership of the company. In reality, the involvement of quality venture investors typically *raises* valuation in the long run.

Be proactive. Check out potential investors.

When it comes time to get money, don't wait to be picked. *Pick your investors.* How? Figure out what types of investment your company needs (we'll look at these types later on). Then get out your microscope, and take a good hard look. Believe me, investors will do background checks on *you*. Well, you should do the same. Go to their website. Investigate their investment philosophies. Call the other companies in the portfolio, and ask what the relationship is like: In what specific ways have these investors participated in the company's growth? However you go about it, make sure an investor can add value in real, concrete ways.

Search out the right mix.

Five characteristics define smart money. Look for *all* of them as you do your investor due diligence:

- *Domain expertise.* How much does a particular investor really know about your industry and market niche? How have they proven their domain expertise within the current portfolio? (In other words, how are *their* companies doing?)
- *Chemistry and staying power.* Is there a personality fit between your team and the investor? Will the investor be available to provide needed support? Will they back your company through the inevitable hard times?
- *Core competencies.* Can the investor's special knowledge and talents help round out your team's execution intelligence?
- *Sophistication.* Is the investor experienced with the ins and outs of startup capitalization and operation? Do they have an awareness and understanding of technology? And—most important—are they sophisticated enough to know that quality returns come from quality companies?

- *Prior successes.* What's the track record? Has the investor worked with startups that went on to be winners?

As we will soon see, Alisa Nessler chose a mix of investors who possessed, between them, all the characteristics of smart money. The investors joined a team that already had a good amount of market savvy and execution intelligence. As a result, Alisa's company, Lane15 Software, is on its way to being a leader in its space. Lane15 is building software that will be used to manage traffic and communication in InfiniBand network environments, which are currently being designed and developed.[13] Because software is critical for operating these new networks, Lane15 is helping to speed InfiniBand adoption.

Startup investors: three common types.

Who typically funds startup companies?

- *Venture investors*—established or "institutional" investment firms, on the lookout for promising business opportunities.
- *Strategic investors*—investment groups within large established businesses, investing in new companies that will provide some strategic business value to the parent company.
- *Angel investors*—wealthy individuals with an ongoing interest in funding and mentoring very early-stage firms.

---

13. In a nutshell, InfiniBand is a collection of new hardware components, such as routers, switches, PC boards, and so on, that will replace the components currently used in computer networks. InfiniBand promises faster, more reliable performance in network environments. InfiniBand architects have divided the environment into "lanes," or communication paths along which the various components interact. Lane15 is named for "Virtual Lane 15," the path reserved for managing traffic in the network.

Your company may require only one type of investor. Or, you may need some combination. Your ideal investor mix depends on your stage of growth, your company's potential in the marketplace, your ultimate goals (to go public, to be acquired, or simply to operate over the years as a private company), and many other factors. Again: *Your combination of investors should heighten your company's execution intelligence.*

Venture investors: $$, know-how to accelerate growth.

Why recruit institutional investors? Because these folks have been through the drill many, many times. They've helped many companies grow. They can help you avoid known pitfalls. They know the capital markets. They understand how to navigate these markets. Their advice and support can be *indispensable.*

Let's take a look at the steps Alisa Nessler and the Lane15 team took to round up their venture investors. Alisa is one of those people who seem destined to run startup companies. When she signed on as CEO of Seattle-based Appliant, for example, she took the helm of a company consisting of "technology and a couple of engineers," she recalls. "It was a very, very early-stage company. They weren't even sure which market to go into."

Alisa quickly sized up the situation—"technology looking for a problem," as she puts it. Then she proceeded to steer Appliant through the major milestones of a successful startup: validating the market, building a team, and raising several additional rounds of funding. In the process, she developed a deep understanding of the e-commerce infrastructure, the underlying technology enabling e-commerce to work. Alisa predicted that as the Internet became more and more critical for doing business, the e-commerce infrastructure would have to evolve. It would need to be faster and more reliable. Perhaps, she figured, she could identify an opportunity for helping to make that happen.

Diving into the middle of Austin's early-stage deal flow seemed a good way to proceed. Alisa joined AV Labs as a Venture Fellow and got a "glimpse into the crystal ball, a view of what might be happening in the future," she says. Pretty soon, she caught wind of an interesting development in the hardware world: InfiniBand. Austin Ventures had invested in hardware companies that were building components of the new architecture. But, Alisa recalls, "there was no software player yet." Determined to explore opportunities on the software side of things, she teamed up with Bill Leddy, an experienced engineering executive who signed on as CTO of a new company. Together they read, strategized, and talked with practitioners and experts in the field.

Venture funding: the highest hurdle.

From the get-go, Alisa and Bill knew they'd need venture money to proceed. Developing software for a brand-new network environment would be an intense, multiyear undertaking. What would it take to get a product to market in a rapidly evolving, highly competitive space? Computer and network equipment, to start with. Plus, high-dollar engineers, sales and marketing experts, and a complete support staff. Who has pockets deep enough to fund such a project? Venture investors. For a technology company starting out to create a complex solution, venture investors can be among the most valuable assets.

At the same time, getting venture financing is tough. As I've mentioned, AV Labs seed-funds a small percentage of the companies that approach us. Larger follow-on investors—venture firms that hand over anywhere from $10 million to $30 million over the life of an investment—fund an even tinier percentage. Why? Because (as I've said before) by its very nature, a startup is an incredibly risky proposition. Given today's volatile, fast-paced (and unpredictable) business climate, even when you thoroughly validate the market, build a great team, and otherwise execute well, *there is still a big chance that you will fail.*

That's why venture firms set such a high bar. That's why they require all the early-stage execution milestones you're reading about in this book. These investors have learned the hard way: The only way to mitigate risk is to validate the market, build a great team, and all the rest.

Which leads me to an important point. *Even if you opt—for whatever reason—not to seek venture financing, launch your business as though you were.* Clear the hurdles of raising venture money, and you dramatically increase your chance of success. Even if you never lay your hands on a cent of venture funding.

Requirement #1: Prove the opportunity.

Alisa Nessler had raised several rounds of venture financing at Appliant. So she knew how demanding these investors could be. Before she and Bill Leddy—who had signed on as CTO—even approached them, they used a small seed round from AV Labs to get their ducks in a row. They recruited a senior architect to design the Lane15 product. They brought on experienced product and marketing directors. Most important, they spent a great deal of time determining what a viable software solution would look like in the InfiniBand world.

During this early period, they "worked hard on developing the business model and understanding the market opportunity," Alisa says. To validate whether it made sense to build management software for the new InfiniBand networks, they met and talked with all the big hardware vendors involved in the then-newly formed Infini-Band Trade Association (IBTA).[14] They visited companies creating complementary technology, such as semiconductors, test equipment, and network devices. In addition, they met with vendors who were

---

14. This association is dedicated to developing standards for emerging InfiniBand technology; the IBTA steering committee includes Compaq, Dell, Hewlett-Packard, IBM, Intel, Microsoft, and Sun.

visible in the fiber channel market, a highly specialized adjacent market segment dedicated to building fiber technologies.

The Lane15 entrepreneurs armed themselves with a great deal of information about these hardware companies' needs. Then they attended an IBTA meeting—and achieved a market validation breakthrough. "As we talked to hardware vendors about their software needs and software plans," Alisa recalls, "we began to understand that many of them were very concerned about time to market. They had a *massive pain:* They needed software to get to market, but they didn't have dedicated software organizations to provide it."

This insight gave Lane15 its focus. As the IBTA event progressed, says Alisa, "every meeting turned into more meetings, relationships began to evolve, and we received great feedback on product planning, product timing, and the kinds of relationships these companies wanted." In the process, the team perceived its core opportunity. They would create InfiniBand management software that could be embedded in the InfiniBand hardware systems. What would drive Lane15's revenue? Their relationship with the hardware vendors— their customers.

"After the IBTA meeting," says Alisa, "we understood our business model much better, and we understood timing issues." Most important, the team saw that since the Lane15 software would be embedded in the hardware vendors' products, "we had essentially been talking to our first customers about their needs. We got a real grasp of the product requirements."

This *deep-down knowledge* of customers' needs, coupled with their newly forged *business strategy* and *relationships,* gave Lane15 the ammunition it needed to approach Series A venture investors. The team received substantial funding led by Austin Ventures. The round included Lightspeed Venture Partners, a West Coast fund whose portfolio includes a number of complementary businesses. AV Labs invested additional capital as well. So did three strategic investors: Compaq, Dell, and Intel. The founders were ecstatic about these three strategic investments—nothing could have validated their market more strongly at this stage of development.

All the investors knew that InfiniBand had just *begun* to evolve. As Alisa predicted that afternoon at The Oasis, Lane15 would likely *not* generate substantial revenue for a number of years—not until Infini-Band itself generated market share. The investors understood this. At the same time, they believed Lane15 had market awareness and customer focus for executing successfully in the InfiniBand space.

Strategic investors: synergy through relationships.

Strategic investments can be pivotal for your startup. This type of financing comes from large, established businesses with an interest in your technology or market. Landing a strategic investment gets you two major benefits, in addition to the money:

- *Market validation.* Lasso a strategic investment, and you've reached a huge milestone. A big player is saying, yes, this solution is strategically important to our core business. In Lane15's case, these investments went a long way toward mitigating the risk of a long revenue ramp.
- *Industry insight.* Strategic investors give you a critical, otherwise unobtainable view into what's happening in the industry. Sometimes, dominant players like Compaq, Dell, and Intel are the only ones privy to this information. A strategic investment puts you on the inside track.

Why was it so important for Lane15 to land investments from major InfiniBand hardware players? The company "needed early access to engineering resources and technical information," says Alisa. "We needed close relationships, so that some of the key players would disclose their plans to us." Lane15 also required access to early InfiniBand hardware as it emerged, enabling Lane15 engineers

TIVOLI SYSTEMS AND ITS INVESTORS: AN IDEAL ALIGNMENT OF INTERESTS

One of Austin's well-known high-tech success stories, Tivoli Systems was founded in 1989 to pioneer the management of computer systems across large enterprise networks. Tivoli's early days involved Austin Ventures. The relationship between these organizations perfectly illustrates the role of a quality investor in helping to steer a high-growth startup.

Austin Ventures was the lead investor in the infant Tivoli Systems, joined by Kleiner Perkins Caufield & Byers, a premier Silicon Valley venture firm, and by the East Coast firm Matrix Partners. The company IPO'ed six years after its founding and was acquired by IBM in 1996. Today, the multibillion-dollar, 5,000-employee corporation is one of IBM's fastest-growing divisions. Leading companies around the world use Tivoli's products and services to manage their networked PCs and distributed systems from a single location.

Did those early investors want their money back quickly? No. "They put in three rounds and six years before they ever saw a return," says Chris Grafft, an Austin Ventures venture partner and AV Labs Master Entrepreneur, and a VP at Tivoli from 1992 to 1997. "Not only that, but they hung in there through a couple of management teams as well."

The investors were "very active on the board," Chris recalls. "They always weighed in on strategic directions. We were trying to make the company bigger than life—and that was where they participated the most."

Early on, Tivoli's business depended on revenue-generating consulting contracts with Sun, IBM, and others. "We made a lot of money from these contracts," says Chris, "but they weren't going to make us a big business. We had to make a transition from that business plan to one where we wrote and sold applications to *Fortune-* and Global-class companies." The early board meetings, then, centered around how to "get out of the early contracts in a safe way and transition the company to a high-powered sales force that could sell all these huge companies on the systems management concept."

The investors were indispensable for driving the transition forward. What's more, as the team executed on the new model, the investor advisors were invaluable for sparking strategic partnerships—alliances with companies like Intel and IBM—that helped Tivoli outmaneuver the competition. "Bill Wood at Austin Ventures was particularly helpful in this regard," Chris says. "He could give you the names of people to talk to, explain the companies' personalities, and tell you what language would get their attention and drive them toward the results you wanted." One of these partnerships led, of course, to the acquisition by IBM.

"Our top-tier venture investors were instrumental in making Tivoli a very large business," Chris says. "They drove Tivoli to be more than just a really good company on a small scale. A board of that magnitude makes it hard *not* to grow successfully."

Not only did the relationship between Austin Ventures and Tivoli Systems help produce Tivoli's phenomenal success, but it serves, in retrospect, as "a milestone in Austin's venture industry," as Chris puts it. "Tivoli's success was instrumental in helping Austin Ventures establish its reputation, while also putting Austin on the map."

to start testing their software as early as possible. "We felt like financial relationships would facilitate that," she says.

Another key factor? The nature of the InfiniBand market itself. "InfiniBand was being driven by a bunch of huge, powerhouse businesses," Alisa says. "We were a little startup. To get traction and credibility, we needed some of these companies as backers."

Obtaining strategic investors.

How can an infant startup like Lane15 accelerate the process of getting these investments? Remember the partnering process I outlined in the third kick? This was the process that helped Newgistics, the return logistics company, land its partnership with R.R. Donnelley and USFreightways. Alisa used the exact same process to line up Lane15's strategic investors. First, as we saw above, she figured out what she needed from them. She knew they would have to be Infini-Band hardware players. Then she performed additional steps. Both are *crucial* for obtaining a strategic investment:

- *Identify the strategic funding organizations within the target investor businesses.* Many large enterprises now have internal venture groups. These groups' sole purpose is to find and fund new businesses with synergistic products and markets. Intel, one of Lane15's strategic Series A investors, operates just such a group, called Intel Capital. Dell Ventures is the strategic investing arm of Dell. Other big companies, such as Compaq, leave it to the lines of business whose strategic interests intersect.

  The Lane15 team initially hooked up with Intel and Compaq at the InfiniBand Trade Association meeting. Both were excited about Lane15's software solution and business strategy. Shortly afterward, Alisa met with the appropriate representatives and sparked a high-level discussion about investment possibilities. Dell Ventures came aboard later.

- *Outline the benefits to the investor.* How will the investment help accelerate the large companies' success? All three of Lane15's strategic investors saw investing as a way to directly affect the evolution of InfiniBand management software. Working closely with Lane15, they could help ensure that the software integrated smoothly with their own hardware components. The result? Faster time to market, which would translate to a clear competitive advantage.

Manish Mehta, a director at Dell Ventures, puts it this way: "We aim to drive Dell's long-term growth by creating a competitive advantage. Our strategic and commercial ties with the companies we invest in are key to that mission."

Lane15's strategic investors would, as we've seen, also be *customers* of the new company. They would buy the software, then embed it in their own hardware products. To land them as investors, Alisa and the team used the same kinds of strategies you would use to close major customers.

Angel investors: mentors and more.

Angel investors are wealthy individuals who sign on to help get an early-stage company off the ground. Typically, angels contribute to early-stage activities like team building and strategic alliances.

Considering going after some angel money? Keep these two points in mind:

First, an angel should be as market- and technology-savvy as any venture or strategic investor. It's all too easy to take the money from deep-pocketed relatives or friends. Do not—I repeat, *do not*—go there. Your relatives and friends are not industry-aware. They know little or nothing about the capital markets. Their added value? Some 99% of the time, zip, zero, nada. And you want to know something else? They often *do* want their money back quickly. No matter what you might think now, before long they'll be standing over your shoulder asking, continually, when they can expect their return. What happens when there's no return to be had (an all-too-common outcome with startups)? Damage to a personal relationship. Remember: *There is nothing angelic about the non-savvy angel investor!* If you go after angel funding—and often, angel investments are an excellent source of funding—make sure the angels can add real value.

Second, angels can be important mentors. Sophisticated angel investors—such as those in the Texas Angel Investor's program, an organization managed by the Capital Network[15]—can help the early-stage company think through its business model, prepare a good pitch for follow-on financing, and otherwise grow the company.

David Gerhardt of the Capital Network has seen many angel investors contribute immense value to startups. One company, for example, was founded by a doctor who wanted to provide software for managing physicians' offices. By the time he approached the Capital Network for help, the doctor/entrepreneur had brought on an operations person. Very smart. But he hadn't developed the business model. He also lacked a financial strategy. Clearly he needed a healthy dose of assistance.

"We hooked him up with mentors who were particularly savvy about raising money," David recalls. "Originally, he was thinking he needed $5 million right off the bat. We scaled his expectations back to $1 million and encouraged him to hit important benchmarks [value inflection points] before raising more.

"Then we helped him close on a round with an angel who sits on the board of a large pharmaceutical company. That gave his company domain expertise for moving forward successfully."

The key to obtaining a successful angel investment, says David, is to "figure out what core functions you need the most, then try to find people who can advise and steer you in addition to giving you money. You're going for a lot more than just money—you're after *smart* money."

Amen.

---

15. The Capital Network is an Austin organization that (among other things) helps early-stage companies hook up with potential angel and venture investors.

Smart money value-adds: What do investors give you?

If you land quality investors, you can look forward to a wealth of benefits—in addition to the bucks.

Fund-raising: know-how and contacts.

Venture investors have instant access to a wide network of follow-on investors. Increasingly, so do the strategic investment arms of large corporations. That spells *huge value* when you're faced with raising more money.

Peter Huff, an Austin Ventures partner who serves on the Lane15 board of directors, has helped the Lane15 team in this regard. Alisa credits Peter, for example, with helping her bring Lightspeed Venture Partners into the Series A round in record time. "Lightspeed called me and expressed interest in the company," she recalls. "While I worked on Compaq, Peter gave Lightspeed the due diligence he had already done. He told them Austin Ventures was standing behind the company, and explained why. That was pivotal in terms of their entry in the round. It also saved me a lot of time." Austin Ventures' early support of the company helped pull in Compaq and Intel as first-round investors. What's more, Peter Huff played a role in bringing Dell Ventures on board as a third major strategic investor.

This, then, is one of the primary value-adds of quality investors: the *legitimacy* they provide. As David Gerhardt of the Capital Network puts it, a kind of "herd mentality" takes over when a well-known quality investor puts money in a startup. That investor's presence, says David, serves as "substantial due diligence and increased valuation in the eyes of other investors."

Recruiting.

With respect to the team, a quality investor can be indispensable. "AV Labs and Austin Ventures have both been great for recruiting," says Alisa. "They are major clearinghouses for the best résumés in the area. They're totally plugged into the network. They've helped me recruit several of our most valuable team members."

If you're looking to recruit that all-important CEO, investors can be a particular boon. They know how much a CEO should earn, cash- and stock-wise. They can help you negotiate a package that fits your capital and equity structures, while also motivating the CEO to build a world-class company. Most important, they can help sell great candidates on the opportunity: If quality investors stand behind a startup, the best and brightest are more likely to come on board.

Industry contacts, networking.

Investors can introduce you to others in the industry. Her association with AV Labs, for example, gave Alisa Nessler access to a wide-ranging network. Besides the contacts we've already talked about, this network included Brian Smith, founder of Crossroads Systems (a player in the InfiniBand space) and a Master Entrepreneur at the Labs; Stephen Straus of Austin Ventures, who put Lane15 in touch with the InfiniBand player (and Austin Ventures portfolio company) Banderacom; and more. Before Lane15 was even a company, then, Alisa used our network at AV Labs to refine her ideas. The network only grew from there.

Contacts with other companies.

As we've seen, Lightspeed Venture Partners (brought on by Peter Huff of Austin Ventures) was a superb investor for Lane15. Some of the telecommunications and networking companies in Lightspeed's portfolio are valuable contacts. The technologies they're developing bear directly on InfiniBand or complement the Lane15 offerings.

Lane15's strategic investor partners also have strong relationships with a wide variety of companies, large and small. Not only will Compaq, Dell, and Intel be prospective customers, but they have all introduced Lane15 to businesses that "might be complementary in terms of our products," says Alisa.

Manish Mehta of Dell Ventures stresses the importance of such introductions. Dell Ventures has invested *over a billion dollars* in 120 companies. All of them are creating technology that is synergistic to "the spaces we play in," as Manish puts it. "One of the things we contribute is the network effect between companies that could drive profitable alignments or opportunities."

Contacts within strategic partners' organizations.
Companies as large as Compaq, Dell, and Intel invariably have internal departments that can give a startup crucial guidance. What's more, relationships with these departments often lead to additional business opportunities for the startup. "Our strategic partners have groups building InfiniBand products," says Alisa. "We want to target these products for OEM business. From the start, we've been introduced to the product groups by the strategic investors. Without that investment calling card, it would have been much harder to reach these groups."

Contacts with potential customers.
As Manish Mehta points out, investors are often a vital source of *customers.* "Dell Ventures can bring Dell in as a potential customer. We also bring Dell's customers in as potential customers. When you think of the customer segments Dell sells into—consumer markets, small- to mid-size businesses, government and education, and the large enterprise—you see it's a gamut that covers just about every customer combination a startup could possibly need."

Unbeatable market intelligence.

Quality investors can give you market insight that's hard to obtain elsewhere. In this regard, they function as important sources of—you guessed it—ongoing *market validation.*

Take Lane15, for example. At every meeting of the Lane15 board of directors, the team spends "a lot of time listening to the folks from Intel and Compaq," says Rich Goode, Lane15's manager of finance and operations. "These are the InfiniBand industry gurus, and their input is indispensable. They describe the latest InfiniBand developments, what their goals are, how that relates to us, and what they think we should be doing strategically with the product. They also give us important feedback on distribution channels. They've been critical for feedback on both the business model and the distribution channel model."

Lane15 receives market intelligence from its venture investors as well. Austin Ventures, for example, has "people whose job it is to understand what's going on in InfiniBand," says Rich. "At the last board meeting, venture partner Mike Hathaway, who comes out of the networking space, helped us clearly articulate InfiniBand's competitive advantages.

"That helps us technologically. But it's also important with respect to fund-raising," Rich continues. "As we meet with potential customers, we have a convincing story of why InfiniBand is a winning solution."

Redirecting the team, refocusing the business.

As I've mentioned, investors will help rearrange your team when it's necessary. In this advisory capacity, they often help recruit seasoned CEOs, people who've run a business from the ground up, to take the helm. Injecting the DNA of an experienced, seasoned CEO can be critical for maximizing the executive leadership. What's more, when a proven executive is willing to jump in, that helps further validate the concept. It's worth pointing out that no good investors make major team changes arbitrarily—they do so in order to bring a company to the next level and accelerate growth.

Besides recruiting new executives, investors also can help teams *refocus* the business. Manish Mehta of Dell Ventures relates how one of their companies was losing momentum after starting to address a market space other than the one it originally targeted. "We directed them back into our business," says Manish, "and from there, allowed them to test their solutions with Dell internally or with our customers in small pilots. Based on the results of the pilots, they were able to make corrections in course and realign their business focus. They've done very well ever since."

Assisting with partnerships.

Is partnering with other businesses one of your core product strategies, as it was with Newgistics? Is it important with respect to customer relationships and revenue channels, as with Lane15? In either case, quality investors can be critical. "In many of our partnerships," says Alisa, "we do a lot of negotiating in terms of pricing, deliverables, what we're willing to do, what they'll do, and so on. Our venture investors have been fantastic sounding boards for making these decisions and trade-offs. I always feel that if I have a deal in the works and am worried about a couple of things, I can run it by Peter Huff and Rob. They'll think of great ways to make the deal work for Lane15."

Technology know-how.

Strategic investors can be indispensable for helping you build a product the market will accept. "Our strategic investors have been incredibly responsive when we've needed something from them," Alisa says. "Early access to the InfiniBand hardware, for example, has been critical." Intel, which is developing some of the industry's first InfiniBand silicon chips on PC boards, made sure Lane15 got one of the first chip/board components. Lane15 has made good use of this technology for testing its software and speeding time to market.

Both Intel and Compaq have reviewed product plans with

Lane15 engineers. Compaq helped Lane15 understand how the software could integrate with some of their products. The strategic investors have also been sounding boards for the revenue model, enabling Lane15 to establish viable pricing guidelines for their embeddable software products.

A vested interest in the startup's success.

Investors are in the game to maximize return on investment. How do they do that? *By maximizing your company's value.* Investors have a real share in your success. They're committed *for the long haul* to the success of all the companies they're investing in.

Make no mistake. Investors are in it to make money. But that means they'll also make money for you and your team. Align yourself with quality investors. It's one of the surest strategies I know of to mitigate risk and build value for your company.

Value accrues most rapidly, of course, when you start making sales. How do you lay the groundwork for sales? With marketing. A coherent, targeted marketing strategy is a must-have as you proceed. What should such a strategy look like? Figure it has something to do with advertising? Well, there's one way to find out. Forge ahead, and receive your seventh kick . . .

SIXTH KICK: TAKEAWAYS

✴ **"Vulture capitalists" will eat you alive. *Not.***
Quality venture investors give quality companies a wealth of *value-adds.*
Just like quality strategic and angel investors.

✴ **Who's a quality investor?**
- They *do not* demand "quick returns." They know it takes many years—even in high-growth markets—for quality companies to produce quality returns.
- Their motivations align with the team's—to maximize value and make money for everybody.
- All the while, they add genuine *value.*

✴ **What to look for? "Smart money" (as opposed to plain old "green money").**
- *Domain expertise.* The investors know the industry and market space.
- *Chemistry and timing.* There's a fit between the investor and your team.
- *Core competencies.* Investor know-how supplements and extends your own.
- *Sophistication.* They understand the special requirements of a startup: capitalization, operational needs, and time to profitability.
- *Prior successes.* They've been through the drill—successfully—and have a roster of winning investments to prove it.

✴ **Who invests in the typical startup?**
- Venture, or "institutional," investors—firms whose business it is to identify and fund promising new companies.
- Strategic investors—the investment arms of established corporations with a special interest in emerging technology.
- "Angels"—wealthy individuals who help fund and steer brand-new companies.

✳ Investor value-adds: a *lot* more than just the money.

- Deep pockets that can adequately finance R&D, marketing, and sales.
- Advice and support to steer you through various stages of growth.
- Fund-raising expertise for additional rounds of financing.
- Assistance in recruiting a solid management team.
- Referrals, introductions, and contacts with other investors, service providers, and potential customers and partners.
- Assistance in forging strong strategic alliances.
- Feedback on products and technology.

✳ Want angel financing? Great—but be careful.

- Look for an angel who's market and technology savvy—don't get money from a rich uncle! (He probably *will* want his money back quickly.)
- Take full advantage of the value-adds offered by sophisticated angel investors—typically, early-stage mentoring and help with team-building and strategic alliances.
- Remember: Most angel investors don't have deep enough pockets for the long haul.

✳ Again, what are you after? Smart money.

That's what often differentiates a successful startup from an unsuccessful one.

✳ Finally—don't get picked by investors. Pick your investors!

Perform the same due diligence on them that they perform on you. Check them out. And go after *only* the ones who'll add the most value.

ADVERTISING AND MARKETING ARE NOT SYNONYMOUS

We'd been working hard to recruit Larry Warnock to join AV Labs as a partner. We were close. Larry was in town on one of those final trips before making this kind of decision, checking out real estate with his wife. On their last night in town, Michael Rovner and I met the Warnocks at Vespaio, an upscale Italian restaurant on South Congress Avenue.

Michael and I brought our wives along as well. The maitre d' seated the six of us in a casually elegant front dining room whose wide windows overlooked the avenue. As we settled in for an evening of good food and wine—punctuated by some selling by Michael and me—it was clear the Warnocks were having a great time.

Sure enough, during the evening Larry told us it was settled. They'd be relocating from California. Larry would be leaving his position as VP of marketing at a Bay Area startup recently acquired by Siebel Systems. Larry had a great track record in high-tech marketing; he'd worked in senior marketing positions at a number of well-known startups. We were thrilled to be bringing him on board.

Why? Because our companies need all the marketing help they can get. When it comes to marketing, most entrepreneurs are downright inept. Let me give you an example—a story we related, in fact, to Larry at dinner that night. A startup founder I'll call Jim had given a pitch at the Labs a week or two before. Jim was quite bright. His energy was so strong it seemed to fill the small conference room— exactly what you want to see in a founder. You could tell he'd worked hard on his PowerPoint slides, which were full of professional-quality charts and other graphics. True, he was making some common mistakes—heavy emphasis on the technology, not nearly enough on the market. But my initial impression was that if we squinted hard, the concept could morph into something viable. What's more, we could always direct the team to focus more on the customer. We do it all the time.

Gradually I noticed that the body of Jim's pitch contained nothing about a marketing strategy. I made a mental note to probe on this when Jim was done. Then he got to the last slide, headed "Financials." Beside a "Marketing Expenses" bullet was the figure $10,000 and the word "advertising." No marketing hires were mentioned. No product management. No public relations. Just some advertising—accomplished with a $10,000 total marketing budget.

Huh? Say what? Jim would have been better off to just leave marketing out of his pitch. Then, when we asked about it, he could have said, "Honestly, I don't have a clue. I'll need your help with this. Marketing is not my strong suit."

In the end, we gave a thumbs-down to Jim's business. I have to be truthful: It wasn't because of his marketing naïveté. It was because his market simply wasn't big enough to generate sufficient returns for venture financing. If we *had* decided to work with Jim, though, I can guarantee you this: Bringing him up to speed marketing-wise would have taken some work. A *lot* of work. Want to know something else? Jim was not all that atypical. That's why we were so excited to be recruiting somebody with Larry Warnock's marketing savvy.

Marketing = advertising: a misguided notion.

In general, technology startups are founded by technology whizzes. Makes sense, doesn't it? Sure. But at the same time, these entrepreneurs typically know nothing about marketing. Successfully marketing a company and its products involves juggling a host of complex issues and activities. Yet, for reasons I've never been able to determine, people's Pavlovian response to the notion of "marketing" is to think "advertising." If you think this way, maybe you envision ads for your company in the big industry magazines. Or you see ads in trade periodicals, or on the Web or radio. You might even imagine a cool ad on TV (Intel does it, right?).

Get this: *Marketing and advertising are not synonymous.* Advertising is only one facet of an overall marketing plan. What's more, advertising tends to be remarkably ineffective for an early-stage company—no matter where the ads are placed. Advertising is wickedly expensive ($10K? Dream on). Worse, it's been proven, time and time again, to produce *a very low return on investment* at this stage. *Later,* advertising can be effective. But that's usually when a company is several years old. Even then, advertising is only one part of a comprehensive, well-thought-out marketing plan that also includes many other programs and activities.

"Okay, then, what *is* good marketing?" Product, buzz, customers.

This chapter will introduce you to some fundamental marketing activities. We'll take a look at the three core functions of early-stage marketing—operations you carry out, essentially, in this order:

1. *Define the product.* Here you figure out how to design and position your product so that it does what it's supposed to do—you got it, *fix your customers' pain.* Product definition is hypercritical. It's your first marketing must-do.

2. *Create "buzz."* The market must be made aware of your company and its offerings.
3. *Acquire customers.* Finally, you have to generate leads for sales—which is, after all, the revenue-producing lifeblood of your company.

Later on, we will dig into each of these activities. You'll acquire a bird's-eye view of how some of our companies at AV Labs are conducting them. But first, let's explore a concept that's at the heart of the entrepreneurial enterprise: Marketing arises naturally from—you guessed it again—*early-stage market validation.*

Good marketing flows from market validation.

What is marketing's key role? To extend and perpetuate one of your all-important tasks: validating the market. For your company to be effective, you have to stay close to your customers over time. And that is marketing's central function—to ensure this happens. The result? Sales is equipped with the products, positioning, and market awareness it needs to produce revenues.[16]

To set the stage for our current discussion, let's go back for a moment to the second kick. As you saw back then, a number of very important things occur during market validation. These outcomes help spark your company's marketing effort. That's why they're worth revisiting here:

- *You uncover the precise nature of the customers' pain.* Remember Ineto? Ineto's customers needed better ways to manage

---

16. Sales, of course, is also critical for fostering and conducting an intimate relationship with customers. In a very real sense, sales serves, like marketing, to perpetually validate the market and keep the company close to its customers. In the following kick, we'll explore the role of sales in obtaining direct feedback from customers in the field and then communicating this feedback to marketing, which uses it to evolve the product, positioning, and core messages.

their customer interactions across various media—phones, e-mail, and the Internet.

- *You identify an initial customer base.* Typically, this subset of the target market has the most vicious pain. Ineto's initial customer base? High-growth technology companies.
- *You learn what features and functionality are needed, right away, to address customer pain.* Ineto's customers were most interested in Web-based solutions for managing phone interactions. They didn't require all the sexy "bells and whistles" the team had envisioned.
- *A community of beta customers emerges.* These customers agree to work closely with your team to create and refine an initial product release. For Ineto, this initial community came to constitute the Customer Advisory Board.
- *You get validation from industry analysts in your market space.* Recall that as Ineto was getting off the ground, it received many awards, including a place on *Red Herring*'s "Top Ten to Watch" list. These awards resulted directly from Ineto's work with leading analyst groups.

Validating the market, then, gives you answers to a set of fundamental questions: Who are our customers? What is their pain? Who has the most brutal pain? How can the product be crafted to address this pain? And how can we heighten industry and market awareness of our company and its products? As your company evolves, these are the exact questions your marketing team keeps answering—over and over again, through product release after product release.

In a very real sense, then, market validation is *a springboard* for your entire marketing effort—not just in the early stages, but throughout your company's entire life. What does marketing do? It validates the market, over and over again. It evaluates customer pain. Identifies target customers. Redefines the product to address the pain. Works with key customers. Nurtures analyst and press relationships. As long as marketing persists with these core market validation activities, *your company will be able to market itself and your products.*

Market validation as fuel for marketing—how Ineto did it.

Ineto is a great example of a company that has continued to use, for marketing, the basic approach it used so well during early market validation. "Back then," says Ineto founder and CEO Mike Betzer, "we were constantly going to customers, finding out what was important to them, coming back and refining our product concept, then going back to the customers, and so on. We've kept doing these things to market the Ineto service." Ineto, in short, has *never stopped validating the market.*

Redefining the product.

Remember Stage 2 of market validation? That's when you create a product prototype, then take it back to customers again and again, tweaking it repeatedly to better meet their needs. *As you market your product later on, you do exactly that.* Take Ineto. Part of the product is its application interface—the screen users see. "For our first release," recalls Mike, "we had the application take up the entire screen. The user had to fill the whole browser window to see if calls were coming in.

"After the initial launch," he continues, "we went back to the field and asked users what changes they wanted to see. They said when they weren't on the phone with a customer, they'd be doing three other jobs—so they needed to be able to use the browser for other tasks while still being notified of incoming calls or e-mails. We needed to shrink the interface to a small toolbar on the browser window, then have the application pop up when a call or e-mail came in."

Redefining product messages.

Customer-focused product definition. That's what led Ineto to fundamentally change its product. The company also integrated the heightened usability into product messages and sales materials (cus-

tomer acquisition activities). Had Ineto not been committed to validating the market over time—listening to customers, then redefining
the product in response—there is no way its marketing operation,
much less the company itself, could have thrived. Again: *Thorough,
ongoing market validation leads naturally to successful marketing.*

Product to buzz to customers: a continuous cycle.

Defining the product, generating buzz, and acquiring customers are
activities that are inextricably intertwined. Product definition—the
most critical of the three—feeds naturally into the creation of market awareness. Market awareness helps you acquire new customers.
Customer feedback helps you redefine the product. Which sparks
the cycle once again.

This continuous cycle is what defines early-stage marketing. It is
part and parcel of ongoing marketing validation. Figure 6 illustrates
the process:

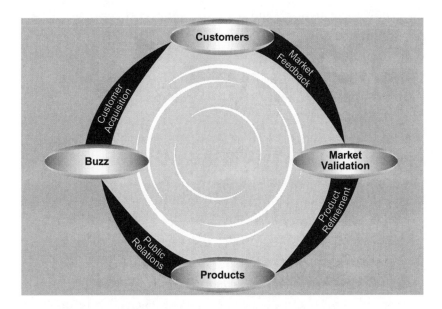

Figure 6. Early-stage marketing: a continuous cycle.

As the figure suggests, you have different kinds of programs for each of the three activities. Different groups within a marketing organization implement these programs (at least after you reach a certain size). But throughout, it is the *interrelationship* of the activities that propels marketing forward and helps it to generate sales—the whole point of marketing, after all.

In your company, then, marketing will serve as the glue that:

- Makes sure sales has the right messages and tools, so that sales can produce revenue.
- Connects key company groups, such as development, with the customers out there, and vice versa.
- Heightens market awareness of your company and its products.

Now, let's take a deeper look at these three crucial marketing roles. Keep this in mind: While we are zeroing in on *early-stage* marketing functions, the same basic operations are at work in later-stage companies as well. The earlier you establish the discipline to define the product, create buzz, and acquire customers effectively, the better your product over time. And the more successful your company!

Define the product: Solve your customers' pain.

What is your most critical early-stage marketing activity? Again: *product definition.* You must define the product before you even think of doing anything else, marketing-wise. Why? A couple of reasons:

- *Addressing customer pain.* Defining the product gives you a way to address customer pain—quickly, and with a product customers will adopt.
- *Building a foundation for further marketing.* Have a product that's ill-defined and vaguely positioned? Then all your other marketing activities are pure BS. Who among us, for example,

has not read the silly, hype-only press releases that flood the technology newswires (thinking all the while, *what does this company do, anyway)?*

Not only must you define the product as your #1 marketing priority from the get-go, but you also have to do so *continuously,* throughout *every* product release, for *the entire life* of your company.

Face out to the market. Face in to development.

Like all marketing operations, product definition is complex and multifaceted. At its core, though, it involves two basic tasks. Both help ensure that customers adopt your solution:

- *Synch the product with the market.* Here, you keep a constant finger on the pulse of the market. You determine exactly what product features customers need most. You figure out how to describe these features and benefits to position the product. You determine pricing.
- *Synch development with product requirements.* As you interact with the market, you obtain a list of product requirements. Then you work closely with development to make sure that what is created matches those requirements.[17]

The former activity is often called "product marketing," the latter "product management." The terminology is not that important.

---

17. Many companies break these two functions into two separate roles, assigning each to a different person. Others consolidate the two tasks into a single role performed by one team member. For better focus and communication, most early-stage startups pursue the latter course. This ensures that nothing is lost in the translation between customers and development. The challenge? Finding the right person to fill this unique position. Rare is the person capable of both the right (market-facing) and left (development-oriented) brain abilities required.

What is? The fact that these two functions play out in utterly unique ways, depending on the nature of a startup, its product, and its customers.

In the sections to follow, you'll see how two of the AV Labs portfolio companies have carried out their product definition activities. You've met them previously in the first and third kicks: Waveset and Salion.

Proactively probing the market—how Waveset did it.

You will recall that the Waveset product lets companies give partners, customers, and other outsiders Web-based access to internal applications, data, and other resources. Waveset customers can also manage this access in a secure manner. Defining this product grew directly out of the company's market validation. The team "took the market validation very seriously" from the start, as marketing VP Kevin Cunningham puts it. "To build a viable company, you have to meet a demonstrable need, build a sizable market opportunity, and generate widespread willingness to pay for the product. Understanding customers' pain is absolutely critical. There is no other way to get that information except to go to the market, ask questions, and listen."

The market requirements document (MRD).

Right after market validation, the Waveset team developed a market requirements document (MRD) outlining how the product would address customers' pain. "We knew we'd identified a problem space," says Kevin, "so we said, 'Now let's think about a solution.' At the end of our market validation survey, we started asking customers about features. We combined their responses with analyst insight and competitive information. Then we crafted a comprehensive document defining the market space, how the product would be positioned, and what we would need to build to be successful."

You should treat the MRD as a must-do for your company as

well. The MRD "keeps everybody on the same page," as Kevin puts it. "Articulating product features in written format ensures there are no surprises at the end of the development cycle. Without an MRD, it's all too easy for a development team to get off track. You wind up at the end of a year-long release cycle with something you're not expecting."

Since (as we've seen) market validation is a continuous process, the MRD "morphs over time, throughout successive product release cycles," says Kevin. "We revise it constantly to reflect new input from customers. Product marketing must stay one step ahead of the development process—so we start crafting the requirements for a subsequent release while they're still working on the current one."

Revalidating the market, release after release.
As Waveset planned for its second release, it went through a second formal market validation from scratch. "We're very proactive about going back to the marketplace and probing customers' needs," Kevin says, "and we're committed to incorporating feedback from both customers and sales. Sales has a good handle on what customers want to see in the product."

As Waveset moves forward, it plans to establish a "lighthouse program"—a program of working closely with a forward-thinking set of customers whose input will help drive the ongoing evolution of the solution. "We'll create close relationships with these customers," says Kevin, "and look to them to be the thought leaders for how the product should evolve." The lighthouse customers will, in short, serve as a primary conduit for validating the market over time.

Make sure your product helps users do their work— how Salion did it.

Salion's approach to product definition helps ensure that the solution matches real, day-to-day needs of customers—both the product's end users and the high-level decision-makers who contend with critical business issues. You'll remember that the Salion solution addresses the staggering pain of suppliers in business-to-business exchanges. With B2B buyers already receiving plenty of help, Salion was one of the first startups to focus on suppliers. What's more, B2B exchanges have not been around all that long. Salion, then, was a trailblazer in this market space—which made their product definition challenge *acute.*

Alpha customers: answering the question, "What do customers really do?"

Salion identified a set of "alpha" customers during initial market validation—early-stage customers who, according to product marketing director William Breetz, "agreed to participate in the product design in exchange for a lower-cost product."

If, like Salion, you're tackling a relatively new market space, I recommend the tactic of recruiting alpha customers. You will find, as they did, that your company's relationship with these customers will be intimate indeed.[18] "To generate detailed user requirements, we have to develop a very deep knowledge of users' work," says William. The best way to get this insight? An in-depth, step-by-step discovery process performed at a customer site, enabling Salion to make sure the product meets customer requirements.

The discovery process.

Salion's requirements-gathering process typically includes the following activities:

---

18. Alpha customers work even more closely with a startup than their better-known "beta customer" counterparts. Beta customers are customers who receive the early, initial releases of a product and then provide feedback, primarily on product quality; alpha customers actually help the startup design and develop features of the product.

- A kick-off meeting with the "economic buyers"—people who understand the business value of the solution and sign off on a purchase. "Here we get a sense of the customer's high-level processes and concerns, the nature of the work that's done, and who's doing this work," says William.
- An interview with actual users, who outline the general process they employ in their day-to-day work. This helps the team understand the context for the work they will observe.
- Two days or more of close, one-on-one observation of this work. Here's where the Salion team comes to truly understand user requirements. "They're the master of their work," says William, "and we're there to learn by observing. We don't ask questions—we just observe, while they perform the work and talk about it." The team also gathers documents and other artifacts that further help them understand these tasks.
- A follow-up session in which the Salion team asks about specific problems. "We stay at the level of talking about their problems, rather than about the software," William says. "If you get users saying, 'We need a button that you press and it does this . . . ,' then you're not learning about their work and their problems. It's fine if they talk about product functionality they'd like, because it hints at their pain, but the pain is what we're after. Here, we dig deeper into the user's opinion. That's important because it affects their perception of the product we'll deliver."

The Salion team performs the process with a number of users and consolidates the information. Then they return to the users and validate whether they're on track. "Invariably, you've got something wrong," William says. "We keep going back and validating again, until we really nail it."

The process is what enables Salion to accomplish three key things, product definition–wise:

- Understand real, actual *user needs.* "They know we understand their work, because we've taken the time," as William puts it.
- Gain insight into the customer's *critical business issues.*
- Design a solution based on *what the team has learned.*

If your business produces enterprise software like Salion's, early customers will almost certainly define your product—not just for themselves but for later customers as well. As William says, "A product should be built around detailed market requirements. Early customers can have a tremendous impact."

Interfacing with development: tying features to benefits.
Like Waveset, Salion also creates an MRD for interfacing with development. "We start with a brief high-level product spec, a 'vision' document outlining the market and business requirements," says William. Once Salion's product planning board reviews and approves this spec, William and his team create a detailed design—also called a functional spec—that ties every product component to a high-level requirement. Finally, they develop use cases, which contain design requirements that are more detailed than the functional spec. Use cases outline exactly how the user will interact with the system.

"You need to know whose critical issue you're solving," William explains. "What does the user have to do, specifically, to meet your customer's business needs? How does a feature help them do it? Even at a startup, where people like to move fast, you have to take the time to do this detailed analysis and document every step. It's the only way to make sure you correctly design and build the product."

Generate buzz: Create market awareness.

After you have defined the product—and remember: *only* after you've defined the product—your buzz-generating activities will commence. Effective buzz creates market awareness of your company and its products. It makes the company seem much bigger than it actually is. What's more, on a local level, good buzz helps you attract good people for the team. Nationally, it promotes the perception that *you're a leader in your space.*

Generating buzz is often very difficult. Unless you're careful, it can also be outrageously expensive. Your challenge? Do it *efficiently,* and do it *affordably.* That involves two main types of operations:

- *Public relations*—typically your most cost-effective way to create awareness and position the company. What are some common PR activities? Press releases, articles in the industry press and periodicals, and other media coverage. If you choose to outsource PR, your agency will likely take on analyst relationships as well.
- *Analyst relationships*—an absolute necessity for any technology company. Industry analyst groups have a high-altitude perspective of the industry, technology developments, and the key players in a given market.[19] Their opinions weigh in heavily with the press. They produce widely read reports on product and market categories. Most critically of all, they recommend solutions to their corporate clients. A positive nod from an influential analyst can be pivotal for your company.

A related, more tactical activity, known as "branding," helps support these core strategic buzz-generating functions. If you were to

---

19. There is a large stable of well-known analyst groups at work today in the technology arena, including Forrester Research, Gartner Group, Giga, Hurwitz Group, International Data Corporation, Meta, and others.

ask twenty people to define what the term "branding" refers to, you would get twenty different answers. In general, I think of it as a set of activities used to create and foster a particular image—everything from the website design to the logo, business cards to corporate colors, graphic images to oft-repeated phrases, such as the logo taglines. Branding is what gives your company its "feel." And, again, it serves to support your strategic PR and analyst-related operations.

Using branding and PR to become the market leader— how Lane15 did it.

Lane15's branding and PR efforts have vastly heightened market awareness of the company. As you will recall from our last kick, Lane15 is building software used to manage the new InfiniBand computer network environments. The startup's market space is dominated by industry giants such as Compaq, Dell, Hewlett-Packard, IBM, Intel, Microsoft, and Sun. Tiny Lane15's buzz challenge is monumental indeed: how to make itself visible and raise its own credibility, so that it can work with these industry behemoths and also engage them as OEM partners.

As senior product marketing manager Brian Borack puts it, "We're dancing with the elephants. We need to make sure we don't get stepped on."

Branding: setting the stage for an impressive market debut.

Right off the bat, it was critical that Lane15 establish market awareness. The company hired a creative-services firm "on pretty much day one" for branding, Brian recalls. "We felt it was important to have our logo, website, folders, and related features professionally put together in a sophisticated way. We wanted a polished image immediately, because we felt it would give us credibility when we approached these large OEM partners."

The branding paid off right away. When the team attended a meeting of the InfiniBand Trade Association, the larger IBTA members received them enthusiastically. "They were shocked that we were only a few months old," says Brian. The IBTA conference sparked several key relationships with OEM partners and others. If Lane15 played its cards right, the team realized, it could quickly be perceived as a leader in the InfiniBand software space.

PR: crafting a "bigger than life" image.
Shortly after the IBTA conference, senior marketing manager Mary Taylor brought on board an established high-tech PR agency, Boston-based Schwartz Communications. "In a space with big industry players, we need a big-name agency," she says. "Schwartz has helped create the perception that we're on the same playing field as the big guys, the de facto leader in InfiniBand software management.

"A high-quality PR firm has so many feet on the street, it's covering many different technologies all the time, and it runs into opportunities we wouldn't otherwise know about," Mary explains. "At our agency, a team of six is totally focused on canvassing analysts, keeping track of the editorial calendars, and more. Internally, we simply don't have time to do that. Even if I could pin down who at *Information Week* writes about InfiniBand, I would have a hard time getting their attention. A PR agency has these relationships already lined up."

Within two months of signing on with Lane15, the agency had arranged for fifteen press briefings and thirteen analyst meetings. What's more, around thirty articles in the industry press—in such publications as *EE Times, Computerworld,* and others—had "lumped the name Lane15 in with Compaq, Intel, and so on," Mary says. "We wanted to stake our claim to being the leader in software, equal with the big companies that are leading in hardware. Our PR agency has been indispensable for that."

BLANC & OTUS: PR FOR A COMPETITIVE EDGE

"Startups have to start with the basics. They have to be able to explain, in simple terms, what they do and why it's important. Many can't do that. They may be smart engineers, and they may have venture money, but they can't clearly articulate their value proposition. Nor can they differentiate themselves from competitors in a compelling way. This is what we help them do." So says Simone Otus, founder and co-chair of the PR agency Blanc & Otus—an agency that has been critical for many of today's well-known technology companies.

Blanc & Otus (or B&O, as it's known in the industry) is based in San Francisco, with offices in nearby Mountain View, Boston, and Washington, D.C. The B&O client roster features an eclectic mix of industry heavyweights like Compaq, Ariba, E.piphany, and E*Trade. Technology-savvy investment firms, such as Sutter Hill Ventures and Technology Crossover Ventures, are clients as well. So are a bevy of emerging players, including Austin's own Motive Communications. In 1999, B&O was acquired by Hill and Knowlton, the world's second-largest PR firm.

Launching a new company is a B&O stock in trade. The agency's near-legendary two-day "positioning workshop" takes four or five of a company's top executives through an intense process of hashing through possible positions. The team then develops and refines a presentation that tells "a clear, concise story that can be used with analysts and the press," says Simone. "The presentation is also indispensable for the sales force. It ensures that every audience gets the same consistent message."

Motive's launch illustrates the B&O positioning magic in action.

"Here was a pedigreed startup," recalls Simone, "a clear-cut winner with great executives and the best venture money. At the start, they told us they were an 'Internet relationship management system.'" As the Motive team worked through the B&O positioning exercise, "we coined the term 'support-chain automation.' At the time, everyone was talking about supply-chain automation—the process of automating a chain of events to make it more effective. We applied the term to tech support." B&O also helped the Motive team quantify the return on investment—another key startup activity—and research the market to validate claims. The results? With the help of B&O, Motive achieved clarity about what it did. It also created a new market niche—"something most companies, especially software companies, must do in order to establish a competitive edge," Simone says. "People bought the story, and Motive became a leader in its field." Now, the company has built on its initial leadership platform, expanding its position to revolutionize service automation.

B&O helps drive companies' relationships with industry analysts. "PR agencies like B&O have been working with analyst firms for years," says Simone. "We have pre-set relationships with them, we know where their specific expertise lies, and we can help make sure they incorporate our clients into their dialog." B&O uses the analysts to develop and test company messages. The agency also sets up agency tours, where the CEO or another company representative "goes out and convinces analysts that the startup has a new market and strong capabilities.

"Once you have the analysts liking you," Simone continues, "we help take the story to the press. It's all about building relationships. Once you've built relationships with a few good journalists, they'll write about you forever. They'll feel like they're part of your inner circle, so when you're ready to announce a product, they're on the team."

Leveraging analysts to penetrate the market—
how Covasoft did it.

Covasoft is a master at using analyst relationships to understand the market and position itself. As you will recall, Covasoft provides software that helps large enterprises manage transactions in their e-business environments. "For my money," says brand marketing VP Pat Colpitts, "we're in one of the most volatile, dynamic markets out there. Not only are people trying to define the category, but they're trying to survive a category churn the likes of which I haven't seen in twenty years. Everyone wants to know where the puck is going to be. It's a very interesting time—and you can't be afraid of the fact that you don't have all the answers."

For help with negotiating this competitive market terrain, Pat and the Covasoft team maintain close rapport with analysts who influence in the e-business market. "Analysts are a mouthpiece to a vast majority of customers, and to the press as well," she says. "You have to find analysts who will champion your cause." Indeed, Pat sees work with analysts as "pretty much the core strategy that takes place, from a corporate-communications standpoint. Everything flows out of these analyst relationships."

Market guidance.

With their high-altitude perspective, says Pat, "analysts can beam a headlight down the road as they view the market. They're able to give sage advice on developing a market strategy. They point out potential land mines. And without violating disclosure agreements, they tell us when somebody's already done something we think is uniquely ours. They touch base with virtually all the players in a given market."

Hurwitz Group, for example, gave Pat, co-founder and CTO

Cody Menard, and a senior developer indispensable guidance for focusing its marketing strategy. Hurwitz "tracks business process development as a category very closely," she says. The analysts helped the team understand the meaning and permutations of the term "business process management," used by vendors to describe many different things. As a result, Covasoft was able to focus its communications and development efforts appropriately.

Recommendations to customers.

"A lot of the customers we're targeting are clients of one or more analysts," says Pat. "Gartner Group and Meta Group, for example, offer software-evaluation services that companies pay for in addition to the analysts' time. If you're a chief information officer or information-technology guy and you've identified a problem having a number of potential solutions, one of your most predictable phone calls will be to an analyst. You'll ask, 'Who's a player, who do you recommend?' So, our relationships with analysts get us on the short list. It's one more very important data point for getting big customers."

Continuing market validation.

What brings the analysts around? Simple: demonstrating that your solution solves a real problem in the marketplace. "At the end of the day," Pat says, "that's what it's all about—showing them we have a solution that works. You can trot out vaporware for a short time. In the beginning, we were in the prototype stage when we met with these guys. But to be successful with them, you have to establish a delivery timeline—and then stick with it."

Pat sees the analysts as an important source of continuing market validation. "I like to get in front of them every quarter, taking the product back to keep showing them how it's evolving to solve customer pain," she says. "For every meeting, there should be newsworthy information for the analysts to use in tracking our development, our customer acquisition and retention, and the status of our financial position.

"The analysts have a real impact on the market—we have to stay current with them."

Acquire customers: Pass good leads to sales.

Your third major early-stage marketing activity? *Pass hot leads to sales.* What's a hot lead? Simple: the name of a prospect who needs a problem solved, *right now.* Hot leads have sizzling pain. These customers are the ones who are most likely to open up their wallets and hand over the cash.

How can you identify hot leads? Early on, of course, through market validation. Market validation shows you the corners of the market with the most searing pain. Over time, you use specific marketing programs to target prospects. These activities reveal promising pockets of additional pain. They give you more and more intimacy with the market. Your prospect list continues to expand.

Programs for targeting prospects.

Here are a few activities you can use to locate hot prospects:

- *Direct-response mailings.* In these mailings, you describe the product and outline how the solution can help. Use mailing lists to go after audiences with *red-hot pain.* Track their responses through a "closed-loop" system (discussed in a moment), which gives you real-time feedback on who's *most* interested.
- *Tele-prospecting.* For some kinds of products, it can be helpful to blanket the target market with telephone calls. This

technique is usually used in conjunction with direct-mail campaigns; you take the responses from the mailers, then develop lists for the tele-prospectors to call.

- *Trade shows.* These industry events can help you identify prospects. They're also important forums for communicating with potential customers. I have seen startups make sales at trade shows on the strength of a product demo alone. When there's a trade show expected to draw a big turnout from your target market, you should arrange to have complete materials and knowledgeable representatives in a booth. Ideally, you can "borrow" this corner of space from a larger, deeper-pocketed partner.

What are you trying to do with these activities? Move prospects through a sales pipeline. When someone responds favorably, you follow up with additional mailings or calls. Then, when a lead is ready to close, you pass the name to sales.

Closing the loop—a sales and marketing necessity.

No customer acquisition operation can be successful without a closed-loop system. Implement such a system, and do it now. Your leads database will contain records of everyone you've contacted, when and how you contacted them, and their response. The results? You can determine how to find and close customers *most efficiently.* You can track *future* sales. You can assess the effectiveness of *specific* campaigns. And you can identify *new* markets.

Figure 7 illustrates the sales and marketing closed-loop system.

Targeting customers with colossal pain—how Ineto did it.

Tele-prospecting has helped Ineto hit the market for businesses needing its customer communications service. Early on, Ineto out-

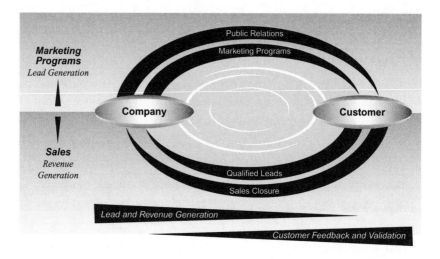

Figure 7. Closing the loop for effective sales and marketing.

sourced its lead generation to a West Coast tele-prospecting company. "Say we have 20,000 logical prospects," explains Mike Betzer, "and we want to find out who's hot, who's in the position to buy our service, who needs to interact with multiple channels. It's a painful process to contact all those people. Simply getting to someone who can make the decision can take forever."

Outsourcing these outbound campaigns has been a huge boon. "The company has already sent back over five hundred leads," says Mike. When a lead comes in, "we call them back to do a Web-based demo. Our demos have gone from twenty a month to over eighty, and our close rate from demo to customer is 25 percent."

Ineto has sprinted ahead on other customer acquisition fronts as well. An example was its response to the change in customer environments brought about by a shifting economic climate. "Our service entailed essentially a $5,000-to-$15,000-a-month contract," says Mike. "Before, we didn't usually have to talk to the chief financial officers. Now that companies have tightened their belts, the CFO is always involved in these decisions. Before, total cost of ownership was about number 12 on customers' priority list, but suddenly it has become number 2 or number 3." As it received this feedback from customers, Ineto morphed its product messages accordingly, highlighting low cost of ownership as a key benefit.

Moreover, the company started developing customer acquisition campaigns aimed specifically at the CFO-level customers. "When we get the lead, we'll hit them with traditional mail that includes an ROI calculator in a little packet. The calculator will ensure that the packet gets opened. If the mailing is going to someone who needs to 'sell up' to the CFO within the customer environment, these tools help him or her do that. We'll also include fact sheets, online pricing tools, and other tools for calculating savings. We arm our internal advocates with whatever they need to move up the chain of command."

Have a strategy. Stay agile.

Defining your product, generating buzz, acquiring customers . . .

How do you put it all together? With a strategy that grows out of market validation. How do you execute that strategy over time? By knowing it will change, just as the market does. You have to stay malleable. You have to develop a *new* strategy when the market demands it.

Newgistics and allmystuff are instructive examples of these concepts in action.

Strategy for positioning oneself in the market— how Newgistics did it.

Recall that Newgistics' return logistics offering streamlines product returns for multichannel retailers and their customers. How did Newgistics go about positioning itself and its offering? By starting with market validation. And, then, by devising a comprehensive strategy for *defining the product, creating buzz,* and *acquiring customers.*

What was Newgistics' biggest marketing challenge? "We were

creating a new service for managing returns in a relatively undefined space," says Deena Byers, marketing VP. "We had to define who we are and what we do, then get out in the market and clearly articulate our value proposition to potential customers."

Meeting this challenge involved, among other things, "defining and segmenting the market, plus profiling our potential customers," Deena recalls. "We asked ourselves: Where is the greatest pain? How and where could we ease the pain while providing the most value?" The Newgistics team determined that catalog retailers—who desperately needed a cost-effective, consumer-friendly returns solution—would be the first target market. "Then, to figure out how to market to these customers effectively, we had to develop a strategic marketing plan. The plan came out of our understanding of the customers' and consumers' needs and behavior, which we identified through surveys and focus groups. We determined how the product and value propositions could address the needs of the audience. Then we packaged everything in such a way that the retail customers would understand the value of the Newgistics solution."

The team sees this strategy as a direct continuation of early market validation. It involved a number of key activities:

- *Developing product requirements.* Newgistics outlined all the product requirements in the market requirements document (MRD). The MRD defined *precisely* what the Newgistics solution would include and what features would best meet customers' needs. Customers said, for example, that they needed a way to issue promotional coupons at the point of return, thereby helping consumers mitigate the costs associated with shipping returns. As a result, "the MRD has an entire section on the coupon solution," says Deena. "It sounds really easy, but this one feature took months to identify and integrate into the product."
- *Creating a brand.* Newgistics knew it would have to create an *identity* for its flagship product. The name they chose—

ReturnValet—crisply communicated the core value proposition. It suggested that the solution would be "at your service," giving customers everything they'd need to outsource returns. The company also envisioned an entire portfolio of future products with names featuring some permutation of the word "Valet." This would extend the notion of comprehensive service and leverage a simple yet highly effective brand.

- *Identifying and forging strategic alliances.* In addition, recall that Newgistics formed strategic *partnerships* with R.R. Donnelley Logistics, a division of R.R. Donnelley & Sons, and USF Processors, a division of USFreightways. The partners' shipping, delivery, warehousing, disposition, and liquidation capabilities would be key to the Newgistics solution. Newgistics also established a strategic alliance with i2 Technologies, a supply-chain management company that agreed to sell Newgistics' return management solution to its customers. "Aligning with established companies already in the supply-chain-management space acclerates our time-to-market. It also builds our credibility in this market space," says Deena.

In addition, the Newgistics marketing team developed a public relations plan to create awareness, co-marketing initiatives to leverage its partnerships, and more. All these activities derived directly from the company's continuous market validation.

Revamping the mission, rearticulating the value proposition—how allmystuff did it.

Very early in its life, allmystuff proved itself able to roll with the punches. As you recall from the fifth kick, this company gives manufacturers and retailers solutions for generating profitable downstream, or post-sale, relationships with their end consumers.

As mentioned, allmystuff originally set out to provide personal Web pages where individuals could collect all their product ownership information. Prior to obtaining Series A financing, the company rethought this initial vision. A leading consulting firm helped, and so did feedback from the market, analysts, and advisors. Based on all the input, the team decided to develop and market the technology as a set of tools for manufacturers and retailers, who would offer the ownership pages on their own sites. The team crafted a strategy document to define its new mission.

"The mission statement articulates the core of what allmystuff is doing," says Jeff Johnson, the company's director of marketing communications. "It puts the management team on the same page. They share a common vision. This has been a huge focusing exercise for the entire company."

Among other things, the newly articulated strategy enabled Jeff and others on the marketing team to craft *consistent, effective communications materials*—a clearly worded mission statement, a value proposition, features and benefits statements, and so on. The materials "translate the business strategy to words, pictures, and copy," as Jeff puts it. The result? A foundation for more specific, tactical artifacts such as product brochures and white papers.

Jeff and his team relied heavily on customer feedback in developing their marketing plan and associated documents. "Once we get messages to a point where we think they're right," he says, "we go see customers, potential customers, and analysts. The process helps us get the messages down and figure out what to emphasize, what words to use, and so on."

What is the ultimate purpose of all these activities? *Sales.* That's what marketing is about—to heighten sales. In the next kick, you'll find out a lot more about this critical operation . . .

SEVENTH KICK: TAKEAWAYS

✹ **Think ads cut it for marketing? Not even close.**
In fact, advertising—with its high expense and low ROI—typically has *little* or *no place* in an early-stage marketing strategy.

✹ **What does good marketing flow out of?**
You've got it—*market validation.*

✹ **How does market validation feed into marketing? By providing . . .**
- Knowledge—precise, *intimate* knowledge—of the customer's pain.
- A target customer base.
- Understanding of how product features and functionality solve the pain.
- A community of beta users.
- Relationships with industry analysts in the market space.

✹ **Marketing: It's a continuous cycle.**
Good product definition leads naturally to buzz in the marketplace, which supports the acquisition of new customers, who provide feedback that helps redefine the product, and so on. The cycle repeats itself endlessly, *throughout your company's life.*

✹ **Three main activities of early-stage marketing: product, buzz, customers.**
- Define the product—your #1 priority.
  - ▫ Synch the product with the market. Listen to customers—and define the product based on what you learn. Revalidate the market release after release.
  - ▫ Synch development with the product requirements. Use a market requirements document to keep everybody on the same page.
- Generate buzz.

- ▫ Cultivate relationships with key industry analysts for the target industry.
- ▫ Engage in effective public relations (PR) activities.
- Acquire customers and cultivate leads.
  - ▫ Direct-response mailings.
  - ▫ Trade shows.
  - ▫ Tele-prospecting.
  - ▫ Other lead-generating activities.

✸ Important! Close the loop for effective sales and marketing.

A closed-loop system keeps track of all customer contacts. It is vital for:

- Tracking future sales.
- Assessing the effectiveness of specific campaigns.
- Identifying new markets.

✸ In marketing, strategy and agility are must-haves.

What are your overriding goals? Know in advance—and plan activities to further your objectives. And when the market shifts, be able to reposition the company *fast*.

NOBODY ELSE CAN SELL YOUR PRODUCT FOR YOU

I had arranged to meet Dale Howe at the Hideout, a coffee shop adjacent to a small theater a few blocks from AV Labs. Dale had been talking to Covasoft about signing on as vice president of sales and service. I was helping them with the recruiting. This would be our first conversation—an up-front visit to set the stage for the more rigorous, in-depth discussions likely to occur over the next couple of weeks. At the Hideout, we'd have a bit of privacy—often hard to come by in the Labs' open loft-style space—and a nice view of bustling Congress Avenue.

It was critical that Covasoft recruit a strong, experienced VP to spearhead sales. The company would be targeting *Fortune*-class business with enterprise software costing well into the six figures. That would require a sales leader with insight, vision, and a deep awareness of customer needs.

As we talked over a cup of coffee, I had a hunch Dale would fit the bill. He was an intelligent, plainspoken Virginian with three decades of high-tech sales and leadership experience. He obviously grasped the problem Covasoft had uncovered. Businesses had *immense* pain around managing their complex online environments.

They needed better ways to monitor the performance of e-commerce applications. As more and more companies shared data and applications over the Internet, Dale predicted the problem would only get worse. For five years he had steered sales at Dazel, a startup (eventually sold to Hewlett-Packard) whose product helped companies manage their printers, fax machines, and similar "output" devices— so he knew information technology organizations and their needs. He also understood the Covasoft value proposition: technology for monitoring and managing e-transactions.[20]

As the waiter refilled our coffee cups, Dale made a particularly astute remark. "Right off the bat," he said, "we have to develop momentum in the market with direct sales. We need to adjust to what we hear from customers, then continually tweak the positioning and value proposition."

A *customer*-focused attitude. Market *awareness*. And a *commitment* to refining the selling proposition based on customer response. Certainly, it seemed Dale Howe had all the attributes Covasoft (or any startup, for that matter) needed in a lead sales executive. There was one question, though, that nagged me. I ran it by him while we finished our coffee.

"I've heard rumblings from the company about counting on a partner to sell the product," I said. "What do you think about that?"

Dale smiled. "Well, I've heard that too," he said. "I asked them, 'Why do you think a partner would do that? You've barely got market traction. You have no market clout. The partner already has their

---

20. In its initial phase, Covasoft is going after customers of BroadVision and Vignette, both of which provide platforms for building complex websites. With Covasoft, companies can monitor interactions and interrelationships among these platforms' database, Web server, application, and operating system components. As Dale puts it, this strategy gives the company a chance to "focus the sales force on a select set of customers to determine whether we hit the mark." This is an excellent example of limiting the initial target customer base, so that sales can be used for continuing market validation.

own quota and plans for making that quota. They need their sales force to focus on their own products.'

"Covasoft's job right now is to create market momentum for the product," Dale continued. "Covasoft is the only one that can do that."

Bravo. Covasoft had the right person. Not only did Dale understand the company's business, but he knew something a lot of people don't: *A startup has to completely own its sales process.*

Using partners as a sales force? Big mistake.

I can't tell you how many entrepreneurs tell me that partners will sell their products. It floors me every time. If you buy into this fallacy, maybe you think you'll just ink a deal with some established industry player—IBM, Microsoft, Dell, Cisco, or whomever. They'll add your solution to their product list, and you'll be all set. Does your product require special system integration work or customization? Then maybe you fantasize that it'll be taken on by some big system integrator, like Accenture, EDS, KPMG, or Pricewaterhouse Coopers. Either way, you'll be free of the need to build and operate a sales force. You and your team can just sit back and work on the product—while waiting for your partners' sales reps to deliver great big chunks of revenue.

You're deluded. It'll never work. Here's why:

- *Big companies' reps sell hundreds of other people's products.* A classic example is IBM, whose sales force carries around thick binders listing hundreds of "partner" products. These companies have so many reseller agreements that few salespeople even have time to keep their binders updated—let alone stay informed about all the products.
- *The reps' priority? Sell their own company's products.* There's typically little incentive to proactively sell other products. In

fact, those sales usually only follow a customer's request for a
particular solution.

- *Before a big system integrator will incorporate a solution, it
  has to be deployed successfully in many, many environments.*
  Early customer successes will prove your technology and
  shape your positioning. You're the only one who can make
  that happen.

- *Partner sales are worthwhile only when there's market pull.*
  Don't even think of signing on sales partners until there's
  widespread market demand—or, as Dale puts it, market
  momentum. How can you create that demand? By owning
  your own sales process.

If you've learned anything from this book, I hope it's this: *You
have to stay close to your customers.* In the last kick, you saw how
marketing extends and perpetuates ongoing market validation.
Well, sales does the same—maybe even more so. What happens
when you rely on others to sell your product? You *create a gap*
between you and your customers. If you're not selling your own
product, you can't listen to them. You can't respond to their requirements. And in the early stages especially, it is absolutely critical that
you do both these things.

Mark McClain, president of Waveset, once said it very well: "In
the early days, you're in a mode of absorbing feedback from the market. If you rely on a third-party selling organization, you risk losing
some of it in translation. That's a very bad idea."

True, partners can be useful, even early on, for *augmenting* sales.
Covasoft, for instance, has a partner program enabling a variety of
partners—e-business application providers, consultants, system integrators, and others—to leverage Covasoft's offerings in their own.
Partners can provide introductions. They can give you much-needed
credibility.

But (and this is a *big but*) you should never see partners as an
alternative to owning your sales process. Nor should you rely on

them as a primary source of revenue. *You* are responsible for getting customers to open their wallets and buy. *Everyone in your company is responsible*—not just sales, but development, marketing, operations, finance, you name it. Everyone has to focus, all the time, on doing whatever's needed to lasso paying customers. *A startup does not earn the right to expand until people start buying.*

After you've created market pull—typically, years down the road—partners may be able to step in as significant revenue producers. Even then, the best companies continue to maintain close customer contact through their own sales organizations. What do these companies do? They keep using sales to validate the market.

Think of sales as ongoing market validation.

Once again: *Sales is the ultimate form of market validation.* Sell your product, and you prove you have viability in the market. You extend and perpetuate the market validation process. You do so in three main ways, each of which is explored in the following sections:

- *Expand your customer base.* Early market validation yields an initial base of customers. Subsequent sales grow that base.
- *Evolve the product.* Constant customer contact enables sales to provide critical feedback for defining and redefining the product.
- *Communicate the vision.* Salespeople are vital for communicating your long-term vision and enrolling customers in the vision.

Use customers to validate and revalidate your market.

When you take on alpha and beta customers during early market validation, that's what ignites your sales process. Cody Menard, cofounder and CTO of Covasoft, puts it this way: "A nice side effect of our early validation was an initial customer base. We had to demonstrate that there was indeed a market. As we came to understand our customers' major pain points, we identified a subset of customers. They've stayed with us ever since."

One of these early Covasoft customers had such sizzling pain that they asked the team to come do an on-site demo. That just goes to show: Do your market validation right, and you're guaranteed to find the people with the worst pain. Prove to them that the solution fixes that pain, and they'll sign on as alpha or beta customers. As you work with these customers, you will likely:

- Provide pre-release product versions, then incorporate their feedback in the first release.
- Give them product discounts—after all, they're investing time and money to help propel development.
- Use them as references for selling to new customers.
- Enroll them to participate on customer advisory boards or similar customer groups.

As you create successive releases, these early customers' feedback can help you sell to an ever-expanding base of customers. Then new customers provide new feedback. What do you have? A continuous cycle of market validation, sales, further market validation, more sales, and so on.

To make the product evolve, sell it!

As we've seen, product definition is a core marketing activity. What gives marketing the information it needs to define the product? *Sales.* Sales is your front-line interface with customers. Customers vote with their money. And they will tell your sales force *exactly* what they like, what they don't like, and what they'd like to see.

In short, sales is critical for what University of Texas business professor John Doggett refers to as your "constant ear on the market." Over time, good salespeople get to know customers extremely well. What's more, they develop keen intuition about what feedback constitutes a product "must-do": *If we don't do this, my sales will drop off.*

Waveset co-founder Mark McClain puts it this way: "Customers help you rank, order, and prioritize what to do. As we were selling early on, customers told us they wanted our product to help them manage their back-end systems, such as mainframes, Windows NT environments, and so on. When enough customers told us the same thing, we realized the product *had* to incorporate that functionality."

This kind of feedback continues through every release. Sales passes the feedback on to marketing's product definition people. Then marketing uses it to redefine the product. Not only does sales repeatedly validate the market, but it also validates your product directions.

Communicate your long-term vision.

Through sales, customers come to know your long-term product vision. They also see how the current, shipped product fits into that vision. In short, sales helps deliver your marketing message. It helps customers understand the future—not just current—value of your solution.

Dale Howe of Covasoft explains it this way: "It's easy to find people selling products into the system management space. What's unique about our product is that it works across applications and becomes more valuable as its knowledge base grows. Our engine has the capacity to expand as Web applications get more complex and you add more to them. So the benefits of the product expand over time."

More than selling a product, then, Covasoft is "selling a vision," says Dale—a life cycle of ever-increasing benefits, beginning with customers' initial purchase.

Four sales models for the startup.

How should you go about designing a sales model? That will depend on your product and customers. However you proceed, though, keep this in mind: *Once you start selling the product, sales becomes the primary conduit to customers.* For that reason, your sales model should be the one that maximizes customer contact.

Here are four common sales models, which I'll explore in some depth a bit later on. Each model is used by at least one of the AV Labs companies you've already met earlier in the book:

1. *Direct face-to-face sales.* Teams of high-powered salespeople call on corporate executives to close sales. This model is suitable for enterprise software, which is used by organizations to improve fundamental business operations. Covasoft and Waveset are selling enterprise solutions, so this model is ideal for them.
2. *Original equipment manufacturer (OEM) sales.* The product is embedded as one component of a larger solution, which is designed, built, and sold by the manufacturer. Lane15's Infini-Band management software lends itself to the OEM model.
3. *Sales with consulting services.* To be effective, some enterprise software requires customers to rethink and reengineer established processes. Training, special implementation services, custom development, and similar services are needed. Mediaprise and Newgistics offer solutions like these.
4. *Telesales.* This "inside sales" model is ideal when a product is relatively inexpensive, or when customers must be educated before being contacted by a direct sales force. In its early stage, Ineto fits this model.

Figure 8 illustrates the four sales models.

As the figure shows, you will have the most direct customer contact with the direct sales and telesales models. When you use

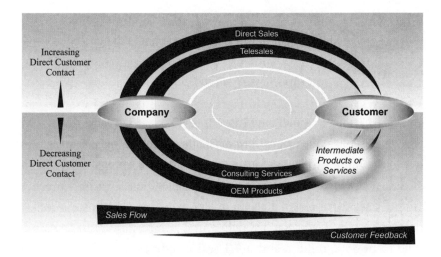

Figure 8. Four sales models for the early-stage company.

consulting services, a professional services organization will interact most directly with customers. Similarly, when a product is
embedded within a larger OEM solution, the OEMs sell to the end
consumer. No matter which model is best for you, you should
strive to develop strong channels for receiving and using customer
feedback.

Option 1: Direct face-to-face sales: Covasoft and Waveset.

If your product costs six figures and above, you will probably use
this model. As you're about to see, customers will tend to be large,
well-established *Fortune*-class or Global 2000 enterprises. You'll
have a lengthy sales cycle—three months, minimum. Your face-to-
face sales force will most likely be a small, well-compensated, geo-
graphically dispersed cadre of experienced professionals.

Where might partners come in? Again, not as your primary "sell-
ers." At the same time, though, partners can help build your *market
presence* and provide *introductions.* If you're tackling the large enterprise market, you need buy-in and support from market influencers.

Otherwise, creating market momentum will be tough. So—leverage partners for introductions and credibility.

Large-enterprise customers.

Covasoft's *Fortune*-class customers rely on e-business as a significant source of revenue. Slowdowns and failures in these systems can cost them a bundle. With the Covasoft solution, they can monitor and manage a huge variety of technical and business components. With Waveset, the large enterprise can give partners and customers secure Internet access to internal applications, data, and other resources.

Covasoft and Waveset are selling into companies whose revenues tend to be $500 million and up. These customers have sophisticated computing and e-business infrastructures. They also have the budgets and resources to implement new technologies. "With a couple of exceptions, our customers are Fortune 100 companies," says Waveset president Mark McClain. "We are initially focused on the high end of the market, because the product is designed to handle the thorny issues that arise in complex, multifaceted environments."

Dale Howe of Covasoft echoes Mark's comments, noting that "the Covasoft product operates across many different applications. The benefits accrue as applications are added and the environment becomes more complex. Our customers will spend the money to avoid e-business failure and increase performance. For them, that translates into customer satisfaction and bigger profits."

A word to the wise: Before these *Fortune*-class customers will buy, they require a great deal of intensive, person-to-person contact. Sales has to prove that the product applies in their environment. Not only that, but they must be convinced that they'll see real, measurable improvements, such as cost savings and greater productivity.

A lengthy sales cycle.

As previously noted, it usually takes at least three months for a *Fortune*-class customer to part with the big bucks we're talking about here. The cycle involves multiple presentations and technology demos. You typically have to reach a variety of audiences: the groups (IT organizations, in the case of Covasoft and Waveset) who will actually implement and operate the new solution, others whose work will be affected, and the decision-makers who control the purse strings.

Covasoft conducts "test drives" that put the solution to task in prospects' environments. "The test drive proves we can help customers predict problems and solve them before they even occur," says Dale Howe. "Customers can *see* how the product meets key business requirements."

This sales model is prone to a host of complications, which can extend the cycle further. A contact might leave the company or change jobs, for example—which means you have to restart the cycle with a new contact. What's more, you can count on these customers to do significant due diligence. They may want to see references from reputable customers. They may want proof of your company's financial stability. This due diligence can take time. So your direct face-to-face sales force has to be *patient, persistent,* and *professional.*

A small group of experienced salespeople.

There are few sales tasks as challenging as selling into the large enterprise. That is why you have to hire a top-notch sales force. Find people with experience in your market space. Recruit those who already understand the customers you're targeting.

Typically, your direct face-to-face sales force will include a sales VP, a small cadre of regional managers, and (often) an equal number of sales technicians, sometimes referred to as "systems engineers." The technicians serve as the technical arm of the sales force. They support the regional managers with product demos, test-drive implementations, and the like.

Both Waveset and Covasoft have a good mix of VPs, regional managers, and systems engineers. In addition, Covasoft has a technical salesperson at its Austin headquarters who's responsible, says Dale, for "institutionalizing and packaging best practices—compiling what works from a demo point of view, refining the test drive, and so on."

Hiring a top-flight direct sales force can be tricky—particularly for an early-stage startup. Most critical of all is the VP. When recruiting a VP, says Mark McClain, "it's important to hire someone who can tap their own network to bring in other people. If a known sales leader goes to a young company, that provides the credibility needed to attract good salespeople. A great VP will bring in a handful of great people. You can tap into a vein of talent without having to recruit every salesperson blind."

Waveset hired as its VP of sales Mary Morgan, who had years of leadership experience at BMC Software, a $1.5-billion enterprise software company with offices worldwide. Similarly, Dale Howe brought Covasoft an extensive network of industrywide contacts and associations.

In terms of early regional manager hires, Mark McClain astutely points out that a company should "focus on hiring 'player/coaches' for these positions. You want someone who's comfortable with being a rep but can also grow a team under them. You need people who sell extraordinarily well but also can manage other people. That way you won't have to hire sales managers later."

Another hiring consideration? The direct face-to-face sales model requires a $1 million-plus per-rep sales quota to make the economics work. The reps can accomplish only a few sales in a year, but the total value of these sales needs to exceed $1 million. Be sure, then, to hire people who are used to working with high-priced products and are not intimidated by multimillion-dollar quotas. In addition, implement a leveraged, commission-based pay structure to reward them well for making quota.

Option 2: Original equipment manufacturer sales: Lane15 Software

If your product is built to be embedded in larger product offerings, then an OEM-oriented sales model makes sense. In fact, it is the only model that will work. As we've seen, such is the case with Lane15.

Recall that Lane15 is creating software for managing the new InfiniBand network environment. InfiniBand's core hardware components are being built by industry giants Compaq, Dell, Intel, and others. These hardware providers—original equipment manufacturers—are, in effect, Lane15's likely customers. As it develops its software, Lane15 is working closely with the manufacturers to meet their needs. Later on, when the InfiniBand solutions go to market, these products will contain the Lane15 software component.

Lane15 is perfectly suited to the OEM approach. "This model is successful," says VP of business development Brian Hairston, "when a product meets a huge horizontal requirement in the marketplace—when it provides some feature many others will have to have for their own products to work." Management software, in other words, is not simply an add-on to companies building InfiniBand products. It is a critical piece of the product infrastructure. Without it, the manufacturers will be unable to get their solutions to market. For Lane15, that translates into "an extraordinary OEM opportunity," says Brian.

If your product lends itself to the OEM model, you'll enjoy some unique advantages. First, it is inconvenient for a manufacturer to switch component providers—meaning an early sale often locks out competitors. For similar reasons, these sales typically lead to multi-year deals. Challenges? Serving both the OEM and the end customer is tricky. What's more, your sales force needs special skills. Let's take a closer look at each of these issues.

Competition lock-out with early sales.

Once Lane15's software is embedded in an InfiniBand solution, changing over to competing software will be tough. The manufacturers will have to spend a lot of time and money to switch. They will also have to perform substantial redesign and other rework. The higher costs like these are, the less likely an OEM will be to change providers. While "the manufacturers may want agreements with multiple software providers, to keep everybody on their toes if nothing else," says Brian Hairston, "as long as the first one to the punch keeps executing well, there will be no valid reason for switching."

Multiyear deals from single sales.
It takes time to integrate a sub-component in an OEM product—particularly in a brand-new market like InfiniBand. Partners have to work closely together for many months. In addition, prior to releasing the InfiniBand products, companies will engineer and test them extensively. According to Brian Hairston, this could take "up to a full year after the initial products are available." Finally, companies are more comfortable when they know their partners have long-term commitments to mesh the technologies successfully.

At a minimum, then, most manufacturers typically want at least a two-year relationship with their suppliers. That gives startups like Lane15 a degree of revenue predictability you just don't have with other sales models.

#1 challenge: maintaining contact with both your OEM partner and the end consumer.
As Brian Hairston puts it, "This model can be a very tenuous, tightrope-walking situation. Your number 1 priority has to be satisfying the manufacturer partner. But you also want to make sure the end user of the product set has a good experience as well." In Lane15's case, end users will be the IT people who implement and operate the new InfiniBand networks.

Why worry about the end consumer? After all, they're not really your customer—the OEM is. Here's why: A satisfied end consumer ultimately translates to long-term sales. At the same time, says Brian, "because the product set moves to the consumer through the OEM, the company in Lane15's position has limited ultimate control over how the product is positioned and used by the end consumer. To some extent, at least early on, we'll depend on our manufacturer partners to do the job right for us. We'll count on them to pass on any feedback they get from the field."

Down the road, Lane15 itself will create and maintain visibility with end consumers. "We have to figure out ways to evangelize Lane15 with the end user," says marketing manager Mary Taylor. "We'll submit articles to the press. In fact, we've already queued up *Network World,* which has a strong IT focus, to do a possible cover on us. Plus, because we're in the InfiniBand Trade Association marketing working group, we get to invite IT managers to InfiniBand trade shows. They can give us feedback and create end-user pull with the OEMs.

"That's the ultimate goal: to reinforce, in the end user's mind, that the OEMs need to use Lane15 software in their products."

#2 challenge: a unique skill set needed by the sales force.

If you have an OEM-based sales situation, you need a lithe, technology-savvy sales force. With a dynamic market like Lane15's, this is particularly critical. "Our salespeople have to be able to deal with fluctuating product situations," Brian Hairston explains. "They have to stay cool, because things are changing fast."

In early 2001, for example, the Lane15 sales force attended the annual Intel Development Forum. "The interest and excitement around InfiniBand was amazing," says Brian. "It confirmed our expectation that we'd need to involve ourselves with a large number of companies. We'd have to staff up very quickly. Plus, we'd need to make sure our salespeople had the needed skill set."

In a nutshell, the Lane15 salespeople have to know how to deal with two different kinds of customers: the OEM customers and the individual end-consumer IT organizations. They have to be aware of high-level strategic business concerns, but they must also understand the nitty-gritty day-to-day work of implementing and running network products. They need the technical know-how to fathom the complexities of chips, routers, switches, and other hardware components. They also need to understand how software can be used to manage these components.

MICROSOFT: MASTER OF OEM SALES

Microsoft is a dramatic example of a company that has successfully implemented the OEM sales strategy. They took what had been a relatively insignificant component of microcomputers—the operating system—and transformed it into a competitive advantage that has made them the world's most powerful high-tech company.

You may or may not have aspirations of becoming Microsoft, but you can certainly learn from their example. Really, Microsoft did exactly what is described here—and they did it to perfection.

Microsoft's operating system:

- Meets a huge horizontal need in the marketplace.
- Is necessary to make a larger product (the PC) work.
- Is implemented so widely that changing over to a competitor's software product (some other operating system) would be, to say the least, time-consuming and expensive.
- *Most important,* end-user demand drives the OEM partners' demand for Microsoft's product.

A U.S. government attorney had this to say about the effectiveness of Microsoft's OEM sales strategy:

For almost a decade Microsoft has retained an extremely high market share—consistently in excess of 70 percent. Substantial barriers to entry and expansion exist in the relevant market. One barrier to entry and expansion is the considerable time and expense required to develop, test, and market a new PC operating system. Other interrelated barriers to entry . . . include:

a. The absence of a variety of high-quality applications that run on a new operating system, and the difficulty of convincing independent software vendors . . . to develop such applications;

b. The lack of a sizable installed base of users; and

c. The difficulty in convincing OEMs to offer and promote a non-Microsoft PC operating system.

(Source: U.S. government's complaint submitted in the antitrust lawsuit *U.S. v. Microsoft Corporation.)*

The moral? You know you've executed your OEM strategy well when the government accuses you of having and exercising too much market power!

Option 3: Sales tied to consulting services: Mediaprise and Newgistics.

The consulting-based sales model is similar in some respects to the face-to-face direct sales model. It often involves selling into *Fortune*-class enterprises. It usually requires a small, well-compensated cadre of experienced sales reps, supplemented by systems engineers for product demos and the like. The key difference is this: The consulting model is used when customers must rethink or reengineer *an already established process.* These customers need more than just the product. They need consulting, custom development, training, process reengineering, and similar services. These *services* are part of the sale.

Consulting services are integral to sales for both Mediaprise and Newgistics. As we've seen, the Mediaprise product enables manufacturers to manage their brand resources in a centralized, consistent way, so that they can easily distribute promotional material, graphics, streaming audio and video, 3-D models, and similar resources to channel partners. "We move far-flung data and resources into a centralized repository," says Steve Keys, VP of business development and sales. "So we have a strong impact on existing business processes. We affect the day-to-day work of many users within an organization." Reengineering, custom development, and training are needed to deploy the Mediaprise solution, called Mediaprise Brand Resource Manager.

Consider Newgistics' reverse logistics solution for streamlining product returns. This solution includes neighborhood locations, shipping and delivery, and warehousing and disposal. Each merchant who adopts Newgistics' ReturnValet service is, in effect, reengineering its entire returns process. The new process is embodied in Web-based software developed and hosted by Newgistics.

Like OEM sales, the consulting-based model presents you with a unique set of challenges and opportunities. To make a sale, you must analyze an environment up-front. *Your product is changing the customer's life.* In addition:

- Professional services can be an important revenue stream.
- When you create custom solutions for one customer, you can often reuse them in other customer installations.
- Reference accounts (important with *any* sales model) are particularly crucial for this type of sale.

Let's look more closely at each of these points.

Revenues from professional services.

Often, consulting provides its own revenue opportunity. Such is the case with Mediaprise. "Our Professional Services organization is a key part of the sales methodology," says Steve Keys. "Plus, these consulting dollars translate into significant revenue."

The Mediaprise Professional Services group produces revenue on three fronts:

- *Environmental analysis.* Consultants help customers understand their current operating environment. Product info, for example, may be in one repository, user guides in another, and images in yet another, with everything in a mix of digital and paper form. The analysis helps customers see how the Mediaprise solution can save time and money by moving these resources into one central repository. "It's an eye-opening experience," Steve says.

- *Custom development.* All enterprise customers have their own enterprise systems. The Mediaprise solution is designed to integrate with these systems, consolidating data from a variety sources into the central repository. The Professional Services team develops custom software to implement a customer's repository.

- *Training and education.* Finally, the team trains customers to access, augment, and otherwise use the Mediaprise repository efficiently to manage their brand resources.

While Mediaprise obtains revenue directly from its Professional Services fees, Newgistics' model works a little differently. In this case, Newgistics performs custom development to enable the Return Valet website to process a particular merchant's returns. This development effort does not serve as a separate revenue stream; rather, it is sold as part of the overall Newgistics service.

Reuse among customer installations.

Reuse is a big benefit of the consulting-based sales model. You can take what you've learned in one customer environment and reuse that knowledge in other environments. "As we work with more and more customers," says Steve Keys of Mediaprise, "our solutions will be able to scale. Particularly in vertical markets, such as consumer electronics, we'll be able to leverage work from installation to installation.

"Say, for example, that Customer A is using an Oracle database. That requires us to build a connector to extract data from Oracle and move it into the Mediaprise repository. The next time we encounter a

VIGNETTE CORPORATION: ADDING VALUE THROUGH SALES + CONSULTING

Vignette Corporation's Vignette Professional Services (VPS) organization is an illuminating example of the sales-with-consulting model . . .

Using the products provided by Vignette, e-businesses can rapidly assemble and deploy their customer-driven Internet applications. With a focus on content, integration, and analysis, Vignette's products enable these businesses to use the Internet effectively to maintain customer relationships.

Vignette markets its products primarily through a direct sales force consisting of hundreds of sales executives and support personnel. So that customers will have an innovative and comprehensive *solution*—one that truly meets their needs—the products are supported with services provided by the VPS organization. Considered a critical part of the Vignette sales and service process, VPS offers everything from strategic planning to project management, implementation to training. The organization's worldwide consultants have extensive experience in software project management, development, and deployment. That helps make sure customers can use the Vignette products to plan, design, and rapidly implement successful Internet businesses.

What are the VPS goals? Mitigate client implementation risks. Improve a solution's time to market and integrity. Share best practices with customer project teams. As for profitability, Vignette earns substantial revenues from its consulting services, charging on either a time-and-materials or a fixed-fee basis.

customer using Oracle, we'll already have the connector and won't have to build it again."

And as the consulting part of your business becomes more efficient through reuse, it also produces more revenue.

The importance of reference accounts.

Any adroit sales executive will tell you this: Customer references are a sales must-have, regardless of your sales model. When you tie sales to consulting, however, references are absolutely critical. After all, you're asking customers to reengineer basic business processes—a daunting (not to mention expensive) undertaking. When they see evidence that the solution has been implemented successfully in other, similar environments, they're much more likely to bite.

"When we call customers," says Steve Keys, "they immediately ask, 'Who else are you working with?' The minute we tell them, we have instant legitimacy. The reference gets us in the door."

Obtaining early reference accounts—or "lighthouse" accounts— is crucial for startups such as Mediaprise and Newgistics. These early customers tend to be leading-edge risk-takers. They're eager to adopt new technology before their competitors do so. "These are the customers you want early on," says Steve. "You sign them up as beta sites, give them special pricing deals, and work with them in a partnership-type arrangement to ensure that the solution works effectively for them. Then you can use them as references to get other customers on board."

In proposals and contracts with early customers, Mediaprise is arranging for these reference customers to accompany the sales force on customer visits. The customers also speak at trade shows and lend their quotes to brochures and sales presentations. Finally, they're written up as success stories distributed to prospects. Again, *any* company—regardless of its sales model—should have a comprehensive program for obtaining and using customer references.

Option 4: Telesales: Ineto.

Do not confuse the telesales model (one form of "inside" sales) with what we typically think of as telemarketing. Here, you're not cold-calling vast numbers of people who might or might need your solution. Rather, you're using a well-thought-out sales approach that relies on salespeople to call a qualified list of prospects.

Here are the situations that call for telesales:

- If you have a direct face-to-face sales force, you can use telesales to screen prospects prior to a visit from a sales rep.
- If your product is less expensive or non-complex, telesales can be your primary form of sales.

Telesales offers a number of benefits. A centralized, inside sales group reduces *costs.* It makes *communication* more efficient. It provides an ongoing *view* into the target customer base: On a daily basis, these salespeople hear customer feedback. Plus, as markets change, you can easily and efficiently *redirect* the efforts of a telesales force.

Ineto uses telesales very effectively—and creatively—to sell its Web-based customer communication service. In its early stages, the company is targeting an audience of mid-market businesses who pay a few thousand dollars a month for the Ineto service. Ineto's telesales force is normally sufficient for closing these deals. When a face-to-face visit is required, one of the company's executives steps in.

"Right now," says Mike Betzer, "we don't have regional salespeople on board, so I and the other managers function in that capacity when we're needed. Later on, we'll be signing up enterprise customers who will pay $25,000 and more a month for the service. We'll evolve to a staff of regional reps to close these bigger deals."

An interactive, dynamic process.
In the past, telesales involved simply picking up the telephone and calling a prospect or customer. Today, the model has evolved to use the Internet, e-mail, and other technologies as well.

Take Ineto, for example. In the last kick, we saw how Ineto pre-qualifies prospects by using a tele-prospecting firm to identify leads. Once the prospects have been identified, Ineto's inside salespeople send out e-mails with attached video clips, links to relevant portions of the website, product demos, and more. "We do all our demos over the Internet," says Mike Betzer. "That gives us more control and enables us to change the demos in response to market conditions."

Inside sales, then, are often the way to go. This model is cost-effective for the early-stage company. It provides an avenue for rapid customer feedback and response. And it continues the validation efforts that are at the heart of a company's sales process.

Regardless of which model you adopt for sales, if the model works you'll eventually grow beyond a startup. You'll evolve into a large, established business with many different groups and departments. What happens then? If you're smart, you'll keep applying the lessons you've learned in this book. The fact is, big companies should act more like startups. Which is exactly the topic we'll explore in the next kick . . .

EIGHTH KICK: TAKEAWAYS

✴ Partners as a sales force?

Sounds great—but isn't. You *must* own and manage your sales process.

✴ Why *not* use partners as the primary sales vehicle?

- Partners' sales reps sell hundreds of other people's products—and most don't know what all of these products are.
- Their priority? Sell their own company's products—not yours.
- Many early customer successes are needed before system integrators will incorporate your product in their customer environments.
- *Market momentum*—pull from the market—is the only thing that makes partner sales strategies work.

✴ What is sales? The ultimate form of market validation.

People are opening their wallets and parting with their money. That proves your solution has validity. How does sales perpetuate market validation? In these three ways:

- Building a customer base.
- Evolving the product through customer feedback.
- Communicating the vision.

✴ Four sales models for the startup:

1. Direct face-to-face sales. Go this route if the following describes your company:

- Product: enterprise software costing in the six figures.
- Customers: large *Fortune*-class enterprises.
- Selling to multiple decision-makers in complex environments.

2. OEM (original equipment manufacturer) sales. Go this route if this describes your company:

- Product: built to be embedded as a component of a larger product.
- Customers: OEMs, who take the larger product to market.
- Challenge: creating pull from the end consumer, who buys the OEM product, and staying close to the end customer's needs.

3. Sales with consulting services—if this describes your company:

- Product: high-dollar enterprise software requiring process reengineering in customer environments.
- Customers: *Fortune*-class enterprises.

4. Telesales—if this describes your company:

- Product: relatively inexpensive, *or* requires customer education prior to direct sales.
- Customers: a qualified list of prospects with a need for the solution.

BIG COMPANIES NEED TO ACT MORE LIKE STARTUPS

I was getting ready to head home one spring evening when I got a call from Mike Turner. He and Mark McClain were downtown. They'd just gotten out of a long meeting with the Waveset attorneys, and now they were hoping I could meet them at our old haunt, Louie's 106, for a beer. I readily agreed, remembering another time we'd gone there—a year ago or more, back when they were still developing their ideas for a startup. Lately they'd been buried over at Waveset, building up the team and getting ready for the first big product launch. I hadn't seen them in weeks. It would be good to hear how things were going.

I guess I expected them to be exhausted (from a long meeting with lawyers, if nothing else). But the minute I saw them saunter through the door at Louie's, it was clear they were anything but. They were laughing, and they looked totally energized.

"Rob, I've had a breakthrough," said Mike as they slid in across from me in the black leather booth.

"Not another one! What is it?"

"Agility is *the* key to business success—whether you're a big, market-leading company or a new startup trying to claw your way to the top."

"No kidding," I said. "That's one of the lessons you definitely learn in the startup world."

"We can't believe how fast we've been able to move, adapt, and morph our plans," he said. "We've gotten done in a month what we thought would take at least a quarter—and that's even adjusting for the speed a startup usually operates at. Big companies have a harder time doing this, trying to balance organizational processes against flexibility and innovation. Too often, the processes take over—and creativity suffers."

Then Mike and Mark turned the conversation to the exhilarating and hectic day-to-day experience of running Waveset. Later on, though, I found myself thinking back to what Mike had said about big companies. What is it, really, that lets a startup move so fast? Why is it so *hard* for *larger* organizations to do the same thing?

To defend or to grow? That is the question.

When you're a big, established company, you enjoy a huge set of advantages over a startup. Advantages like economies of scale. A well-managed infrastructure. Brand equity. Most important of all, substantial market share. It's really no wonder you'll be tempted to hang on to the status quo and *defend your market position.* "What we've done has produced all this success," you'll think. "Let's not mess with it—let's just hold onto our market share."

That's all fine and good. Except for one thing: There are a lot of startups out there, and they have no market share to defend. No brand equity. Nothing, in short, to lose. So while you're trying to defend your position, the startup is trying to *grow.* It has, in fact, no choice but to grow. Its only option is to try and knock "the big guy" out of his market share. Trust me: When you grow into a mature enterprise, *you'll have multiple startups nipping at your heels.* The larger and more successful you are, the more entrepreneurs there'll be who are bound and determined to bite off a share of your market.

Your lesson? If you do nothing but defend your position, startups will hurt you. If you stop growing, stop innovating, stop replacing your own products with new ones, stop listening to what customers want *now*—not a year or two years or five years ago but *now*—then some startup out there will do it for you. The result? A loss of the very market share you're trying to defend.

The trick is this: As a big company, you must continue to focus on principles like the ones we've explored in this book. Somewhere along the way, you'll be tempted to start believing that what works for a startup simply doesn't apply to you. If you think that way, you're wrong. Act like a startup, and you will avoid complacency. Act like a startup, and you'll renew your focus on growth. Act like a startup, and you'll *strengthen* your market position—rather than merely defending the status quo.

How can you do these things? How can a big company act more like a startup? For an answer, I turned to a group of the startup founders and executives you've met in this book. Before they took the entrepreneurial plunge, each of these people spent a decade or more in leadership positions within large high-tech organizations. They became intimately aware of what makes a big company tick. And as they moved into startup environments, they were often surprised by the difference.

I thought it would be helpful, then, to close this book by letting you hear directly from these entrepreneurs. I sat down with them and asked: "What have you learned from being in a startup that you wish you'd known back then? What behaviors—behaviors that are *imperative* for an early-stage company—can help a mature enterprise act like an adroit startup?"

I think you'll be intrigued by what they had to say. Read on . . .

Alisa Nessler, CEO, Lane15

Alisa Nessler, whose company is profiled in the sixth kick, spent almost ten years at IBM, where she worked as a sales representative, a marketing manager, and a brand manager. She was also at BMC Software for a number of years, managing a product marketing group for a set of BMC products. Before joining AV Labs as a Venture Fellow and founding Lane15, Alisa served as CEO of two other startups: Seattle-based Appliant and Austin's Haystack Labs. Here, she contrasts her experience at IBM and BMC with the experience of running Lane15 and the other startup companies.

ADVICE FROM ALISA:
Remember that every hire counts.

"One of the first things you learn in a startup is that it's very expensive to make a bad hire. In a large company, people sometimes tend to think that when you have somebody who fits into the bucket labeled 'Heart's in right place,' or the one labeled 'Good attitude but just not getting it done,' you can work around it. Maybe it's because in an established organization, it's easier to lose sight of individuals' value-adds.

"In a startup, you simply can't do that. Everyone is important. *Every team member's work has to have a direct impact on value, or the person has to go.* That mind-set would make large companies a lot leaner and meaner—and a lot more effective.

"At the same time, just as there are people who don't carry their weight, there's also a certain class of people who are very achievement-oriented. No matter what, they'll be over-accountable and do absolutely anything it takes to get the job done. *Often, large companies don't necessarily reward those people the same way a startup does.* In a startup, you're aware every moment that all your hard work is what creates value. As the company grows, the entire employee base gets to participate in an increase in value. This is one of the things that makes start-ups so attractive for great people: If you're going to put that much of yourself into something, it's nice to participate in the upside opportunity as a result. Mature companies need to aim *constantly* at *rewarding great people* with bonuses, promotions, and other things that recognize their individual efforts.

"In a similar vein, smaller companies are able to let people step up to the highest level they can achieve. You're never held back by tenure. The best people can have a huge influence on the company, regardless of their experience or job title. I've known many superior people in big companies who had great ideas—but were never able to run with them, simply because of their position in the company. *Big companies need to figure out ways to reward outstanding employees and give them a voice.* Open-door policies could help. So could flatter organizational structures, more autonomy, and the like."

ADVICE FROM ALISA:
Never stop validating your market.

"Some big companies evolve toward a very engineering-driven product management process. The engineering team often doesn't communicate much with people in marketing about whether there's a market for a product. They simply come up with their own ideas, then develop a product and see if it sells. Not surprisingly, because there's often insufficient market validation, some products don't sell that well. In the meantime, the company has spent a lot of money and resources on them.

"Why isn't the market always validated? Because if market validation gets done, it's usually marketing that does it—and sometimes marketing's budget for product planning is limited. Engineers will tend to use their budget to hire programmers, not to validate the market. They're sometimes not accountable for producing a product that's successful in the market. As a result, there is often a mismatch between the values of the organization and where it spends money.

"If being in startups has taught me anything—and it's taught me a lot—it's that this model is like putting the cart before the horse. At Lane15 we spent a great deal of time and energy validating the market for InfiniBand software, making sure we could link up significant OEM partners and customers, figuring out how we could establish an identity that would enable us to play effectively in the InfiniBand space. Only then did we launch the development project. Ever since, throughout the development effort, we have validated and revalidated the solution with our biggest customers to make sure we're on track. *They're* the ones that can tell us that—not our engineers.

"I wish I'd known more about market validation before. *Big companies need to stay market-driven and customer-focused, however they can.* And no matter what size a company is, it should never simply give engineers free rein to build whatever they want to build, without thoroughly exploring the customers' pain and the market's need."

ADVICE FROM ALISA:
Align your team around your company's vision.

"Another big lesson I've learned at startups is this: You can achieve an incredible amount when everybody has a common goal. In larger organizations with many levels of accountability, employees' goal hierarchy is typically this: individual, team, group, division, and finally company. If goals are not properly aligned across this complex hierarchy, the company can lose its effectiveness. It can waste time and energy competing internally, across teams, departments or divisions, rather than with outside competitors. *In a startup,* by contrast, *everyone is on the same page.* Everyone has a common goal: for the company to succeed. That way, you get so much more done.

"Keeping everyone on the same page is relatively easy for a startup, simply because it's so small. This is more of a challenge for a big company. But it's also really important. Established companies have to determine *how they can communicate the overriding strategic objectives to every employee,* and then *align everyone's interests* with those objectives. In a startup, especially one that's venture-backed, you never lose sight of the fact that you can't waste resources on internal competition. You can't afford to waste a single day or a single dollar."

ADVICE FROM ALISA:
Synch new products with your sales model.

"I've been at companies where products went out the door that never should have. Good engineers had built them, and maybe they were good products, but they didn't fit with the sales model. In another company, the products might have been great—but this company couldn't get the sales team to properly focus on them.

"What's the lesson? Product plans should be well aligned with the sales channel. *Everybody*—including engineers— *must be intimately familiar with the sales channel,* the *customers* that salespeople deal with, *price points,* and *other key sales issues.* If the channel has to go call on a different customer or a different department to sell a product, they're less likely to be successful. If suddenly they have to call on a different type of decision-maker, or if a new product has a widely different price point, that makes them less effective as well. So does having to have a lot of training to sell a new product. The point is, new products should align with the core competency of the sales force. Otherwise, *sales will fail.*

"In a small company, where groups interact every day, keeping this alignment is fairly straightforward. The challenge arises as an organization grows. Everyone in a big company should remember a key thing about sales: Sales-people will focus most of their effort on how they can put the most cash in their pocketbook. In a small company, every decision you make is based on how it impacts or motivates the sales force. In startups, sales is just so critical you can't afford to make mistakes. *For a big company, it's imperative to ensure that the salespeople are properly motivated* and have their interests properly aligned with the corporate goals—and also that new products are in synch with their core competency."

Mike Betzer, President and CEO, Ineto

As we saw in the second kick, Mike Betzer was at MCI for thirteen years—most recently serving as VP of information technology. As you're about to see, Mike has some very interesting things to say about his tenure at MCI—and about what big, established companies like MCI could learn from tiny startups like Ineto.

ADVICE FROM MIKE:
Entrepreneurial energy? Use it.

"Now that I've been outside MCI for three years, I'd have to say it was pretty entrepreneurial as big companies go. Still, I've learned a lot from being in a startup that I wish I'd known back then. At a high level, if you look at the cost of doing business the way it's been done the past several years, it's incredibly expensive. A lot of times, you have people in big, mature companies who get an idea, then leave to start their own company. After a certain amount of time, if they're successful, the startup becomes attractive and the big company buys it—often paying a huge premium. *Wouldn't it be easier if big companies could stay fast and flexible enough to develop these ideas internally?*

After all, they often *have* the intellectual capacity to do it. The problem is, people often leave to do it themselves.

"Now, we could be moving into a phase where these huge companies could have a monster leg up if they could harness and capitalize on the entrepreneurial energy of the team. Will they do that? Ninety-seven out of a hundred probably won't, but three may.

"The key is to have an established format for *collecting knowledge,* for *motivating people to share their ideas.* Good ideas should be rewarded through recognition, bonuses, and other incentives. And the people who have the ideas should be given the autonomy to pursue them. *Big companies need to establish safe havens where people can develop next-generation technologies and products.* Otherwise, they will just have to keep paying huge premiums to buy technology that could have been created in-house."

ADVICE FROM MIKE:
Move like a startup: fast, focused, flexible.

"If big companies could stay fast, focused, and flexible, they could generate a huge competitive advantage. And they could save millions of dollars."

Decide and act—fast.

"When I compare my life now with what it was like at MCI, I see that 50 percent of all my management time there was spent in conference calls and meetings. *All too often, leaders weren't listening to customers or leading their people.* There was way too much discussion. When you're not close enough to the customer, it's easy to make the wrong decisions. You have to make sure you keep the business focused on talking to customers and making sure they're satisfied—then you have to act fast when it's time to make a decision.

"In business, speed wins. A great story from MCI illustrates this point. At MCI, I led the venture arm, and we were investing in a lot of startup companies. This is, by the way, another way to help a big company stay fast—it keeps you close to new technology when you set aside a few million dollars and make investments in companies you like. You not only get financial returns, but you get to watch the next generation closely as it develops; when it reaches a critical mass, you can acquire it, or expand the relationship.

"At MCI we made some great investments and realized some tremendous returns. But *sometimes we missed the mark, mainly because of bureaucracy and a lack of risk-taking.* At one point, I was in conversation with Netscape—it was a tiny startup at the time—about MCI making a 5 percent ownership investment. One of my technical guys had hooked up with one of their technical guys and said we should meet with them. We did, and needless to say, Netscape was tremendously excited. But ultimately the corporation couldn't understand why this was such a big thing. The president of our division didn't want to do it—not enough information, not core to the business, and ultimately not an investment.

"This shows how easy it can be for a big company to lose the ability to see beyond its own headlights. If you want to be an investor, you have to move as fast as a venture capitalist moves. *You have to move really, really fast, and you can't wait for a perfect level of information to make a call.* Just watching our venture investors has given me keen insight into how these investment arms in big corporations need to operate."

#1 focus? The core competency.

"Working in a startup, I've learned you have to *figure out what you want to be good at, then do it better than anyone else.* There is a distraction a month—some new twist or turn, from a partnership perspective, a distribution perspective, or whatever. Success comes from figuring out what to focus on, understanding what's in your core competency and what's ultimately lead boots. Then you pursue the core competency and outsource everything else.

"Take partnerships. Sometimes, getting to market involves more than just identifying a market and finding customers who will open their wallets. Sometimes, it requires partnering with the right companies as distribution channels. Some partners look good at first glance, but ultimately if a partner can't move as fast as you need, you're wasting time. You have to ask yourself: With this partner, can you actually *get it done,* or will there be meeting after meeting at which people talk about *theory and ideas?*

"The telecom sector is a good example. When we went out and started Ineto three years ago, we knew one possible partner sector would be the telecom companies. We knew every single telecom company should be offering a product by Ineto, or like Ineto. Our service is outside their core competency, so we knew they needed to partner with us to acquire it. What happened was that we'd have great meetings, but ultimately nothing would come out of it. Every time, they would say, 'There's a budget problem,' or 'We're going through this or that and can't do it right now,' or whatever.

"Finally we decided we wouldn't talk to telecom companies, because they didn't get it. Now, in just the last sixty days, Worldcom has announced a product in this space that they'll launch soon. Sprint and Broadwing are also building products. This competition is great for us—it validates the space. Plus, we're not that worried about the competitors. Since it's not part of their core competency, it's unlikely they will be focused enough to build it on their own. Even if they do, there is a massive $3 billion market for this solution. In the end, most of them will probably find out they can't build it themselves, so the only option will be to find a partner."

Stay flexible and innovate.

"When I think of flexibility and the lack of it in most big organizations, it all comes back to the budgetary cycles. Wall Street is such a weird motivator, with its demands occurring quarter over quarter. This can be too shortsighted, creating many starts and stops. It's hard to develop new, big technologies in an environment like this. *Big companies have to create a way to work the Street* so that the Street will understand, 'Look, we'll be spending a tremendous amount of money on R&D to develop the next thing.'

"For example, look at Dell versus Gateway. Both are big PC producers. Dell, though, spent lots of money moving into the corporate world. They spent many, many cycles outside the quarterly demands, building a presence in the server space. Early on, they were strapped, and they had to decide, 'Should we keep throwing money at this server thing?' They did, and they showed that it worked. Ultimately Dell became the number one producer of corporate servers, while Gateway is still selling PCs mostly to consumers. The Gateway approach is fine, but if you want to own the world, *you have to figure out a way to keep risk alive,* and let these next-generation projects breathe *outside* the quarterly demands of Wall Street.

"Therein lies a great CEO and a great board of directors. It's important for big companies to be able to pull that off. Otherwise, they have to buy companies, which costs hundreds of millions of dollars."

ADVICE FROM MIKE:
Give teams time and space to build value.

"Even though investors have become much more focused on their money than in the recent past, they are still willing to wait it out with a startup if there's *a real market,* a real *management team,* and the proven ability to hit *a validated market* with a needed solution. Is Ineto where I thought we'd be, three years into the company? Not even close. It takes time, energy, and a consistent focus to create a better solution for a huge market.

"Let's look at this issue from the perspective of big, mature companies. For them, it comes down to priorities. *Any big company can make the decision to keep something alive.* In the late '80s and into the '90s, MCI was an incredible place to work. You could figure out better ways to get to market, then take the market. Those were the glory days. I was also there when we went through a couple of bad cycles, times when we weren't growing like we thought we should, and had to correct. But ultimately the company never stopped reengineering and trying to figure out how to make network products and services smarter, faster, and better.

"During those years, MCI defined itself as a top-notch technology and engineering company. To the world, we were a marketing company. MCI was great at figuring out how to acquire customers. MCI knew how to bill millions of customers a month. But there was a tremendous amount of information technology that sat behind that wonderful marketing machine.

"Creating that great technology—and turning it into a solution customers would buy—was a priority. These priorities have to stay priorities. They can't fall victim to the trade winds of the perpetual annual budget cycle of grow it, cut it, grow it, cut it. *Companies that take this shortsighted approach won't survive, because you have to have a continuous process of reengineering.* Intel is a great example—it's been leading its market space for fifteen years. MCI was the same in its glory days. The question is, can a company survive for multiple generations? That remains to be seen."

CISCO SYSTEMS: ENTREPRENEURIAL PRINCIPLES IN ACTION

Cisco Systems was founded in 1984 by a small group of Stanford University computer scientists seeking an easier way to connect different types of computer systems. Today, this multinational, 50,000-employee corporation is a worldwide leader in networking. How does Cisco stay successful? By acting like a startup.

Cisco's passion, according to its own annual report, is "to increase customer satisfaction and to achieve our stretch goal of maintaining the number one or two market share position in every market in which we compete." How well has the company met these goals? Consider the following:

- Cisco does hold the number one or two market share position in sixteen of the seventeen markets in which it competes.
- It controls two-thirds of the global market for routers and switches that link networks and power the Internet.

Market share is not the only evidence of great execution. So are the many accolades awarded Cisco and its management team. A few examples:

- #2—America's Most Admired Companies *(Fortune,* April 5, 2001).
- #7—World's Most Respected Companies *(Financial Times,* December 13, 2000).
- #3—Best Companies to Work For *(Fortune,* December 18, 2000).
- Top 20—Best Corporate Citizens for 2001 as one of America's

most profitable and socially responsible major public companies (*Business Ethics magazine,* March/April 2001).

- CEO John Chambers—CEO of the Year *(Worth,* May 2000).

Just what has made Cisco thrive? Three things: a superior management team, a close relationship with customers, and flexibility. All these features also characterize a successful startup company.

From CEO John Chambers on down, I can think of few management teams that are better able to evaluate market challenges and take advantage of opportunities. As for its relationship with customers, Cisco's annual report tells the story best. The report refers repeatedly to *customer support, customer satisfaction, customer retention, customer service,* and *customer loyalty.* It's obvious that Cisco is dedicated to knowing its customers. What's more, this company strives continually to meet and exceed customers' needs.

What about flexibility? According to Mike Volpi, Cisco's senior vice president of business development and alliances, the company's formula for successful growth changes constantly. Says Volpi: "The adage *If it ain't broke, don't fix it* doesn't apply here." Volpi recently told a group of investors at the Thomas Weisel Partners' Emerging Networks Conference that "quickly moving markets have forced Cisco to demonstrate unprecedented agility for a company its size, just to keep from being left behind by competitors. . . . For its success to continue, Cisco isn't going to get set in its ways."

Not that the picture has always been a rosy one. In the first quarter of 2001, for example, Cisco missed earnings estimates for the first time in thirteen quarters. Clearly, Cisco's performance had been affected by an economic downturn and by customer decisions to curtail technology-infrastructure investments. At the same time, of course, these same factors also affected Cisco's competitors—along with virtually the entire technology sector as a whole.

How did Cisco adapt to the adversity? According to Volpi, Cisco saw it as another opportunity. The company went back to basics, rededicating itself to what made it successful in the first place. It took steps to raise its standing with important telecommunications companies, for example, revamping its telecom business to dedicate more sales and technical-support staff to a smaller number of customers. The aim? To help phone companies develop the value-added services their corporate customers want. Announced senior VP William Nuti, "We're going to get back to basics in terms of listening to our customers and responding to what their needs are."[21]

---

21. Stephanie N. Mehta, *Cisco Fractures Its Own Fairy Tale, Fortune,* May 14, 2001.

Steve Keys, VP of sales and business development, Mediaprise

Before co-founding Mediaprise, Steve Keys spent many years as program director at IBM. (Mediaprise was profiled in the fourth kick.) In these passages, Steve reflects on what his startup experience has taught him about how big companies can behave more efficiently—more, in short, like a startup.

ADVICE FROM STEVE:
Optimize your resources to speed things up.

"One of the main reasons people move from large to small companies is this: *They want to get away from the bureaucracy.* Consider, for example, the policies and practices of many big companies, where very deep hierarchical structures elongate the execution and decision-making process. At IBM, if you wanted to participate in an industry conference and demo an IBM product, you would have to communicate with everyone from public relations to executive support, moving through many different layers of organizations and getting multiple approvals. In a startup, all it takes is a phone call, then you write a check and go. We recently went to the Seybold Conference because we wanted to gain visibility with the 300–500 attendees. We made one phone call to one of the speakers, and they agreed to open up the agenda and give us five or ten minutes.

"Many mature companies are recognizing this and moving toward *flatter* organizations with *fewer* hierarchical levels. This is a good way to get around the inherent bureaucracy of a huge organization and empower individuals to make decisions on their own.

"Along those same lines, a startup's limited resources provide, paradoxically, one of its main advantages. In a startup, you learn to *optimize* your scarce resources by finding *creative* ways to get things done. Contrast this with a huge company, where the infrastructure is provided for you—from administrative support on up. For every possible question, the organization is designed to provide an answer. As a result, people tend to focus narrowly on their own departmental skills and not learn and grow beyond that. *Their minds can get stale and slow.* The small-company environment, on the other hand, generates creativity by not providing such a wealth of infrastructure.

"How can the large company address these issues? By giving people a chance to see, much sooner, how their *individual* contribution affects *the bottom line,* and by breaking up the organization into smaller, *more dynamic teams* where people have more flexibility. Today, big companies talk about promoting and encouraging risk-taking, but the layers of organization and all the internal policies tend not to really be designed to give people that flexibility.

"In a small company, anyone with the business interest or knowledge can call a CEO or executive at virtually any company we can get access to. In many large companies, the hierarchical structure hinders the two-way communication of ideas. Many companies, aware of this problem, are *flattening* their corporate structures to open communication channels and empower *individual risk-taking.*"

ADVICE FROM STEVE:
Fight to solve customers' pain—
not to win internal battles.

"One offshoot of the very large teams you find in big companies is that these large groups have their own ways to measure progress—and it sometimes has little do with the customer, or specifically with how they are addressing customer needs.

"At Mediaprise, we are very committed to ongoing competitive analysis. We constantly evaluate new companies on the radar screen, attending trade shows and forums where the competing products are being demo'ed. Plus, we talk to customers *every day* about what their pains are, what solutions they want to see, and what is motivating them to buy a solution like ours. We have a sales demo that we take with us on every sales call—so we get feedback not just on the idea but on the real product.

"At the execution level of big companies, where people like program directors function, there tends to be as much *internal competitiveness as customer focus.* If you were to ask a CEO, he would undoubtedly say he and his staff talk to customers every day. But this customer focus is hard to maintain at lower levels in an organization, where there is so much competitiveness between groups. At IBM, for example, there was a constant competition, between IBM Global Services and the internal service organization.

"What's more, at big companies, managers and workers sometimes tend to spend as much time convincing vice presidents and supervisors they're on the right track as they do dealing with the customer and solving the customer's problem. In presentations, you often try to get the general managers to perceive you in a positive way. It's often a CYA exercise, having nothing to do with how your work ties directly to the customer.

"*Established companies should insist that every presentation be built around how customer pain is being addressed.* Every project should be designed with that in mind. At Mediaprise, we are committed to remaining engaged with customers, and to making sure everyone is aware of how their work meets customer needs. We realize this will become more challenging as we grow. But it's a process that must never stop. Understanding where customers are going, and what solutions they need, is a mainstay of our business. All companies should think this way, no matter how large they become."

ADVICE FROM STEVE:
Create a customer-first culture.

"At Mediaprise, we communicate every week with the troops in what we call 'town hall' meetings. Everyone meets in the hallway, and the CEO gives an update. We also have plenty of written communication.

"*This type of regular, ongoing communication helps everyone know how they're contributing.* A big part of our culture, for example, is to put the customer first. Everyone from marketing to sales to HR to engineering has direct visibility into what's important to customers, what customers are saying, and how each individual's work helps meet customer needs. This fosters the idea in people's minds of what they need to do, every day, to help acquire customers—which is, after all, what will lead to the company's success.

"We even have a VP with the title 'Customer Success.' That's how committed we are to making sure, as a company, that customers can use our product successfully.

"Given everything we have learned in a startup, *it would be a wonderful program for IBM to require all of its change agents*—top contributors, people who have an impact on the company—*to spend six months at a startup.* The downside, of course, would be that they'd have a comfortable job to go back to—a safety net that startups just don't have. Still, they'd gain *a whole new perspective* in terms of what's important and what's not."

Mike Turner, CEO, Waveset.

As we saw in the first kick, Mike was for many years an executive at Tivoli Systems. He helped usher Tivoli from its early stages through an intense period of growth—culminating in its purchase by IBM and its development into an enterprise software powerhouse with thousands of employees. What Tivoli experiences stand out in his mind? How might Tivoli have continued to build on its startup success? Find out, as you read Mike's comments over the next few pages.

ADVICE FROM MIKE:
Execute intelligently with small, focused teams.

"'Lean and mean' is a huge competitive advantage. As Tivoli became larger, we tended to rely on more people to do more things. Being a startup has taught us how to do more with less. We've learned that *what works is to keep teams as tight as pos-*

sible. Instead of using eighty people to develop a product—even a complex enterprise software product—you can do it with dozen. At most, you can have pockets of teams focused on different things. The key? Keep your eye on the end goal and leverage resources appropriately.

"Tivoli did this well early on, building the first management product for the Internet phenomenon with just four or five engineers and a few test people. The whole team had around eight or ten people on it, and we took the product from zero to delivery in three months.

"Later, as product teams grew to fifty or more, it took longer and longer to get product releases out. Some of this was due to a more complex product and more stringent requirements. Still, if you can compartmentalize and keep teams small and independent, there's much less communication overhead. It's easier to synchronize team members. As a result, they can spend more time solving problems and developing products, *rather than tracking organizational processes.* That's been our experience at Waveset, where a very small, very tight group of engineers has built a complex product in just a few months' time.

"From a big company's perspective, it's not about hiring fewer people; *it's about compartmentalizing them into small, focused units.* Even a huge, well-established organization like the U.S. military understands the value of small teams. The military uses sixteen-person teams, knowing you can get a lot more done with these smaller units that can act independently."

ADVICE FROM MIKE:
Maintain direct customer contact.

"As a startup, you really spend a lot of time engaged in primary, *customer-focused* market research. You interact with prospects *directly*, on a one-to-one basis at the highest levels of the management team. This is something that larger companies tend to forsake.

"I can think of several instances where more direct customer interaction would have made a huge difference for us at Tivoli. Instead, the larger we got, the more we relied on secondary research and industry analysts to drive our decisions. In addition to listening to Giga or Meta, we could have spent more time listening to the customers themselves. What did *they* need? What were *their* next big issues?

"For example, IBM built the security management application for Distributed Computing Environment [DCE was a computing infrastructure in the 1990s] based on the widespread analysts' belief that DCE would be the next big thing. According to our secondary research, the market should have materialized. But it never did. DCE was never widely adopted. *Had IBM talked to a large number of prospects directly, things might have turned out differently.* If we had been a startup, we would have *had* to know this to survive.

"In a startup you're interacting *all the time* with customers, trying to understand their needs and build a responsive product. This becomes even more important as a small company grows into a big company. *Customer-centered market validation should remain a critical part of a company's culture, no matter how large it becomes.*"

ADVICE FROM MIKE:
Get a product to market—when it's needed— and iterate quickly.

"A startup teaches you a lot about product development. No one can predict what the market will need in three years. When there's extreme focus on the customer and a commitment to sales, you learn you have to do a six- or nine-month project, take it to customers, find out what works, then rev it again.

"For a bit company to be effective, it has to have a significant R&D function. Still, it's easy to get caught up in lengthy, large scale projects that often take many years to deliver. The market may be validated in the beginning, but *you must keep checking in to make sure the project evolves as the market does.* Otherwise, you run a big risk that the product will miss the mark when it's released.

"We've learned it's often better to get to market quickly with a subset of features customers need the most, then grow and iterate on the product, based on customer feedback. Otherwise, you risk having hundreds of engineers working on a project that won't necessarily drive success in the field when it is launched—if it gets out the door at all.

ADVICE FROM MIKE:
Remember—create value in every step.

"In a startup, all you think about is creating value, and you think of it as a continuous process. *Everyone* in the company is *focused* on making the company *more valuable.* As companies grow, they can easily lose sight of what creates the most value at a given point in time, forgetting that's why they're in business in the first place.

"The venture financing process—and the overriding importance of that process for a startup—is what helps align a startup team around creating value. The first thing that creates value is the team and the concept. You get enough money to validate the market, and if you validate it successfully, that means you're more valuable. Then, using the Series A funding, you design and test the product, develop partnerships, and ship a solution. From there, with the next round, it's a matter of scaling up, revising and shipping the product again, growing the sales force, developing the right sales channels, and so on. As the company continues to grow, the focus on creating value is ever-present.

"In a startup this process is very stark. It progresses from funding event to funding event, with each financing round signifying some set of milestones. Everyone is completely aware of the process, the milestones, and everyone knows exactly how his or her work contributes to the rise in value. *Larger companies can easily get sidetracked,* concentrating on *product creation* as opposed to *value creation.* If the customer-feedback loop is lost, for example, products can sink like lead balloons in the market. *Big companies must continuously validate the market* and focus on delivering value during a development project. That way, a product is more likely to be successful."

ADVICE FROM MIKE:
Communicate the big vision, all the time.

"It sounds like an oxymoron, but when you're a small company, you have to think really big, and when you're big, you need to be able to still think small. What I mean is: In a small organization, everyone on the team has the big picture. *When a company gets very large, people tend not to be able to grasp the complexity of where they're going.* They tend to compartmentalize and carve off a small piece of the world. Because their focus is on only one small part of the overall company, it's easy to develop myopic vision. People often don't understand how everything fits together to create a large picture. More important, they don't see how what *they* do helps the *company* succeed.

"*Big companies have to help people understand the larger*

vision and how their work aligns with the overall goals. Break-throughs happen when people comprehend the whole picture and their unique role in contributing to the vision.

"As a startup, this is easier. Everyone communicates on a day-to-day basis. Everyone's always in synch. It's a living, breathing process. Big companies tend to communicate more formally, at big company meetings—typically, on a quarterly basis. But things change day to day, and all the interesting work gets done between the formal meetings. When you're limited to providing snapshots in time every twelve weeks, you don't capture the living part of the market and the environment. As a result, people end up operating on old data.

"As an example, we'd been doing really fantastic in systems management at Tivoli, and we wanted to move toward application management—managing business data and information rather than systems-management components. We'd identified application management as a new market opportunity. Yet talking about it at company meetings wasn't enough. People didn't understand how the new direction fit in with the overall picture, or where it plugged in to the day-to-day scheme of things. Without regular, proactive, close communication, it is very difficult to say, 'We are doing so great right now that we need to change.' But that's what you *must* do to continually innovate and grow the business.

"In contrast, look at what happened at Microsoft in '96 and '97. Bill Gates wanted the company to focus on the Internet, and he said, 'You can't meet with me unless you're talking about the Internet and how Microsoft can leverage the Net successfully.' This forced a huge company to get serious about a new direction and to see it as more than just a fad. Gates was able to turn a huge ship right around and steer it in a brand-new direction. He simply refused to communicate about anything *except* what needed to happen."

NINTH KICK: TAKEAWAYS

✳ **So you're a large company now. Want to keep growing?**
There's one way to do it—act like a startup!

✳ **Defend or grow—that's the choice.**
The mature company typically wants to defend its market positions. The mantra? "If it ain't broke, don't fix it." Makes sense, doesn't it? Sort of. Except for those pesky startups.

- Startups have no market share to defend.
- Startups have no choice but to grow.
- Startups have nothing whatsoever to lose.

✳ **When you're a big company, what happens if you do nothing to grow?**
Startups will hurt you. Startups will do *anything* to steal your market share.

✳ **How can the mature company act more like the adroit startup?**

- *Make sure everybody is creating value.* Every hire counts—and dead-weight needs to go.
- *Get back to market validation.* Stay market-driven and customer-focused. Talk about customer pain *all the time,* and make sure everybody knows they're fixing it.
- *Communicate a common vision.* Do whatever it takes to make sure everybody is on the same page.
- *Align new products with the sales model.* New products have to synch up with the sales force's core competency. Otherwise, sales fails—and we know what that means.
- *Harness entrepreneurial energy on the team.* Reward great ideas. Give people the autonomy they need to pursue them. Establish safe havens for next-generation R&D. The alternative? Pay through the nose to purchase yet another startup.

- *Make decisions, and act fast.* Cut the bureaucracy. Take risks. Grab opportunities when they come up. If you have an investment arm, run it like a venture capitalist.
- *Stick to your core competency.* Partner up for the new technologies your customers need. Don't try to build it yourself.
- *Create smaller, dynamic units.* A few people can get things done much faster than huge teams.
- *Keep R&D alive. Some* projects have to exist outside the quarterly demands of Wall Street. Work the Street—and make them understand the value of your next-generation R&D.

THIS ONE'S YOURS TO GIVE IN THE MARKETPLACE!

Whew! You've survived basic training. When you opened this book, you undoubtedly had a lot of misconceptions about the entrepreneurial enterprise. Just about everybody does. Now, though, you've lost your illusions, dropped your misguided assumptions, and gained new insight. Now you know what's *really* needed to build a foundation for a successful business.

You're aware, for starters, that a "great idea" means little when it comes to founding a great company, or spinning out a great business unit, or pursuing any other new path in a great way. What matters most? *The quality of your team.* Surround yourself with A plus players. Infuse your company with execution intelligence.

Then, apply that intelligence to the single most important thing you'll ever do as an entrepreneur: *learning about your customers.* Who are these people anyway? What problem is making them really crazy? Learn what your customers' pain is and learn how you can solve it. Then, as you devise a solution, adopt this as your mantra: *Solve the pain. Solve the pain. Solve the pain.*

Once you find out what your customers' pain is, you'll be tempted to play the hero. You'll want to deliver a product that fixes *all* the pain, all at once. When that thought crosses your mind, think of one of this book's most important messages: *Get to market! Now!* Either by partnering up with companies whose solutions complement your own, or by delivering some subset of the functionality your customers ultimately need. *But do it now.*

And don't obsess about money. I know it's one of the thorniest issues facing an entrepreneur, but if you're not careful, financing can become your Waterloo. Especially if you insist on the buckets of cash many early-stage startups think they need. Get the big bucks too early, and you lose too much ownership. Dilution kills motivation and it kills companies. So, *get enough to get your company through the next set of value inflection points.* When it comes to financing, *always* think in terms of value inflection points.

I hope this book has driven these lessons home. I also hope it's made you drop what's probably been a heavy-duty focus on the business plan, which you should think of as a corporate brochure! Don't worry about your business plan. Instead, think *execution intelligence. Customers. Product to market.* Handle those issues, and the plan writes itself. Not only that, but your presentation before investors will be sharp, thorough, and compelling. The investors will be all the more likely to hand over the cash you *really* need.

Once you've raised smart money, maximize its value. Market your company and its products not through advertising—a tactic guaranteed to drain your resources while producing little return—but by *positioning and marketing* your product, *generating buzz* in the marketplace, and *acquiring customers.* Those are the key activities of effective early-stage marketing.

Finally, keep in mind that complacency has no place in a great company. An entrepreneur is not just someone who sparks a new business; it's someone who lives these lessons every day, and whose entrepreneurial spirit deepens and extends as the years go by. Find a great business, and you'll find an entrepreneur at its helm.

That's my hope—that someday someone who's read this book will look back and say, I thought I knew what the deal was with starting a company. I thought I knew exactly what to do. Then I read this book. I found out what it *really* takes. And I applied those principles. Look at my company now!

At AV Labs, we're interested in hearing about your experiences on the entrepreneurial path. Tell us your story. Start by visiting the Good Hard Kick section of the AV Labs website: www.avlabs.com.

My final advice to you? You've got the foundation. Now do what matters—go out there and make something happen.

APPENDIX 1

CAPITALIZATION PRIMER

For those readers who are unfamiliar with the equity life cycle, Figure 9 illustrates the funding stages of the typical technology company. Following the figure are definitions of key terms used throughout the fourth kick and in various other parts of this book.

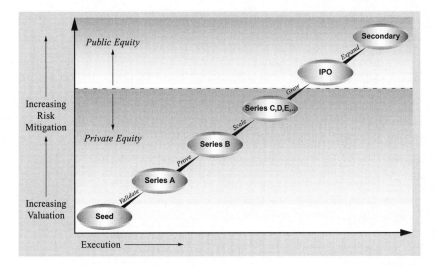

Figure 9. The equity life cycle: raising money in today's market.

Valuation. The value of a company, normally set by investors or the market. Most venture-backed companies have no hard assets in a classic accounting sense. Valuation, then, is set based on the company's potential. The less risky the potential, the higher the valuation. Valuation rises as the team hits "value inflection points"—milestones such as validating the market, developing a profitable business model, acquiring customers, and delivering a product.

Risk mitigation. The progressive lowering of the company's risk. As key value inflection points are hit, risk is mitigated and valuation rises. In the earliest stage, of course, the risk is highest—it has yet to be mitigated by market validation and other fundamental value-increasing activities.

Dilution. The degree to which current owners, such as the founding team, employees, and existing investors, see their ownership percentage cut as new investors put money in. When a company receives a large investment early (when its valuation is low), dilution is larger. That's why it is so crucial for the team and on-board investors to manage dilution by optimizing capitalization.

Seed round. Funding of (usually) less than $1 million in a typical software company, provided in the very earliest stage. Validating the market and developing a profitable business model—thereby mitigating the initial startup risk—are key goals for this period. Many companies forgo the seed stage. Big mistake.

Series A round. The first substantial financing event, usually in the range of $5–10 million for a software company. How is this money used? Typically, to get the first product to paying customers, which proves the market. In addition, the management and professional teams are built out.

Series B round. The next (or "follow-on") round after Series A. The amount raised depends on the nature of the business—classically between $10–30 million for technology companies. These funds are used to scale the company after it has proven its first product is on track. It represents increased investor confidence that the company will succeed: Team- and product-related milestones have been achieved; customers are on board; and there is market visibility, along with an accelerating revenue ramp.

Series C, D, E . . . rounds. Companies usually need additional capital to continue growing the company before risk is mitigated enough to tap the public capital markets. The capital is used to capture new markets, build additional products, develop new product lines, and more. These rounds are typically raised at increasing company valuations; they reflect the successful penetration of larger and larger market segments, and the risk mitigation that comes with them. Depending on the nature of the company's financial requirements, many rounds of private equity (venture capital) can be raised here.

Initial Public Offering (IPO). Financing via the public markets, enabling the company to expand its operations. At this stage, the Securities and Exchange Commission (SEC) has determined that risk has been quantified sufficiently to allow investment by individuals participating in public markets. The company acquires a stock symbol and begins being traded on Nasdaq, the NYSE, AMEX, or some other securities market. During an IPO, founder and investor shares are typically "locked up" for a minimum of six months; this ensures that the company continues to perform and a stable trading environment is established before larger shareholders start liquidating their positions.

Secondary Offering. Once a company has gone public and established a track record of reliable financial performance, it can continue to tap the public equity markets at higher valuations through secondary offerings. Not only do these offerings infuse money for continued growth, they also provide an environment in which large shareholders (investors, founders) can liquidate portions of their holdings in an orderly manner.

CAST OF CHARACTERS

allmystuff

www.allmystuff.com

Founded: 2000, by Jens Tellefsen, joined by Scott Miller, Brennan Carlson, Bryan Koontz, and Brian Dainton.

Primary market: Makers of computers, computer peripherals, and consumer electronics.

Pain: Manufacturers and retailers have a hard time getting to know their customers. They're even more at sea when it comes to post-sale interaction. As for customers, they're frustrated by the inconvenience of keeping track of receipts, warranties, and other information about products they own.

Product: A platform used by manufacturers and retailers to offer end consumers "product ownership pages" on their company websites. Consumers use the pages to track and manage information about their products. The businesses use them to communicate with consumers about product updates, special offers, additional products, and more.

Solving the pain: Increased "downstream" (or post-sale) revenue for manufacturers and retailers, along with improved customer service and relationships.

Covasoft

www.covasoft.com

Founded: 1999, by Cody Menard, Kim Evans, and Gary Neill.

Primary market: Companies that are heavily engaged in e-business. Initially, Covasoft is targeting customers of BroadVision and Vignette, both of which provide platforms for delivering custom content and conducting e-commerce over the Web.

Pain: When a company relies on e-business as a significant source of revenue, it simply can't afford for the e-business environment to fail. Yet these environments are so complex—and contain so many interdependencies among various components—that managing them is extremely difficult. The companies need ways to proactively identify and resolve problems before they affect business activities and affect the bottom line.

Product: A comprehensive solution that manages all elements of online business systems, including IT components, applications, and business processes. The system efficiently collects and correlates data and quickly predicts, diagnoses, and corrects problems that affect uptime and performance.

Solving the pain: More reliable performance of the e-business infrastructure, leading to fewer outages and a corresponding rise in revenue.

Ineto

www.ineto.com

Founded: 1999, by Mike Betzer, Alasdhair Campbell, and Stephen Michael.

Primary market: Companies seeking to add or integrate communication channels or avoid capital expenditure, treat multiple locations as one, and find solutions for their customer communication challenges.

Pain: Today's customers want a choice in how to contact companies: telephone, e-mail, Web collaboration, or chat. But each new communication channel brings with it high costs—both in dollars and in the technical talent needed to integrate the channels into a contact center. Businesses are left with an unhappy tradeoff: customer satisfaction, or capital conservation.

Product: A hosted, or Web-based, customer communication service offering telephone, e-mail, and chat/co-browse.

Solving the pain: Integrated voice, voice mail, chat, and e-mail interactions are routed to the right representative—for vastly improved customer service with no infrastructure investment.

Lane15

www.lane15.com

Founded: 2000, by Alisa Nessler.

Primary market: Original equipment manufacturers (OEMs) of hardware components for the emerging Infini-Band computer network architecture.

Pain: To get to market with their InfiniBand products, hardware manufacturers must include software for managing the components' behavior in the network. OEMs typically don't have the software expertise to develop these capabilities.

Product: InfiniBand management software, which will be embedded in routers, switches, and other Infini-Band network components brought to market by OEMs.

Solving the pain: The manufacturers are assured of reliable software management capabilities for their InfiniBand products. The Lane15 software will also help speed adoption of the new network.

Mediaprise

www.mediaprise.com

Founded: 1999, by Anurag Kumar, Mohan Warrior, and Steve Keys.

Primary market: Companies and organizations with global brands.

Pain: As the global marketplace continues to expand, companies must efficiently build and manage corporate standards and brand assets across many partners and locations. For example, they need ways to streamline collaboration and approval processes among marketing partners. They also need project management tools that tie into a project's related brand assets.

Product: A set of project management and workflow applications built on top of a "Marketing Workbench." The Workbench includes a central repository where companies can store and manage brand assets.

Solving the pain: Improved management and delivery of relevant brand assets, which ultimately accelerates time to market. The bottom line result is increased revenue opportunities.

Newgistics

www.newgistics.com

Founded: 1999, by Phil Siegel.

Primary market: Catalogers, direct marketers, and multichannel retailers.

Pain: The product returns process is cumbersome for retailers and inconvenient for their customers. Many retailers' processes also provide little product visibility or business intelligence, and make disposition difficult. Supply-chain performance suffers, and costs rise. End customers need convenient ways to return goods, face-to-face service, competitive shipping rates, and faster refunds.

Product: ReturnValet, a comprehensive returns management solution, includes neighborhood return locations, a convenient home label program, a scalable technology platform, and cost-effective returns processing.

Solving the pain: An enhanced customer experience, streamlined operations, and lower processing costs.

Salion

www.salion.com

Founded: 2000, by AV Labs and McKinsey & Co.

Primary market: B2B suppliers: manufacturers of custom and semi-custom products built to customer specifications and sold through business-to-business exchanges.

Pain: Most B2B solutions ease buyers' pain in the e-commerce world—search engines, reverse auctions, and more—but little exists to help suppliers. Long on the losing end of the B2B equation, the suppliers are desperate for help.

Product: A comprehensive solution for B2B suppliers, offering a search engine for finding requests for proposals; tools for plotting timelines, tracking due dates, and internally collaborating on proposals; and a proposal information repository enabling suppliers to determine what is winning business.

Solving the pain: Because they can now win a higher percentage of business, the B2B suppliers can transition from low-margin business to high-margin business.

Waveset

www.waveset.com

Founded: 2000, by Mike Turner, Mark McClain, Kevin Cunningham, and Bill Kennedy.

Primary market: Fortune 500 enterprises—starting, in Waveset's early days, with the finance, manufacturing, and transportation verticals.

Pain: The Internet is an ideal vehicle for large companies to share applications and data with partners, customers, and other outsiders—but businesses lack good ways to manage this access in a controlled, secure manner.

Product: A product to help customers pinpoint, centralize, and enable data access across an enterprise to multiple parties, including partner and customers.

Solving the pain: Businesses can now use the Internet to open up their internal data systems to outsiders, with the assurance that the access is secure and well-managed.

ACKNOWLEDGMENTS

Writing a book is a little like founding a startup—a *lot* like it, in fact. I don't know whether I would have taken it on without a good hard kick from Simone Otus, Bill Meyers, and Cindi Johnson of Blanc & Otus, who made me believe it was doable and helped me shape the idea. My agent, Daniel Greenberg of James Levine Communications, helped me see what the customers—in this case, book publishers— were looking for. Better yet, he steered me to the perfect publisher for this book. Crown Business's John Mahaney's vote of confidence ignited the project for real. And Ruth Mills, my senior editor, displayed grace, good humor, and sheer editorial brilliance to help bring it to fruition.

I also thank Austin Ventures, the dominant venture capital firm in the Southwest and one of the largest in the United States. Without Austin Ventures, AV Labs would not exist. Particular thanks are due Joe Aragona and John Thornton, general partners of the fund and the godfathers of AV Labs, for their ongoing support.

My colleagues at AV Labs are the best group of people I've ever worked with. At AV Labs, people talk all the time about the principles explored in this book. It's a rich, incredibly fertile environment for deepening one's understanding of the entrepreneurial task. I especially thank Tommy Deavenport, Kim Paschall, Michael Rovner, and Phil Siegel for their support, encouragement, and insightful reviews.

I thank Nancy Gore, who handled the day-to-day interviewing, writing, and editing. Thanks also to Greg Bashaw and Harry Kline for their research and reviews, Cheryl Latimer for her graphics work, and Paul Hurdlow of Gray Cary Ware & Freidenrich for legal advice. For their willingness to be interviewed and for the special insight and knowledge they lent this effort, I am grateful to Brian Borack, William Breetz, Deena Byers, Pat Colpitts, Brent Currier, John Doggett, David Gerhardt, Rich Goode, Chris Grafft, Rick Hahn, Brian Hairston, Guy Hoffman, Dale Howe, Jeff Johnson, Penny Lane, Manish Mehta, Chris Oakes, Tiffany O'Brien, Bruce Roberson, Charles Sansbury, Peter Simon, Mary Taylor, Neil Webber, and Elaine Wetmore.

From the bottom of my heart, I thank the entrepreneurs whose stories form the core of this book: Jens Tellefsen of allmystuff; Cody Menard, Gary Neill, and Kim Evans of Covasoft; Mike Betzer, Alasdhair Campbell, and Stephen Michael of Ineto; Alisa Nessler of Lane15; Steve Keys, Anurag Kumar, and Mohan Warrior of Mediaprise; Phil Siegel of Newgistics; and Mike Turner, Mark McClain, Kevin Cunningham, and Bill Kennedy of Waveset. I learn from them every day and am incredibly grateful to be sharing their journey.

Finally, my thanks and love to my wife, Anne.

INDEX

ABOUT THE AUTHOR

ROB ADAMS is the managing director of AV Labs, which he founded in 1999 when the firm raised its first fund of $60 million. A second fund of $125 million closed in March 2001. AV Labs is an early-stage venture fund providing seed and Series A financing to technology startups. With a view toward accelerating companies through their early-stage development, it combines a bench of experienced industry executives with a proven acceleration and validation methodology.

Before he started AV Labs, Adams was a partner at TL Ventures. Prior to the venture business, he was a technology executive for eighteen years. He started his career with Lotus, joining the company shortly after its IPO, and he was instrumental in launching 1-2-3 for Macintosh and Notes. He subsequently co-founded and was CEO of Business Matters, a venture-backed developer of financial forecasting and modeling products. He then ran sales and marketing for Pervasive Software, a company he helped take public in 1997.

Adams has a B.S. in engineering from Purdue and an M.B.A. from Babson College, and he serves as a top-ranked adjunct professor at the University of Texas Graduate School of Business. An avid skier, private pilot, and runner, Adams lives in Austin, Texas, with his wife, Anne, and children Kyle and Megan. He can be reached at rob@avlabs.com.